When We Pray

When We Pray

The future of common prayer

Edited by
Stephen Burns &
Robert Gribben

Stephen Burns, Peter Campbell,
Bryan Cones, Mark Earey, John Francis Fitz-Herbert,
Robert Gribben, Amelia Koh Butler, Jason McFarland,
Glen O'Brien, Bosco Peters, Carmel Pilcher, Stephen Platten,
Charles Sherlock, Elizabeth Smith, Robyn Wrigley-Carr

COVENTRY
PRESS

Published in Australia by
Coventry Press
33 Scoresby Road
Bayswater Vic. 3153
Australia

ISBN 9780648725107

Compilation Copyright © Stephen Burns and Robert Gribben 2020
The copyright of individual chapters remains with the authors

All rights reserved. Other than for the purposes and subject to the conditions prescribed under the *Copyright Act*, no part of this publication may be reproduced, stored in a retrieval system, or transmitted in any form or by any means, electronic, mechanical, photocopying, recording or otherwise, without the prior permission of the publisher.

Scripture quotations are from the *New Revised Standard Version Bible*, copyright 1989, Division of Christian Education of the National Council of the Churches of Christ in the United States of America. Used by permission. All rights reserved.

Cataloguing-in-Publication entry is available from the National Library of Australia http://catalogue.nla.gov.au/.

Cover image by Peter Kline
Cover design by Ian James - www.jgd.com.au
Text design by Megan Low (Film Shot Graphics FSG)
Set in Century Schoolbook / Gothic

Printed in Australia

Contents

Acknowledgments

Contributors

With Others
Stephen Burns 15

Part A: Prayer Book Traditions 27

The Spirit of Prayer Books Past
Robert Gribben 29

Revolutionary Liturgy and the Prayer Book Tradition: What revolution?
Stephen Platten 43

John Wesley's *Sunday Service*: A Methodist Urtext
Glen O'Brien 65

Ecumenical Beauty: Evelyn Underhill's *Prayer Book*
Robyn Wrigley-Carr 89

The 'Prayer Book Tradition': Back to the Liturgical Future
Charles Sherlock 113

The LORD's Song in a Foreign Land
Bosco Peters 137

Liturgical Authorisation in Australian Anglicanism: Who still cares?
Elizabeth J. Smith 159

Beyond *Common Worship*: Imperatives and Hindrances for the Church of England
Mark Earey 179

Part B: Liturgical Themes and Foci 201

Creation is also our Prayer Book
Carmel Pilcher 203

Ritual Apologies and Reconciliation in Australian Society
John Francis Fitz-Herbert 229

Looking for the Body's Language
Bryan Cones 257

Confessing More than Sin
Stephen Burns........................... 277

Thou Shall Not Chant': Prayer Book, Musical Authority and Parish Practice
Peter Campbell 303

'Becoming We': Exploring Liminality
Amelia Koh-Butler 333

Response................................355

A Roman Catholic Response
Jason J. McFarland 357

Acknowledgments

This book has its origins in a symposium day on 'the future of the prayer book tradition' hosted by the editors at Trinity College Theological School in Parkville, Melbourne on 4 May 2018. We are grateful to the college for its hospitality and to the presenters on the day whose papers are collected here.

One presenter, Gerald O'Collins SJ who reflected on his robust engagement with the current Roman rite, had already published his presentation (with John Wilkins) in *Lost in Translation: The English Language and the Catholic Mass*, Liturgical Press, 2017.

As the idea for this book clarified, we sought out other writers, both from around Australia and overseas, to add their voices to our explorations—and we appreciate the work that each one has offered.

Among the academics, parish pastors, cathedral deans and bishops present on the symposium day was Deidre Palmer, President of the Uniting Church in Australia, and we thank her very much for her Foreword. We also offer grateful thanks to Peter Kline, whose art — based on the witness to Christian worship in ancient catacombs — graces the cover. The original painting now hangs on Stephen's study wall at home.

Editorial work on the book was completed during breaks at Pilgrim Theological College, where Stephen teaches and where, at an earlier time (and under a different name, Uniting Church Theological College) Robert taught for many years. Stephen thanks his colleagues and students for such an enjoyable place to work, where faith and intelligence combine all the time.

Last but by no means least: also present at our original symposium day was Hugh McGinlay of Coventry Press, to whom we offer our thanks for his valued encouragement and expert work in shepherding the book that has emerged here.

Stephen Burns
Robert Gribben

Contributors

Stephen Burns is a presbyter in the Church of England. A British-Australian citizen, he works as Professor of Liturgical and Practical Theology at Pilgrim Theological College, University of Divinity. His books include *Christian Worship in Australia* (co-editor with Anita Monro, St Paul's, 2009), *Presiding Like a Woman* (co-editor with Nicola Slee, SPCK, 2010), *Christian Worship: Postcolonial Perspectives* (co-author with Michael Jagessar, Equinox/Routledge, 2011), *Worship and Ministry* (Mosaic, 2012), *Liturgical Spirituality* (editor, Seabury, 2013), *Pastoral Theology for Public Ministry* (Seabury, 2015), *Postcolonial Practice of Ministry* (co-editor with Kwok Pui-lan, Lexington, 2016), *Liturgy* (second edition, SCM Press, 2018) and *Liturgy with a Difference: Beyond Inclusion in the Christian Assembly* (co-editor with Bryan Cones, 2019).

Peter Campbell is a lay member of the Uniting Church in Australia. He is registrar of Trinity College Theological School, University of Divinity, Melbourne, and an Honorary Associate of the Melbourne Conservatorium of Music. He has recently published in *Musicology Australia* and *Diversity in Australia's Music* (Cambridge Scholars, 2018, edited by Dorottya Fabian and John Napier).

Bryan Cones is a presbyter in The Episcopal Church, Diocese of Chicago. A US citizen, he is former editor at Liturgy Training Publications and U.S. Catholic, he has recently published articles in *Anglican Theological Review*, *Australian Journal of Liturgy*, *Pacifica*, and *Worship*, and two collections: *Liturgy With a Difference: Beyond Inclusion in the Christian Assembly* (co-edited with Stephen Burns, SCM Press, 2019) and *Fully Conscious, Fully Active: Essays in Honour of Gabe Huck* (co-edited with Stephen Burns, LTP, 2019) as well as *This Assembly of Believers: The Boundless Riches of Christ in the Church at Prayer* (SCM Press, 2020).

Mark Earey is a presbyter in the Church of England. A British citizen, he is Tutor in Liturgy at The Queen's Foundation for Ecumenical Theological Education, Birmingham. His publications include *Worship That Cares* (SCM Press, 2012), *Beyond Common Worship* (SCM Press, 2013), and *Liturgical Worship* (second edition, Church House Publishing, 2018).

John Francis Fitz-Herbert is a presbyter of the Roman Catholic Archdiocese of Brisbane, and parish priest in Maroochydore. He is a doctoral student at Charles Sturt University and has recently published in *Indigenous Australia and the Unfinished Business of Theology* (Palgrave, 2014, edited by Jione Havea).

Robert Gribben AM is a Minister of the Word in the Uniting Church in Australia. He is Professor Emeritus of Worship and Mission at Uniting Church Theological College, United Faculty of Theology, and Honorary Research Fellow at University of Divinity, Melbourne,

Australia. He is a past editor of *Australian Journal of Liturgy*, and his books include *Uniting in Thanksgiving: The Great Prayers of Thanksgiving of the Uniting Church in Australia* (UAP, 2008). He has served on the Council of Societas Liturgica, was chair of the English Language Liturgical Consultation, and is an active participant and author in bi- and multi-lateral ecumenical dialogues.

Peter Kline is a lay member of the Anglican Church of Australia, Academic Dean at St Francis Theological College, Brisbane, and Lecturer in Systematic Theology at Charles Sturt University. A US citizen, his publications include *Passion for Nothing* (Fortress Press, 2017). Peter is an artist (http://peterklineart.virb.com/). His painting *Catacombs Worshipper* is used on the cover of *When we pray*.

Amelia Koh-Butler is a Minister of the Word in the Uniting Church in Australia. A recent graduate in doctoral studies at Fuller Seminary, Pasadena, she is currently Interfaith Chaplain at the University of Western Sydney, having held roles in synod leadership in New South Wales and South Australia, and involvement in national committees on cross-cultural ministry and theological education. Her publications include *Wide and Deep* (MediaCom, 2017) and *Sisters in Scripture* (MediaCom, 2018).

Jason J. McFarland is a lay Roman Catholic and Assistant Director of the Liturgy Centre of Australian

Catholic University, where he teaches liturgical and sacramental theology. A US citizen, his publications include *Announcing the Feast: The Entrance Song in the Mass of the Roman Rite* (Liturgy Training Publications, 2012) and *Doing Liturgical Theology: Method and Context* (co-edited with Stephen Burns, Peeters, 2020).

Glen O'Brien is a Minister of the Word in the Uniting Church in Australia, and Associate Professor at Eve Burrows College (Salvation Army), University of Divinity. He has recently published articles in *The Journal of Religious History*, *The Journal of Ecclesiastical History*, and *Pacifica*, and his books include *Christian Worship: A Theological and Historical Introduction* (Uniting Academic Press, 2013) and *Methodism in Australia: A History* (co-edited with Hilary Carey, Ashgate, 2015).

Bosco Peters is a presbyter in the Anglican Church of Aotearoa New Zealand and Polynesia, and currently serves as Chaplain of Christ's College, Canterbury. A New Zealand citizen, his book *Celebrating Eucharist* (Auckland: DEFT, 1995) was the first commentary on the acclaimed *A New Zealand Prayer Book* (1995), and he runs one of the first blogs on liturgy (www.liturgy.co.nz) to have been developed, which has long attracted a wide international readership.

Carmel Pilcher is a Sister of St Joseph, and was Director of Liturgy in the Archdiocese of Sydney, Roman Catholic Church. She is a past member of Council for

Societas Liturgica, and has recently published articles in *Australian Journal of Liturgy* and *Worship*. Her books include *Vatican Council II: Reforming Liturgy* (co-editor with David Orr, OSB, and Elizabeth Harrington, ATF, 2012).

Stephen Platten is a bishop in the Church of England, and the chair of its Liturgical Commission. A British citizen, he currently serves as assistant bishop in London, Southwark, and Newcastle (UK) dioceses. The author and editor of many books, these include *Anglicanism and the Western Catholic Tradition* (editor; Norwich: Canterbury Press, 2000), *Dreaming Spires? Cathedrals in a New Age* (editor; London: SPCK, 2008), *Comfortable Words: Polity, Piety and the Book of Common Prayer* (co-editor with Christopher Woods; London: SCM Press, 2012), *Holy Ground: Cathedrals in the Twenty-first Century* (Durham: Sacristy Press, 2016), *Oneness: The Dynamics of Monasticism* (editor; London: SCM Press, 2017), and *Animating Liturgy: The Dynamics of Liturgy and the Human Community* (Durham: Sacristy Press, 2017).

Charles Sherlock is a presbyter in the Anglican Church of Australia. He taught at both Ridley College, Melbourne, and Trinity College Theological School, Melbourne. He compiles the Daily Lectionary for the Anglican Church of Australia and was a member of ARCIC. His books include *Words and the Word* (Mosaic, 2012), *Performing the Gospel: In Liturgy and Lifestyle* (Broughton, 2017) and *Performing A Prayer Book for Australia* (Broughton, 2018), forthcoming.

Elizabeth Smith is a presbyter in the Anglican Church of Australia. She is parish priest in Kalgoorlie, Western Australia, and serves as Secretary to the Liturgy Commission of the Anglican Church of Australia. Her publications include *Bearing Fruit in Due Season* (Liturgical Press, 1997), and many hymns and liturgical resources.

Robyn Wrigley-Carr is an Anglican deaconess and Senior Lecturer in Christian Theology and Spirituality at Alpha Crucis College, Sydney. She has recently published articles in *Australian Pentecostal Studies, International Journal of Children's Spirituality, Pacifica,* and *Studies in Spirituality,* and her books include *Evelyn Underhill's Prayer Book* (SPCK, 2018).

Introduction
With Others

Stephen Burns

When we pray, we join with others. Christian traditions say this in different ways: for example, the Roman Catholic tradition calls its evening office 'The Evening Prayer of the Church', with the liturgical documents of the tradition amplifying the point: so the General Instruction on the Liturgy of the Hours echoes the Constitution on the Sacred Liturgy to affirm that 'the liturgy of the hours, like other liturgical services, is not a private matter but belongs to the whole Body of the Church, whose life it both expresses and affects'.[1] Anglicans around the world share the inheritance of *The Book of Common Prayer*, no matter how near or far their current books may seem from the 'definitive' edition of 1662, or its precursors of 1549, 1552, or other variations.[2] The verb that names the Uniting Church in Australia is also central to its liturgical resource, *Uniting in Worship*.[3]

Before all of these examples, the Prayer of Jesus ('Lord's Prayer') teaches address to God in a plural voice ('*our* Father'), and the church's prayer itself finds a wider context in conviction that it joins contemporary voices to 'that hymn of praise sung throughout all ages in the hall of heaven', as the General Instruction on the Liturgy of the Hours puts it.[4] Moreover, Christians of a wide variety of churches proclaim in the *Sanctus* a thrice-fold 'holy' at the heart of their eucharistic prayer, recalling both the gravity of Isaiah's personal encounter with the divine and the depiction of heavenly creatures in chorus in John's Revelation (Isaiah 6:3, Revelation 4:8).

No matter how personal, particular or intimate prayer may be, when we pray, we join with others: uniting, in common, as part of the church, in company with Christians far and near, throughout history and around the world – and maybe even strange and unseen singing 'beasts' by the crystal sea around the sovereign's throne in another realm.

In what follows, at least the more prosaic dimensions of these scenes are a focus – that is, Uniting, Anglican and Roman traditions and the resources by which they encourage prayer with others amongst their members. In their various ways, the following essays address 'common', shared, worship. 'Common worship' or 'common prayer' is a term that echoes in the titles of ritual books of some traditions: so Anglicans have books of common prayer; some Anglicans and also Presbyterians call their books common worship, while others have the variant 'common order', and so on. These terms are not tradition-specific, and point to widespread liturgical resources that have typically been in print, were earlier made by scribes, and are increasingly mediated electronically, and that invite and shape, perhaps direct and regulate worship when Christians gather to pray.

How Roman Catholics, Anglicans and Uniting Christians are shaped by their ritual books differs somewhat from tradition to tradition, as does the status of their ritual books in the respective churches. In the case of Anglicans, this differs again from Christians in the same 'Anglican Communion' around the world. And, increasingly, whatever books are provided by a central source – whether it be in Rome or Sydney or London or somewhere else – what happens in the prayer of one congregation may differ in significant ways from what happens in another, even though the congregations are apparently of like-kind. Some 'Anglican congregations' in Melbourne, for instance, are not only not identifiable as Anglican communities by their signage or literature but do not use any centrally provided liturgical resources or whatever 'common' worship is at their disposal.

Uniting, Anglican and Roman Catholic traditions are each currently stretched by – and sometimes creative in the face of – challenges to their communal forms of prayer. There are also tensions between the traditions, more so latterly perhaps than in the era that followed the Second Vatican Council and the reception of its liturgical vision not only in the Roman Church, where it might have been expected to have impact, but also widely among Protestants.[5] In more recent times, though, the current translation of texts used in Roman Catholic liturgies has turned them away from 'prayers we have in common'[6] which through at least a stretch of the twentieth-century meant that assemblies in many traditions all used the same English translation. The greeting

The Lord be with you.
And also with you.
once held in common is no longer so. Nor are a range of other once-shared English translations.

Within the Roman tradition, the introduction of the current English translation of the texts for Mass (2011) was met with widespread consternation – as well as praise from some others – for further reasons, enacting as it does a more literal translation of Latin texts than the previous approach of 'dynamic equivalence'[7] in which the sense of the original could be rendered in ways which are not so precisely tied to earlier Latin constructions. While the current translation has faced questions from various quarters, one of its most trenchant critics is the Australian Jesuit Gerald O'Collins, whose challenge to the current texts is paired with an appeal for rehabilitation of the sacramentary prepared for use in the 1990s and suppressed by the Vatican. O'Collins' appeal for retrieval of this 'missal that never was' caught a possible window of opportunity in Pope Francis' pronouncement of October 2017,[8] reorienting decisions about liturgical use less centrally with the Vatican and more under the authority of local bishops.[9] While it remains to be seen how this shift may stall, or be propelled, or what it may mean for Roman Catholics around the world, it suggests a significant modification of practice with respect to uniform texts, and may signal a new appreciation of the Second Vatican Council's Constitution on the Sacred Liturgy and its teaching on what came to be called 'inculturation'.[10]

The massive diversity of global Anglicanism, whatever its differences, can all track its roots through a book of common prayer (BCP), though over time there have been many iterations of the BCP, with provincial books differing from one another in quite significant ways, and the earliest of such books themselves representing significant differences: so that of 1552 shunted the rites of 1549 in a more protestantising direction, while 1559 pushed back some of its predecessor's initiatives. A striking feature of the current situation is that Australia was the first province of the Anglican Communion to revise the resources which emerged through the liturgical renewal contemporaneous with the Second Vatican Council in the Roman Church: that is, *A Prayer Book for Australia* (APBA, 1995) is a revision of *An Australian Prayer Book* (1978).

But after the twenty-five and more years since APBA, Australia has become the tardiest at least among 'global western Anglicanism'[11] to revise its book. The notorious divisions of the Australian Anglican scene – Sydney diocese and its conservative evangelicalism, the brittle anglo-catholicism which prevails in some other places in counterpoint to Sydney – have made moving forward with prayer book revision very difficult,[12] with less than half of Australian Anglicans now using the closest thing they might have to a book in common.

Elsewhere – at least around the global west – new patterns of worship now pertain which adjust and develop what common prayer means in practice, with a lurch away from identical texts to common shape and 'family resemblance' indicated by means other than the words that are or are not said.[13] Perspectives from both England and the US at more of a distance, and NZ closer to the Australian context out of which most essays here come, are represented in what follows.

The move in many parts of Anglicanism to a more 'directory' approach to liturgical resources, to be best-fit to local mission circumstances makes for a kind of allegiance in approach to that of the Uniting Church in Australia. This tradition, forged from merging Australian Congregationalist, Methodist and some Presbyterian precursors has developed some of the most wide-ranging liturgical resources anywhere in the world. While sharing with a range of Protestant traditions an emphasis on 'ordered liberty', and representing the ecumenical centre, drawing on Roman and Anglican materials, it also includes orders that draw on the Christian East and more tentative provisions that push forward feminist liturgical concerns.[14] For the Uniting Church, its liturgical resources act as a 'standard and norm', not necessarily to be used as is, but as a measure by which to test the doctrine and other merits of more local compositions. Ordered liberty allows for latitude, though attempts to keep permissible liberty recognisably related, in common, ordered in allied ways.

The missional context of Australia – with much of the rest of the global west – has stretched all of these various practices, perhaps close to their limits. The imposition of common texts in English around majority-English speaking regions smothers the massive cultural diversity that marks Roman Catholicism, in part because migrants in all their variety represent more and more the backbone of regular worshipping assemblies in so many places. Whether or not a move to less centralised authorisation of liturgical forms and options emerges, the acute difficulties of the sexual abuse scandals that have afflicted this tradition even more than others presents questions about its attractional power and its ability to direct thought and practice in morality or prayer or anything else among people alienated from it and by it. Anglicanism, also heavily implicated in abuse of the vulnerable, now faces a sharp problem as it squares up to large numbers lately choosing to leave behind their nominal affiliation.

If not much in Australia then elsewhere, an option for what former archbishop of Canterbury Rowan Williams called a 'mixed economy' of church, which a variety of liturgical styles reflect, is emerging in serious engagement in 'fresh expressions of church' alongside more longstanding practice where inherited liturgical services remain viable as attractional events. While variety between 'parties' has long marked the Anglican tradition, the indifference with which the liturgical efforts and predelictions of these parties is met by wider societies may be new and is in any case intense – and as yet the fresh expressions experiment is too new for long term assessment.[15] But the least that may be said is that, given recognition that the platform is burning,[16] it is not just re-arranging the vestments or other kinds of churchy tinkering. The Uniting Church has also seen more piecemeal engagement with fresh expressions, while also, like Anglicanism in Australia, in decline.

What prayer in common in Anglican and Uniting traditions in Australia might mean is quite uncertain, given so much difference in current practice, while the more steady Roman tradition occludes the cultures of many of those who are present. All are missing many contemporary persons from immediately surrounding cultures. Questions of both how liturgy forms worshippers for mission in this context, and how liturgy itself serves as an invitational event press on every side.

The essays that follow track the past, assess the present, and imagine the futures of Christian worship in various ways. Some are concerned with particular ritual books that have shaped the common prayer uniting together Christians over time within and between specific traditions. Others look at what is missing and wanting in current provisions. Others again suggest paths and make projections into the future of common prayer, the prospects of uniting in worship, and for shaping the prayer of the church in different settings, styles, and ecclesial communities.

The essays might be read in any order, but in presenting them to the reader, we have opted for a schema that clusters essays largely focused on particular books or tradition-specific elements, followed by those which take a more thematic approach. So at first particular ritual resources, past and present, come to focus – John Wesley's Sunday service, and *A Prayer Book for Australia* amongst them – and then themes that cross traditions – creation, reconciliation, confession, or whatever – surface. But there are various exceptions: inevitably themes and books can collide (the assembly in the *Book of Common Prayer, 1979*, for instance), while the ecumenical indebtedness of one ritual book to another is repeatedly apparent (and not least with regard to Evelyn Underhill's fascinating personal compilation).

In whatever order they are read, then, the essays will bounce off each other. Convictions are sometimes alternate and in counterpoint as well as other times allied and in harmony. Given the flux of the contemporary conversation about patterns of praying together to which this collection makes a contribution, this 'bouncing' is apt, as we in no way wish to suggest that issues we try to face here can be neatly tidied up, nor compromises easily achieved, tensions resolved, solutions simplified, outlooks firmly certain. That said, it will be clear to the reader that commonalities – of concern, of appreciation, of emphasis – emerge across the essays, and ideas, suggestions, and clues abound about the future of praying with others.

So despite the many changes and divergence that this book narrates, sense is shared between authors, and across traditions, and from around the world. Our anthology of essays will no doubt spark many more questions than answers, though we hope it asks good questions, uplifts durable resources, queries conventions ill-fit to contemporary settings, and invites hope that communal prayer will one way or another continue to flourish in Christian assembly.

Endnotes

1. Para. 20, Celebration in Common', referring to *Sacrosanctum concilium*, 26.
2. See Charles Hefling and Cynthia Shattuck, eds, *The Oxford Guide to the Book of Common Prayer: A Worldwide Survey* (New York, NY: OUP, 2006) and Stephen Platten and Christopher Woods, eds, *Comfortable Words: Polity, Piety and the Book of Common Prayer* (London: SCM Press, 2011).
3. *Uniting in Worship* (Melbourne: Uniting Church Press, 1988), *Uniting in Worship 2* (Sydney: Uniting Church Press, 2005). See Robert Gribben, *A Guide to Uniting in Worship* (Melbourne: Joint Board of Christian Education, 1990), Stephen Burns, *Pilgrim People: An Invitation to Worship in the Uniting Church* (Adelaide: MediaCom, 2012).
4. Para. 16, 'Celebration in Common'.
5. Don E. Saliers, 'Christian Spirituality in an Ecumenical Age', Louis Dupre, Don E. Saliers and John Meyendorff, eds, *Christian Spirituality III: Post-Reformation and Modern* (London: SCM Press, 1989), 52-544, 538.
6. See http://www.commontexts.org/publications/
7. See Keith Pecklars, *Dynamic Equivalence: The Living Language of Christian Worship* (Collegeville, MN: Liturgical Press, 2003). See more widely, James F. Puglisi, ed., *Liturgical Renewal as a Way to Christian Unity* (Collegeville, MN: Liturgical Press, 2005).
8. See https://press.vatican.va/content/salastampa/en/bollettino/pubblico/2017/09/09/170909a.html
9. Gerald O'Collins with John Watkins, *Lost in Translation: The English Language and the Catholic Mass* (Collegeville, MN: Liturgical Press, 2017). See more widely, Edward Foley, et al, eds, *A Commentary on the Order of Mass: The Roman Missal* (Collegeville, MN: Liturgical Press, 2011), noting criticisms in particular from Anscar Chupungco.
10. *Sacrosanctum concilium*, 37-40. See also Anscar Chupungco, *Cultural Adaption of the Liturgy* (Mahwah, NJ: Paulist Press, 1983), and Paul Turner, *Whose Mass is It? Why People Care so Much about the Catholic Liturgy* (Collegeville, MN: Liturgical Press, 2015).
11. This nomenclature is used in Jeremy Morris, ed., *The Oxford History of Anglicanism, Volume VI: Global Western Anglicanism, c.1910-Present* (Oxford: OUP, 2017), which includes important discussion of the term's weaknesses, especially when paired with 'global Anglican' as a reference to the so-called third-world.
12. See Stephen Burns, '*A Prayer Book for Australia*: That Was Then, This Is Now', Australian Journal of Liturgy 17 (2018): 20-40. For global diversity, with respect to daily prayer, see Stephen Burns, "Learning Again and Again to Pray": Anglican Forms of Daily Prayer, 1979-2014', *Journal of Anglican Studies* 15 (2017): 9-36.
13. See Hefling and Shattuck, eds, *Guide to the BCP*; on *(New) Patterns for Worship* and its influence in the Church of England, see Stephen Burns, *Worship in Context: Liturgical Theology, Children and the City* (Peterborough: Epworth Press, 2006), and subsequent developments, especially Mark Earey, *Beyond* Common Worship: *Anglican Identity and Liturgical Diversity* (London: SCM Press, 2012).

14 The Service of the Lord's Day 3 has many Eastern Christian elements, the experimental Service of the Lord's Day 4 is cast in expansive language and strongly influenced by Christian feminist literature. Both services are found on the CD which accompanies and expands the printed material in the UiW2 book.
15 None the less, emerging research from the Church of England suggests that fresh expressions of church represent numerically the equivalent of two new dioceses, and in terms of participation by young people, the equivalent of seven dioceses – therefore not to be dismissed. The contest about fresh expressions of church has sometimes been acid and shrill, e.g. Andrew Davison and Alison Milbank, *For the Parish: A Critique of Fresh Expressions* (London: SCM Press, 2010), though more balanced views have emerged: e.g. Julie Gittoes, et al, eds, *Generous Ecclesiology: Church, World and the Kingdom of God* (London: SCM Press, 2015). See also Louise Nelstropp and Martyn Percy, eds, *Evaluating Fresh Expressions: Explorations in Emerging Church* (Norwich: Canterbury Press, 2009) and with respect to worship in particular: Steven Croft and Ian Mobsby, eds, *Fresh Expressions in the Sacramental Tradition* (Norwich: Canterbury Press, 2012) and Phil Potter and Ian Mobsby, eds, *Doorways to the Sacred: Developing Sacramentality in Fresh Expressions of Church* (Norwich: Canterbury Press, 2017).
16 The image of the burning platform appears – alongside that of crossroads, time bomb, and boiling frog – in Anglican Church of Australia, *Building the Mission-shaped Church in Australia* (Sydney: General Synod, 2007). For discussion, see Stephen Burns, 'Pastoral Ministry Today,' in Bradley Billings, ed., *A Pastoral Handbook for Anglicans* (Alexandria: Broughton, 2018).

Part A:
Prayer Book Traditions

1

The Spirit of Prayer Books Past

Robert Gribben

The 'prayer book tradition' is often read as being exclusively Anglican. The identification of the term with the *Book of Common Prayer* (chiefly that of 1662) is perhaps understandable, since it was singled out in English history as the rule of prayer and liturgy in that realm. That would explain alternative prayer books being given different titles: *A Directory of Public Worship* (making a liturgical distinction clear), or the Scottish (and general Presbyterian) *Book of Common Order*, or the Church of South India's *Book of Common Worship*, or even *The Methodist Worship Book* – and variations on the theme. But are not all these 'prayer books' in any ordinary use of the term, authorised liturgical texts to guide the worship of the people? Our aim in this chapter is to address the range of such prayer books.

The first Prayer Book in English was a radical step away from the inherited patterns of the Holy Roman Empire, when King Henry VIII removed his nation and the faithful from its authority. The governing principle at the time was *Cuius regio, eius religio,* that the religion of any realm was the religion of its monarch. Despite outward continuity – Latin continued in the English Church while Henry was alive – a great deal of other change occurred, the despoliation of parish churches and the destruction of monasteries, and all the piety associated with their furnishings, art and music, as Eamon Duffy has movingly brought to our attention.[1]

The two first English Prayer Books

What it meant to be an *English* Church awaited his successor, the boy king Edward VI, openly influenced by guardians whose policies echoed the Protestant reformation, and in a span of five years, two prayer books in English were composed and issued at the hand of Henry's and Edward's archbishop of Canterbury, Thomas Cranmer. I would like to think the debate as to whether 1549 or 1552 was Cranmer's real liturgical goal is over; in my opinion, he intentionally took two steps forward in a chosen direction. (Sadly, these two books became the banners of opposing forces within the Anglican tradition, to our own day. I am often tempted to think that there is a fundamental divide among human beings between those who prefer things plain, and those who find them complex. At the heart is a dispute over what constitutes 'beauty'—but that is another topic.) In any case, the invention of the printing press meant that they were uniform texts, and their use could be uniformly insisted upon. That insistence divided the English church.

Anglican liturgical history thus proceeded through the exigencies of Tudor and Stuart rule until 1662. *That* prayer book, however, followed an interval with neither monarch, nor episcopate, nor uniform prayer book. Alternative views of ecclesiology and liturgy held sway for almost twenty years, under a Commonwealth and Parliament - and a new kind of prayer book was invented to meet the needs.

The Directory of Public Worship

The *Directory of Public Worship* of 1644[2] set out the structure of each rite, describing the theological purpose of each prayer and action, but allowed the presider to offer the prayer in his own words. Someone has described the Directory as a prayer book consisting entirely of rubrics.[3]

The Directory ignored the fact that not every parson is capable of composing a theologically cogent prayer in reasonable public language. We might recall the church order once ascribed to Hippolytus, *The Apostolic Tradition*, at this point, where he makes that very point, at a time when bishops at the altar still offered prayers 'according to their ability'[4]:

> It is not at all necessary that he prays with the very same words given above, as though by an effort of memory giving thanks to God. Each shall pray whatever is according to his ability. If someone has the ability to pray a lengthy and solemn prayer, that is well. If someone else, in praying, offers a short prayer,

this is not to be prevented. That prayer must only be correct in orthodoxy.

There are limits to the creative literary skill of most of us, as we seek not vainly to repeat ourselves every Sunday.[5] In 1644, an order, and its theologic were provided, but freedom was preserved. This is the background to the Uniting Church's 'ordered liberty',[6] but we should perhaps also note *The Apostolic Tradition's* final caveat, '...that prayer must only be correct in orthodoxy'.

1662 and Nonconformity

The experiment of a republic had failed in England by 1660 and the powers that be, in state and church, moved to return to the *status quo ante*, to heal the wounds which civil war had inflicted. King Charles II himself hoped for some compromises which would have kept the best of the Puritans in public office, to no avail. The Puritan Richard Baxter provided, within a fortnight, an entire compromise book now known as the Savoy Liturgy,[7] but it was simply rejected. In the newly re-established Church, the book was to rule.

The requirement of the oaths by clergy to use the Book of Common Prayer (hereafter BCP) without variation or omission gave it an authority which many Christians of the time could claim only for the Scriptures.[8] Even those who welcomed the Restoration itself could not, on principle, accept an imposed liturgy. Two thousand clergy lost their livings in the 'Great Ejection'.[9]

A new kind of church status was invented: 'Nonconformity', which included all who would not so use the BCP, which meant Roman Catholics, Presbyterians, Congregationalists (including Baptists) and many other smaller groups, only Jews (!) and Quakers being excepted. It was another two decades, and more in the case of Catholics, before Nonconformists could worship without fines, imprisonment or exile. The worldwide impact of this twist of English history can be seen among many examples in that it provided the denominations that formed the Uniting Church in Australia.[10]

Nonconformist texts for worship

The Westminster Assembly of 1644 authorised and insisted on the use of the Directory of Public Worship as a *replacement* for the BCP. Presbyterians and Congregationalists were perforce minorities and never large in England. The situation in Scotland was different but is beyond our scope in this essay, but the wordy and dreary worship of the Nonconformist churches by the late 18th century gave rise to a new liturgical movement in Scotland which bore fruit in new scholarship, a Church Service Society (1865) and the *Euchologion or a Book of Common Order* in 1867 which created a renaissance in the following century. The rights of local congregations were respected, but more ordered patterns of worship emerged, and the *Book of Common Order* was (and is) the guide.[11] The most recent *Common Order* (1994) says the successive books 'have never been prescriptive, making "this and this only" mandatory on ministers and congregations'. English Presbyterians and Congregationalists tended to look over the border for liturgical guidance. Nevertheless, such Ministers had a book in their hands.[12]

Methodist use of authorised books is traced in another chapter of this book (see O'Brien).

Uniting in Worship

The Prayer Book controversy of 1662 remains in living memory. The Uniting Church in Australia consciously based its new liturgical provisions (the two *Uniting in Worship* books of 1988 and 2005) on the *Directory of Public Worship* but went further and provided complete prayers for each rite, for which, with rare exceptions (e.g. marriage vows) a prayer *with the same theological intention,* drawn from other sources, could be substituted. It is a prayer book consisting largely of models.[13]

Some have missed this liberty and have invented a new kind of uncharacteristic rubricism, but it still holds promise. Equally, some have taken liberty to mean freedom from doctrinal constraints. Nevertheless, UiW has been widely used, and significantly opened the Uniting Church to the liturgical renewal of the 1970s and beyond.

Australian Anglican prayer books

So, what of modern Anglicans in Australia? I need only to make a simple point. There was *An Australian Prayer Book* of 1978; then *A Prayer Book for Australia* of 1995. Anglican presiders are required to use them, but with permissions and possibilities undreamed of in 1662. Thus, extempore prayer, and texts from sources other than the authorised prayer book are frequently and unapologetically offered in Anglican worship.

If the liturgical freedoms of these modern books were possible in 1662, the ecumenical world would be – simpler. And it a matter of profound thanksgiving that almost every liturgy in the English-speaking world from the 1960s to 2010 was written together with direct consultation with a range of other churches, drawing on the same scholarship. Blessed be God for the international English Language Liturgical Consultation, The Australian Consultation on Liturgy and its national counterparts elsewhere.

The internet and copiers

But we are now the recipients of inventions even more powerful than the printing press, but no friends of uniformity or even unity: *the internet,* and *the copier.* The internet allows an electronic text to be available instantly, across the globe, in any language, in any script. Almost every church's liturgy is online, with further resources and commentary. Most of us do not now depend on books in pews or in worshippers' hands, but rather expect a pew-sheet prepared for the day, or a single small service booklet. Hymns and other words may well appear on a screen.

So, it is now a fact that any worship leader can find any prayer anywhere on the 'net, from theological sources of any quality; they may copy it and edit it as they drop it into the Sunday bulletin for their congregation. It is actually almost impossible *not* to edit, alter or generally fiddle with the text on the way. Uniformity is inconceivable. Copyright, though much insisted upon, regrettably provides a very weak barrier to the worst aspects of such changes. Is there a future for a 'prayer book tradition'?

The ecumenical questions

What now provides the link between the churches' tradition of faith, and their local liturgy? In a culture which is loath to exercise discipline or to curb 'creativity', how do we deal with a never-ending overabundance of alternative resources? Will we no longer be able to discern anything of the unique genius of our inherited traditions? What will indicate the doctrinal integrity of a prayer? What makes our liturgies *Christian*? Who has the authority to decide what is a near-equivalent to the way we used to say something? Not even the Uniting Church's 'ordered liberty' can guarantee faithfulness, if (as it seems) it tends more in the direction of liberty, and liberty without order. What of the faith of the One, Holy, Catholic and Apostolic Church, expressed in prayer and praise? The critical issues are both liturgical and doctrinal. These are new – and ecumenical – questions.

The Church of Rome has its responsible Congregation for Divine Worship and the Discipline of the Sacraments, and other bodies, who are currently in an interesting phase. Pope Francis, in *Magnum Principium*[14] has recently returned authority to the national bishops' conference to decide liturgical issues.

The Anglican Communion has given a high place to its Inter-Anglican Liturgical Commission (IALC), whose members represent the whole range of contemporary scholarship and practice, with an impressive list of publications, but it cannot act as police officer. They have ventured that:

> In the future, Anglican unity will find its liturgical expression not so much in uniform texts as in a common approach to eucharistic celebration and a structure which will ensure a balance of word, prayer, and sacrament, and which bears witness to the catholic calling of the Anglican Communion.[15]

That is a high hope in the present cultural mood, and its states the problem rather than suggesting a way forward. What is the likelihood of wide acceptance of whoever defines the 'common approach'?

And for the 'non-liturgical' churches?

There have been plenty of calls from liturgiologists, in the face of this dilemma, for the recovery of liturgical studies in the normal curricula for clergy training (and, given the new respect for the role of all the baptised, the assembly, in worship, for lay students as well). Such a call must face the fact that for some decades, theological faculty curricula have been overloaded, the great traditional disciplines of Scripture and theology, languages and church history, have had to juggle in timetables and required courses with new disciplines such as those from the social sciences, and pastoral theology and practice, and even music and the arts (strong companions of liturgies though the latter be). Changes in tertiary education as a whole affect the shape of theological learning, and decisions about time and tasks are dictated increasingly by managerial and bureaucratic considerations. And who will speak for liturgy, who have never studied it?

By all means, let battle commence.

But the issue concerns the Church, not only academe. It is precisely the *baptised* who must understand the crisis and call for change. The general ignorance among congregations as to why we do what we do in Sunday worship is so profound that they do not even know what they have lost. So we do not so much need to give information about liturgical renewal (let alone explain or comment on it) as lead the assembly to experience it, so that new expressions in liturgy find their own authentication in practice. The spirit (or Spirit) of a baptism or a eucharist affects its own change in our spirits (cf Romans 8:16), but those spirits must also be tested. Perhaps the whole task is summed up by Charles Wesley:

> *Unite the pair so long disjoined,*
> *Knowledge and vital piety:*
> *Learning and holiness combined,*
> *And truth and love, let all men [sic] see...* [16]

The resources of the Church of Rome after Vatican II were better marshalled than the others' and had a tradition of authority in such matters the rest of us lack. And such education usually falls to the clergy – but I have often seen it happen as a result of lay questions ('What is 'Great' about the Great Prayer of Thanksgiving? Why are we offering communion to children? Are we becoming more Catholic – or more Baptist – or more Pentecostal? - and why not?) The production of new educational material even at this late stage (and online!), and the encouragement of clergy to share boldly and frequently what they have discovered in liturgical theology and practice, may help, but we are still talking about the need for a total reconversion of the Church – the holy ordinary people of God – to the deep things no longer illuminating and sustaining the way of faith, through a true *catechesis*.

We ought to remind ourselves that the Church's future has been under threat before – and probably to leaders no less theologically aware than we are; I think of the disappearance of that great African Church of St

Augustine. The sober truth for our contemporary western Church is that churches, *qua* organisations, institutions – can die and are dying. That is not what the Lord's promise to Peter challenged. The Church of God will be there to welcome the *Parousia*, we should not doubt, but in what form and where? Not spread in great numbers across all the nations of the earth, it would seem, by present lights.

Nor, soberly, should we think the answers to our problems be bureaucratic, didactic, systematic, or the result of a program or a curriculum. Why, indeed, write a book about it? Because we who believe do not have the luxury of giving up, for the One who leads us is alive and active. The issue at heart is faith. And that is a gift of God, not a creation of ours – but we must be willing to discern, discover, be surprised by things unfamiliar, unexplored, unpredicted from the human perspective, in the gift of that stormy Spirit. And if we also need to begin with ourselves, let us also remember that in Christian faith, the context is communal: one, holy, catholic and apostolic.

But if we do not find fresh ways to hand on the substance of the *depositum fidei* in the assembly of God's people when they worship - then Professor McGrath's prediction may come true:

> ...the four movements which are most likely to dictate the shape of a future Christianity [are]: Roman Catholicism, Pentecostalism, evangelicalism and Eastern Orthodoxy. It will be obvious that there is an omission here.

Mainline Protestantism seems very unlikely to survive the next century in the west, at least in its present form.[17]

Endnotes

1 See Eamon Duffy, *The Stripping of the Altars: Traditional Religion in England, 1400–1580* (New Haven, Conn.: Yale University Press, 1992), and Saints, Sacrilege, Sedition, Religion and Conflict in the Tudor Reformations (London: Bloomsbury, 2012).
2 The full text may be read in Bard Thompson, *Liturgies of the Western Church* (London: Collins/Fontana, 1962).
3 It was not an English invention: Guillaume Farel, the reforming pastor of Neuchâtel, composed one in his *Le Manière et Fasson*, See Thompson, *Western Church*, for the text, 216--.
4 See translation by Kevin P. Edgecomb athttp://www.bombaxo.com/hippolytus.html, (at 9.1) accessed 3/5/18.
5 The effects of Directory worship are traced in Horton Davies' study, *Worship and Theology in England, From Andrewes to Baxter and Fox, 1603-1690* (Princeton NJ: Princeton University Press, 1975).
6 See Uniting Church in Australia, *Uniting in Worship 2* (Sydney: Uniting Church Press, 2005), 13f. Note also related notions in others'/other books: 'form and freedom' as key value in The Methodist Church of Great Britain, *The Methodist Worship Book* (Peterborough: Epworth Press, 1999) and The Presbyterian Church (USA), *The Book of Common Worship* (Louisville, TN: Westminster John Knox Press, 2018).
7 See Thompson, *Western Church*, 375.
8 The oath, or Form of Assent, read: 'I. A. B. doe declare my unfaigned assent and consent to all and every thing contained and prescribed in and by the Booke intituled The Booke of Co[m]mon Prayer and Administration of the Sacraments and other Rites and Ceremonies of the Church according to the use of the Church of England togeather with the Psalter or Psalmes of, David pointed as they are to be sung or said in Churches and the form or manner of making ordaining and consecrating of Bishops Preists and Deacons.'
9 They included a great-grandfather and both grandfathers of the Wesley brothers.
10 More precisely, two of the denominations, since the Methodists did not exist at the time. Methodism after Wesley was more and more drawn into the Nonconformist camp.,
11 One older but trustworthy guide to Presbyterian history is W. D. Maxwell, *A History of Worship in the Church of Scotland* (Oxford: OUP, 1955), but see also, e.g. Duncan Forrester and Douglas Murray, eds, *Studies in the History of Worship in Scotland* (Edinburgh: T & T Clark, 1984), and the exploratory Bryan D. Spinks and Iain R. Torrance, eds, *To Glorify God: Essays on Modern Reformed Liturgy* (Edinburgh: T & T Clark, 1999).

12 At the point of union in 1977, Australian Presbyterians used the *Book of Common Order* (Scotland, 1940) in a local edition, and the Congregationalists had to hand *A Book of Services and Prayers* (London: Independent Pres, 1959) edited by the late Dr Harold F. Leatherland.
13 The rather grand binding in which some printings appeared immediately aroused the old fear of 'Anglican' and imposition. The 'People's Book' of *Uniting in Worship* (1988) which provided resources for worshippers to use in church and beyond failed to sell as well as hoped probably due to this fear.
14 Apostolic Letter in the form of Motu Proprio "Magnum Principium" *Quibus nonnulla in can. 838 Codicis IurisCanonici immutantur*, 9 September 2017, see text http://press.vatican.va/content/ salastampa/en/bollettino/pubblico/2017/09/09/170909a.html.
15 See the essay by Pierre Whalon, in Charles Hefling and Cynthia Shattuck, eds, *Oxford Guide to the Book of Common Prayer* (New York: OUP, 2006), online at https://ebookcentral-proquest-com.divinity .idm. oclc.org/lib/undiv/detail.action?docID=430580#. Gordon Lathrop's investigation of the underlying ordo of Christian worship is important in this discussion, also see Dirk G. Lange and Dwight W. Vogel, eds, *Ordo: Bath, Word, Prayer, Table, A Liturgical Primer in Honor of Gordon W. Lathrop* (Akron, OH: O[rder of] S[aint] L[uke] Publications, 2005), especially Chupungco's essay, and Lathrop's final response.
16 In his 'Hymns for Children', where is it rather a petition or prayer for parents and teachers. The first lines are: *'Come, Father, Son, and Holy Ghost,/To whom we for our children cry'* and the last *'In those whom up to thee we give,/Thine, wholly thine, to die and live':* Hymn XL. At the Opening of a School in Kingswood', at https://divinity.duke.edu/sites/divinity.duke.edu/files/documents/cswt/65_Hymns_for_Children_%281763%29.pdf   (p. 35)
17 Alister E. McGrath, *The Future of Christianity* (Oxford: Blackwell, 2002), 99.

2

Revolutionary Liturgy and the Prayer Book Tradition: What revolution?

Stephen Platten

There are moments in people's lives when new perceptions form or when their world is viewed from a dramatically different perspective. The distinguished philosopher of religion, and later Bishop of Durham, Dr Ian Ramsey, talked of moments when the 'penny drops' or the 'ice breaks'.[1] Somehow one's world, at least some aspect of it, is re-fashioned. Just one such moment remains vividly in my mind in relation to how I understood the power and significance of the liturgy. As members of staff at the former theological college in Lincoln, in the 1980s, we all welcomed a new lecturer in liturgy, one Robert Gribben. It was a twofold welcome since he would also be filling the slot of Lincoln's Methodist Ecumenical Lectureship. Gribben nurtured as a Methodist, was now de facto a minister in the Uniting Church in Australia.

Robert brought to his new role at Lincoln a panache and creativity admired by all. So, for example, almost everyone was helped to see the liturgical journey from

Candlemas to Easter in an utterly new light.[2] The dramatic contrasts in the use of colour for the seasons, the use of light and darkness and an imaginative choreography of the liturgy radically affected people's perception. It was a fascinating irony that catholic-minded Anglicans had their perceptions of the liturgy re-focused by someone who ostensibly came from a church that had come to birth through a sharp historical divorce from the Church of England, during the 18th century with the eventual birth of Methodism.

The impact of these new perceptions was sharply focused in one season after another, in different festivals and even sometimes in the manner in which the daily office and eucharist were celebrated. It was during this time at Lincoln that the Paschal Vigil and Eucharist were first reintroduced in their fullness with the dramatic contrasts using different genres of music interspersed between the solemn readings recounting creation and redemption. The college, in successive years, celebrated the Vigil after dark on Holy Saturday and next time at dawn on Easter Morning. An Ulster Anglican, who had never experienced such a celebration before, reflected that it was the most *missionary* service he had ever attended.

Gribben's impact must, of course, be partly put down to both his scholarship and to his extraordinary talent as a teacher. The phenomenon described, however, was also effectively part of a far wider shift whose roots are traceable back well before the nineteenth century. In the twentieth century, however, a shift, a burgeoning liturgical movement flowered. It effectively ushered in a liturgical revolution. Such a revolution is not unique to liturgical nor indeed even to theological development. In 1962, Thomas Kuhn, the American physicist, historian and philosopher of science, wrote a ground-breaking book[3] about the nature of scientific development. He argued that, over the centuries, science has continued within one paradigm and without significant change; he called this *normal science*. Every so often, however, a series of breakthroughs, coming together, result in a paradigm shift, this heralds *revolutionary* science: examples would include the Copernican revolution in astronomy, Newton's work on gravity and the laws of motion, Darwin and Wallace on evolution and Einstein on relativity. Many of the old patterns either break down or morph, producing a new paradigm.

Liturgical development can, to some degree, be seen in a similar light. Effectively the first revolution was the earliest *evolution* of the liturgy, as we now understand it, in sub apostolic times. Elements of liturgical worship appear to be caught in the aspic of the New Testament, but it was in the *Didache* and other texts within sub-apostolic literature that this development emerged and contributed to Patristic patterns. Another limited example would include the *Iconoclastic* controversy in the east, with the subsequent restoration of icons at the second Council of Nicaea in 787.

Putting to one side the slow but dramatic drifting apart of the eastern and western traditions, following the schism of 1054, the next liturgical revolution must be that provoked by the sixteenth century Reformation.

45

This led to the development of new liturgical patterns and theological matrices. Within the Church of England, Thomas Cranmer was effectively the architect of a liturgical revolution. Here indeed was the wellspring of the 'Prayer Book Tradition' which this book explores. Using Kuhn's instrument of analysis, the western catholic tradition (albeit developing, changing and adapting to local custom) was *normal liturgy*. Cranmer's work in the 1549 and 1552 prayer books informed the basis of *revolutionary liturgy*. Later revisions (notably in 1662) stood within a tradition which for Anglicans, all the way through until the mid-twentieth century, would now become the accepted pattern. Thus for the Church of England and in the main for the developing family of 'Anglican' Churches, this once again became *normal liturgy*.

Later would emerge, to some degree from the same tradition, Methodist liturgical worship including the Covenant Service. Other more clearly Protestant liturgical patterns included, ironically, the evolution of patterns of worship amongst the Society of Friends.[4]

Anglican liturgical worship, then, was born out of a revolutionary matrix and a matrix against which more Catholic-minded theologians in the nineteenth century would react, and indeed even earlier amongst some Caroline divines, Lancelot Andrews being an interesting exemplar.[5]

The Liturgical Movement

The next example of *revolutionary liturgy* effectively arose from the so-called liturgical movement. It was, perhaps, in Germany that the most crucial work emerged. The Beuronese Congregation of Benedictines, founded in the mid-nineteenth century, under the influence of Solesmes Abbey in France and Maredsous in Belgium were pioneers. This same congregation refounded the Benedictine Abbey at Maria Laach in the Rhineland just before the turn of the twentieth century. Here the key figures were Dom Odo Casel, and the diocesan priest, Romano Guardini. Casel was the crucial figure in underpinning the theological foundations with his so-called 'mystery theology';[6] he sought to re-establish a rich understanding of the eucharist and the manner in which the eucharist both 'makes' and 'manifests' the Church, and is indeed also the foundation of the individual's living and praying of the gospel. Again, in a most subtle manner, the liturgy is ineluctably *missionary* in its performance.

So, here were the seeds for a revolution, a new flowering in liturgical theology, but here too began innovative and constructive practice. These two elements together, provoked a new attitude to both the structuring and performance of the liturgy. In Kuhn's terms, here was a clear paradigm shift, a revolution. It was a shift that would be manifested and flower most richly in the middle years of the twentieth century, and notably with the Second Vatican Council.

Vatican II and liturgical renewal

It is almost impossible to exaggerate the overall impact of the Second Vatican Council not only on the Roman Catholic Church, but also in its 'knock on' effects within other Christian communions.[7] The key Council documents relating to worship and liturgy were the *Dogmatic Constitution on the Church in the Modern World*,[8] the *Decree on Ecumenism*[9], the *Dogmatic Constitution on the Nature of the Church*[10] and the *Constitution on the Sacred Liturgy*[11]: all have been foundational. In an institutional/ ecclesiastical sense they are further manifestations of the paradigm shift already noted. The translation of the liturgy into the vernacular was but the beginning. The recovery of the eucharist as a *celebration* of the entire eucharistic community over which the priest *presides* led to the wholesale re-ordering of churches across the world. The revised liturgies for Holy Week and the Triduum sparked off completely new understandings of the nature of Christian worship, not only amongst Roman Catholics but far more broadly.

Even within the Roman Catholic Church itself, these revisions and changes have not been uncontroversial. The pontificate of Francis has thus far augured well for a recovery of the Vatican II conciliar spirit. Nonetheless, despite these criticisms and critiques, the centralised patterns of authority within the Church have meant that such changes have been universally received.[12] The recent over-literal revised version of the liturgy is a relatively small (albeit highly controversial) shift in contrast to the Vatican II reforms.[13]

Piero Marini was the head of the Office for the Liturgical Celebrations of the Supreme Pontiff from 1987-2007. As personal secretary to Archbishop Annibale Bugnini, he was closely involved in the work of the *Concilium* which was charged with the task of implementing liturgical reform. He later became secretary of the reconfigured *Congregation for Divine Worship*. Marini has documented this entire process in his book describing the development of reform.[14] He notes towards the end of his book, that the *Congregation for Divine Worship* changed its name once again in 1975 to the *Congregation for Divine Worship and the Discipline of the Sacraments*. This was probably one of the first signs of a tendency to return to a preconciliar mindset that has for years now characterised the Curia's approach. As more and more time passes since the Second Vatican Council, an event charged with such hope and renewal, its distinctive contribution seems to be increasingly questioned.[15]

John Baldovin, in his useful response to this critical backlash, reviews a number of different commentators who have questioned the reforms. He concludes:

> ...with regard to the Church's worship there is no going back. Antiquarianism can take many forms and today it seems often to assume that of nostalgia for a beautiful mediaeval dream of a liturgy, a liturgy that took place in the

Ages of Faith. That world – and therefore that liturgy – are gone. It will do no good to try to retrieve them.[16]

Interestingly enough, the Church of England's Liturgical Commission, established by the Church Assembly to review liturgical provision, preceded Vatican II by some eight years. It was set up in 1955 to look to the renewal of worship. Again, the work of the Commission would build upon earlier insights, and notably Anglican scholarship from earlier in the century. Henry de Candole and Gabriel Hebert both introduced some of the work of the mainland continental pioneers, notably Odo Casel and Lambert Beauduin.

Hebert had been influenced by the work of F. D. Maurice. In his book *Liturgy and Society,* Hebert laid out the foundations of his thought, drawing widely on the work of mainland continental theologians. Worship was, he was clear, central to Christian life since the Christian religion is not simply an individualised and private religion. Hebert was concerned to recover the corporate nature of worship; it is the liturgy which identifies the nature of the Church. This combination of a recovery of the corporate nature of worship with the realisation that worship was one of the foundations of the *Parish and People Movement,* which in itself encouraged the development of what later became known as the Parish Communion Movement. Indeed, Hebert's other key book at this point was titled simply *The Parish Communion.* Christopher Irvine comments:

Further theoretical and practical consideration regarding the programme for the renewal of worship were offered in the essays contained in Hebert's symposium *The Parish Communion* (1937), which was arguably the greatest influence on the worshipping life of the Church of England during the middle decades of the twentieth century.[17]

It was undoubtedly this movement that helped restore the Eucharist to its central role within the life of the Church of England. This itself heralded the need for a proper return to liturgical study and liturgical reform. Following reports, then, on the place of the Book of Common Prayer and of saints in the Anglican tradition, a course was set fair for the future. The Church of England acted with wisdom in not *replacing* the Prayer Book with new rites, but maintaining instead that the Book of Common Prayer remains a key repository for Anglican theology, following the principle of *Lex Orandi, Lex Credendi*. Indeed, it was for this reason that its first collected book of revised liturgies was deliberately titled *The Alternative Services Book*.

The first Liturgical Commission included a number of estimable scholars including Ronald Jasper, Geoffrey Willis, E.C. Ratcliff, Geoffrey Cuming, Colin Buchanan and Austin Farrer. The immediate output of the Commission was a set or *series* (as they were known) of experimental rites in separate booklets. Services from the 'deposited' Prayer Book of 1928 were authorised for use and published as Series I. The first entirely new rites in traditional language were titled Series II and the later set of liturgies in modern language became Series III. It would be an edited version of various of these that would be published as the one volume Alternative Services Book in 1980. Twenty years later, a very significantly revised set of liturgies were published as *Common Worship*. These liturgies were the beneficiaries of significant work completed between the publication of the *Alternative Service Book* and the entire corpus of new rites.[18] The final volume of *Common Worship* – Ordination Rites – was published in 2007. But still, the first set of revised rites was a remarkable achievement, although without unfairly deprecating the ASB, undoubtedly, *Common Worship* was a very significant advance on the earlier revision, and benefited from the most imaginative strands of the 'paradigm shift' outlined earlier.

The supplementary volumes focusing on *Festivals* and *Times and Seasons* recovered much of the best traditional material, reaching back to the Patristic Period but it also included much entirely original work. Both the language of this new material and the choreography of the rites offered a richness, a variety and an imagination which has helped transform liturgical practice across the Church of England.

Concealed within all this, however, is one central irony which bears directly on the Prayer Book tradition. The new rites came together under the title *Common Worship*, but there is such variety and permissiveness about their practical use that it has led some to describe the new volume as a 'directory of worship' rather than a Book of Common Prayer. In a most interesting article written to celebrate the three hundred and fiftieth anniversary of the Book of Common Prayer, Paul Bradshaw adverts to the fact that this loss of common practice has a longer history than even the past half century. He points out that 'the first English Prayer Book of 1549 ... (expressed the intention) ... that 'all the realm shall have but one use.'[19] A parliamentary Act of Uniformity was applied on each occasion that a new rite was produced in the sixteenth and seventeenth centuries. Bradshaw indicates how the politics of the Church of England pointed liturgical usage in multi-various directions, from very early on in the twentieth century, beginning with the ritualist controversy, then through the debates on the 1928 Prayer Book. So, after Parliament's rejection of the 1928 book, Bradshaw notes:

> The bishops themselves were partially responsible for encouraging the first of these (deviations) when in 1929 they put out the statement that 'during the present emergency and until further order be taken', they would not 'regard as inconsistent with loyalty to the principles of the Church of England the use of such additions or deviations' as fell within the limits of the 1928 proposals.[20]

Bradshaw concludes:

> there is much more to be said for a shared liturgical experience than is often heard nowadays, when the greater elasticity envisaged by the Letters of Business in 1906 seems to have been stretched to breaking point.[21]

This, then, is a salutary reminder. It resonates with that fear expressed by Guéranger in the 1840s about liturgical variety. We are all the beneficiaries of a hitherto unknown liturgical imagination and variety. At the same time, however, in moving from church to church we may rarely encounter precisely the same liturgy. This is even true to some extent within the Roman Catholic Church with choice of eucharistic prayers and other variable material, but within that communion there remains a tightly drawn compass of doctrine expressed in the *Catechism* and mediated by the Magisterium. Anglicanism, which prefers a *Lex Orandi, Lex Credendi* approach to worship and belief, will find it increasingly difficult to express an agreed doctrinal tradition, without careful reflection upon the kaleidoscopic nature of its liturgical rites.

Recovering a sense of history

As we have already noted, there was a sense of renaissance as well as innovation within this modern liturgical revolution. Much historical liturgical scholarship was radical in its impact. Perhaps the shift to westward celebration of the eucharist is the most potent example here.[22] The accretions of the Middle Ages (some of which bear a great richness in themselves) had obscured many of the theological origins of both the eucharist and other sacraments. Some of the most interesting revivals and rediscoveries here relate to the rites of Christian initiation. The tradition of mystagogical catechesis, relating baptism and confirmation (seen as parts of one rite) to the paschal mysteries are particularly vivid in their impact. The catechumens set out on Ash Wednesday to be catechised – trained like athletes – as they prepare for the glories but also the exigencies of Holy Week and Easter. The work of the Jesuit theologian, Father Edward Yarnold S.J. was very influential here,[23] inasmuch as he was a pioneer in rediscovering the power and practical impact of the early rites.

This specific area of research helped give birth to the Roman Catholic *Rite of Christian Initiation of Adults*. This catechetical approach allows people (it has been adapted for children too) to join a group and gradually learn and be inducted into the key elements of Christian belief in their own time and at their own rate. Hence, there can be a rolling pattern which is repeated and people may join and prepare for baptism and confirmation at different points along this continuous journey.

Anglicans too have embraced the catechetical movement, and the so-called *Pilgrim Course* is influenced by this approach.[24] The catechetical approach allows for a *dramatic performance* of the sacraments. In a contemporary rite derived from the catechetical movement, as in the primitive Church, the preferred time for baptism is Easter and at the Paschal vigil, and so at the heart of the Paschal mysteries. As catechumens (candidates) approach baptism, they are wearing their everyday clothes, albeit not overclad. The priest either immerses them fully, or they stand within a large font (as seen in the baptisteries of late antiquity). They are plunged three times into the water, in the name of Father, Son and Holy Spirit. They are 'drowned', taken down into the tomb with Christ only to be raised with him. The neophytes (those just baptised) then change into an outfit entirely of pure white which symbolises their new status within the resurrection life of the Church. Sometimes, if the church building is close to a river, there may indeed be an attempt to regain the resonances of Christ's own baptism in the Jordan, by John the Baptist, by total immersion in the river.[25]

The prodigious use of oil within the liturgy has equally been recovered and given new currency across all traditions within the Church. At baptism and confirmation, the oil of catechumens and chrism are both used, and the oil of healing is used in the anointing of the sick. This usage has also brought the 'Mass of the Oils' on Maundy Thursday back into the mainstream Christian calendar. At this eucharist, generally in the cathedral, the diocesan bishop blesses each of the three oils. At this same service, deacons, priests and bishops re-affirm their ordination vows and laity are encouraged to attend to emphasise the fullness of God's Church.

This recovery of earlier patterns has been complemented by a similarly innovative approach to the seasons of Lent and Easter, Advent and Christmas. Within the Church of England, during the revision process, material was gathered together within two main volumes for these seasons.[26] These volumes have since become part of the library of liturgical material included within the wider heading of *Common Worship*. The increasing popularity of Advent Carol Processions and Epiphany processions is another manifestation of this double process of recovery and innovation. Throughout, a rich treasury of seasonal material is available for all feasts and special celebrations.

The Christian journey

As we have already seen, with the advent of the *Pilgrim Course*, the image of the Christian life as a journey has become an increasingly important metaphor. It is a metaphor with a good pedigree even within the Church of England. In the confirmation rite of the Book of Common Prayer, the words used at the 'laying on of hands' capture the spirit of the Christian journey perfectly:

> Defend, O Lord, this thy Child (or this thy Servant) with thy heavenly grace, that *he* may continue thine for ever; and daily increase

in thy Holy Spirit, more and more, until *he* come unto thine everlasting Kingdom. Amen.

In *Common Worship*, the prayer is retained, but is now said by everyone. It reminds all present that this rite is but one further episode along the road of the Christian life. Frequently now, dioceses are including cathedral confirmation services which are themselves 'pilgrim', progressive or stational rites. There will be a progression from the font, the place of entry into God's Church, through to the place of the laying on of hands and finally, to the place of communion, where the entire congregation is encouraged to move into the eastern part of the church (that part of the building where we often remember Christ's continuing intercession for all of us). They will receive communion standing and so, they receive it 'in solidarity'. This reminds all that our creation and redemption is not an act of God purely of an individual nature, but instead places our communion within the redemption of all humanity through what New Testament theologians have sometimes described as the 'Christ-event'. Humanity is created and redeemed 'in solidarity'.

Pilgrimage has itself also become more popular within cathedrals. Their shrines are now often the focus or destination of the pilgrimage. Arrival in the cathedral is celebrated in a liturgical act as a *liminal* moment, a crossing of a new threshold and thus an opportunity for the renewal and deepening of a Christian's life and witness. Often specific commemorations of saints can offer a focus for this aspect of liturgical observance.[27] The *camino*, the road /route (or series of routes to Santiago de Compostela (in north west Spain) is the most dramatic and populous of all pilgrim routes. Much literature is now available and even novels have captured the spirit of the journey.[28]

This recovery of pilgrimage and journeying is part of a wider and different aspect of the 'liturgical revolution' in the use of movement, space and gesture. So, there is now an encouragement in the baptism rite, for example, at the point where the candidate states: 'I turn to Christ' to see the candidate physically turning in a new direction. The giving of a candle at baptism also offers an opportunity for candidates to retain a memory of their baptism and perhaps also light the candle annually on the anniversary of their baptism.

Similarly, in the ordination rite, there is now a careful choreography to indicate the drama of the ordinands' commitment at this moment of grace. So, deacons begin seated within the congregation at the start of the rite and are 'called' out from the wider congregation for this specific ministry. Priestly ordinations, in contrast, however, begin with the deacons entering as part of the procession of clergy. The calling this time is to another order, but within the wider 'sacred ministry' of the Church. Sometimes ordinands will prostrate themselves (another example of recovering a practice from earlier patterns) as a sign of their offering. Often a chalice and paten are given to priests. Bishops receive their pastoral staffs from the archbishop or senior consecrator as they are ordained. Such symbolism enriches the drama of the rites.

Occasional offices

It is perhaps too rarely acknowledged just how formative the ministry of the Church of England (notably through the use of the Book of Common Prayer) has been upon English society. Certainly the marriage rite has had a significant impact on patterns of family life over a period of more than four hundred and fifty years.[29] With the increasing popularity of other venues, and notably secular buildings including hotels and stately homes, it would have been easy for the Church to lose its place in the proper formation of married life. For this reason, and because the Marriage Measure 2008 was also on the horizon, the Archbishops' Council, in 2007, set up the *Weddings Project*. The results enabled a teaching project to be established throughout the church to encourage clergy to set out more attractively the possibilities and benefits of marriage in church.[30]

More recently, a further project offers similar support to clergy and laity both with regard to baptisms (frequently known as 'christening') and also funerals.[31] A very large proportion of funerals are still conducted by Church of England clergy simply by dint of establishment: everyone in England lives in an Anglican parish and has the right to request a church funeral. Similarly, all who so desire may ask for baptism for themselves or for their children if they live within a particular parish. The 'birth and death project' seeks to assist and encourage parish clergy in both these areas and indeed to give proper and clear access to laity within a parish. The renewal of liturgy increasingly offers opportunities for shaping a rite to convey both theological depth and pastoral care.

Missionary liturgy

Over the years, different keywords gain popular currency and this is as true in theology as it is in other disciplines. At one point, *ministry* was the focal term and in recent years the emphasis has moved to *mission*.[32] The shift is understandable in a climate which is not overfriendly to religion, Christianity and the Church. Certainly it is an imperative placed upon God's Church to pass on the gospel message as contemporary 'apostles'; the word *Mass* itself implies mission since it derives from the dismissal at the end of the eucharist (the Latin dismissal is *ite missa est*.). We are dismissed to take the gospel to the wider world. Mission, however, is often seen rather narrowly and this has had its impact upon the resources and emphasis placed upon the liturgy. The assumption is that the liturgy is not missionary in nature or function. Although it is true that the offering of the liturgy, the *Opus Dei*, can never be utilitarian, since we worship through God's grace and as a natural response to God's gift in that grace, nevertheless the performance of the liturgy, if performed adequately, can effectively be a missionary act.

So much of what has been received through what we have described as the 'liturgical revolution', the *new paradigm*, has itself increased the missionary power of the liturgy. Staying with this same image of *normal* and *revolutionary* liturgy, Cranmer in crafting the Book of Common Prayer, presumably also had a 'missionary impulse' in mind even though he might not have used those words. The impact of the Reformation on his theology was such as to create a dynamic in his liturgical scholarship. He aimed at bringing the laity more effectively within the compass of 'common prayer' and also at re-capturing a greater sense of the penitential throughout his new liturgical diet. Thus, the prayer book tradition was itself born out of a *revolution*. In appreciating this, we can see that tradition is itself patient of development and subject to further revolution – as indeed in the case of the 20th century liturgical movement. Perhaps the question with which we are left is 'Is the prayer book tradition still clearly identifiable and indeed resonant within the contemporary liturgical patterns currently existing throughout the Anglican Communion?'

Endnotes

1. See, for example, Ian Ramsey, *Models for Divine Activity* (London: SCM Press, 1973) and Ian Ramsey, *Models and Mystery* (Oxford: Oxford University Press, 1964).
2. cf. Rite on Time: Robert Gribben, *Recovering the Roots of Christian Worship Today* (Melbourne: Forum, 1993).
3. Thomas S. Kuhn, *The Structure of Scientific Revolutions* (Chicago, IL: University of Chicago Press, 1962).

4 Interesting insights into this counter-intuitive notion of Quaker liturgy are collected together in Pink Dandelion, *The Liturgies of Quakerism* (Aldershot: Ashgate, 2005).
5 cf. Stephen Platten and Christopher Wood, eds, *Comfortable Words: Polity, Piety and the Book of Common Prayer* (London: SCM Press, 2012), especially 49-68.
6 Odo Casel, *The Mystery of Christian Worship* (London: DLT, 1962). Casel's work is notoriously opaque and the translation here does not help. A interpretation of Casel's theology lies at the heart of George Guiver, *Pursuing the Mystery* (Mirfield: Mirfield Publishing, 1996).
7 See here Stephen Platten, 'Selling a Tiara, Giving a Ring: Paul VI's Jewelled Legacy', *Theology*, 119 (2006): 407-416.
8 Vatican II; The Conciliar and Post-Conciliar Documents, vol. 1 (New York: Costello, rev. ed. 1988) 903ff.
9 op. cit., pp. 452ff.
10 op. cit., pp. 350ff.
11 op. cit., pp. 1ff.
12 For an excellent survey see Piero Marini, *A Challenging Reform: Realizing the Vision of the Liturgical Renewal* (Collegeville, MN: Liturgical Press, 2007). Archbishop Marini was head of the Office for Liturgical Celebrations of the Supreme Pontiff (1987-2007). See also John F. Baldovin, *Reforming the liturgy: A Response to the Critics* (Collegeville, MN: Liturgical Press, 2008), for a balanced review of critics of the reforms.
13 But here cf. Gerald O'Collins with John Wilkins, *Lost in Translation, The English Language and the Catholic Mass* (Collegeville, MN: Liturgical Press, 2017).
14 Marini, ad loc.
15 Marini, op. cit., p.157.
16 Baldovin, op. ci.t, p. 157.
17 Christopher Irvine, ed., They Shaped our Worship: Essays on Anglican Liturgists (London: SPCK, 1998), 69. See also Christopher Irvine, Worship, Church and Society: An Exposition of the Work of Arthur Gabriel Hebert to Mark the Centenary of the Society of the Sacred Mission (Kelham) of Which He was a Member (London: Canterbury Press, 2012).
18 cf. for example *Lent, Holy Week and Easter* (London: CHP, 1984), *The Promise of his Glory* (London: CHP, 1990), *New Patterns for Worship* (London: CHP, 2002), *Enriching the Christian Year*, (London: SPCK, 1993), *Patterns for Worship* (London: CHP, 1989).
19 Paul Bradshaw, 'Liturgical Development: From Common Prayer to Uncommon Worship', Platten and Woods, eds, *Comfortable Words*, 121.
20 Ibid. pp. 126-127.
21 Ibid. p. 131.
22 Interestingly enough a certain element of liturgical fundamentalism crept in at this point. Every altar in every church and every chapel must become westward facing. It is clear, however, that some buildings are so designed to preclude anything other than an eastward celebration. Furthermore, there is a perfectly respectable theological raison d'etre for such a practice as priest and people look forward, offering praise to the transcendent God, who in the glorified Christ is ever before us and interceding for us.
23 Edward Yarnold S.J., *The Awe Inspiring Rites of Initiation* (Collegeville, MN: Liturgical Press, Collegeville, 1971, 1994).

24 Pilgrim Course: A Course for the Christian Journey (London: CHP, 2013).
25 The present author was indeed prevailed upon to baptise in the sea at Spittal, just south of Berwick-upon-Tweed, where the parish church is just 100 yards from the beach cf. *Berwick Advertiser* 14th October 2016 and also Newcastle Diocesan Newspaper for October 2016.
26 *Lent, Holy Week and Easter* and *The Promise of His Glory, New Patterns for Worship, Enriching the Christian Year*.
27 One of the most extensive examples of this was *Pilgrims' Way*, in 1997, a celebration/commemoration of the arrival of St Augustine in Canterbury and the deaths of St Columba on Iona. Pilgrims travelled from Rome across to Canterbury and then four separate routes radiated from Canterbury, finally arriving in Derry, close to the birthplace of Columba.
28 See David Lodge, *Therapy* (London: Secker and Warburg, 1995).
29 Platten and Woods, *Comfortable Words*, especially 1-19.
30 cf. www.yourchurchwedding.org
31 cf. www.churchgrowth.org
32 For a moderate rant on this subject, see Stephen Platten, 'The Grammar of Ministry and Mission', in *Theology*, 875 (2010): 348-356.

3

John Wesley's *Sunday Service*: A Methodist Urtext

Glen O'Brien

The nineteenth-century British Methodist statesman Hugh Price Hughes (1847-1902), in a rather effusive mood, once said he desired nothing more than that 'Methodism should be sufficiently elastic and comprehensive to satisfy every legitimate method of Christian worship.'[1] While that elastic has often stretched to breaking point, it is possible to affirm twin traditions in Methodism that combine a love for the *Book of Common Prayer* (BCP) with an enthusiasm for extemporary prayer and freedom of religious expression, often expressed by the term 'ordered liberty'. Wesley's 1784 'Sunday Service for the Use of the Methodists in North America' functions as an 'urtext', an original text to which other later liturgies have been compared, and a mode of transmission of Anglican liturgical heritage for Methodists and Uniting/United churches.[2] This paper will survey the use of the BCP as well as Wesley's Abridgment in British, Australian, and American Methodism and conclude with a brief reflection on the Uniting Church in Australia. Space does not allow discussion of the reception and use of the Sunday Service beyond the English-speaking countries discussed here.[3]

John Wesley's 'abridgment mania'

For John Wesley (1703-1791), the 1662 Prayer Book was a virtual *sine qua non* for Christian worship, though he did not hesitate to abridge it for use in both Britain and America. In Wesley's own lifetime, the many who found a new lease on life as a result of hearing the Gospel through the agency of a Methodist preacher or class leader were encouraged to attend the parish church and participate in its liturgy. Relatively few Methodists followed Wesley's pattern of attendance at the preaching house and class meeting coupled with Sunday morning attendance at the parish church. Nonetheless, the liturgy of the Church of England was brought into the heart of (at least Wesleyan) Methodism, both through the use of the *Book of Common Prayer* itself, and to a lesser extent through Wesley's Abridgment.

If I may paraphrase Wesley's stance on the relationship between Anglicanism and Methodism, it would be something like, 'the Methodists will leave the Church of England over my dead body.' And that is pretty much how it played out. He died (in 1791) and the Methodists left. The break, however, was neither decisive nor sudden (no official Minute ever recorded a decision to depart). In fact the question of the relationship of 'Wesleyan Methodism' to the Church of England dogged

Methodists well into the nineteenth century. Broadly speaking, there were 'Church Methodists' who thought of themselves as part of the Established Church and 'Chapel Methodists' who thought of themselves as an independent Dissenting body, sometimes even as a better kind of Anglicanism.

After Wesley had appointed Thomas Coke (1747-1814) as Superintendent of the work in America on 2 Sept 1784, he wrote to the American Methodists telling them that he had 'prepared a Liturgy little differing from that of the Church of England (I think, the best constituted national Church in the world), which I advise all the travelling preachers to use on the Lord's Day in all the congregations, reading the Litany only on Wednesdays and Fridays, and praying extempore on all other days. I also advise the elders to administer the Supper of the Lord, on every Lord's Day.'[4] Along with the newly ordained Richard Whatcoat (1736-1806) and Thomas Vasey (1742-1826), Coke delivered copies of the new prayer book to the preachers in America so that when the Methodist Episcopal Church was formed at the Christmas Conference of 1784, American Methodism was not left unfurnished with a liturgical resource.

Wesley wrote in the Preface, 'I believe there is no Liturgy in the world, either in ancient or modern language, which breathes more of a solid, scriptural, rational piety, than the *Common Prayer* of the Church of England: and though the main of it was compiled considerably more than two hundred years ago, yet is the language of it not only pure, but strong and elegant in the highest degree.'[5]

The overall length of the service was shortened. Feast days of saints were removed 'as answering no valuable end.' The Black Rubric in the Lord's Supper (explaining why communicants should kneel) was also removed. There were no references to clerical clothes, a practical matter, since the vast majority of his preachers dressed in street clothes. References to the *Book of Homilies* were also removed. Also gone were both the Nicene Creed and the Athanasian Creed with the latter's objectionable anathemas, some imprecatory Psalms 'highly improper for the mouths of a Christian congregation', readings from the Apocrypha (except Tobit 4:8-9 retained as an offertory sentence in the Lord's Supper).[6] References to the 'priest' are replaced by the terms 'minister', 'elder', and 'deacon.' Gone are the sung liturgical texts, provision for private baptisms, the language of baptismal regeneration by the Spirit, words of absolution, the use of a wedding ring in the marriage service, and the language of certainty of resurrection in the burial service.

Wesley's precise reasons for these omissions involves guesswork to some degree but it is clear that he stood in a long-standing Puritan tradition in suggesting these kinds of amendments. He had also studied the works of (and discussed with) Non-Juror authors, the abridgments and amendments they had made in seeking a liturgy of a more 'primitive' type. J. Ernest Rattenbury put Wesley's motives for his Abridgment down to his 'abridgments mania' in general ('he used nothing more vigorously than the blue pencil') as well as an expectation that an abridged Prayer Book would be more suited to a context in America that was both Puritan and anti-Anglican.[7] According to James White, 'Every page of the Sunday Service bears marks, not of a casual reviser, but of one who had read or heard the prayer book daily throughout eight decades, and who is determined to retain all that wore well and to discard only that which proved inadequate in his own experience.'[8]

Wesley first began to tinker with the BCP while a missionary in Georgia in 1736.[9] Two decades later at the Leeds Conference of 1755, Wesley was not inclined to defend the answers of sponsors in the baptismal ritual, the office of confirmation, the words of absolution in the visitation of the sick, nor the thanksgiving in the burial service. He also disavowed the damnatory clauses of the Athanasian Creed, reflecting his typically Pietist tolerance for allowing some degree of tolerance of heterodox opinions so long as one's heart was in the right place.[10]

Wesley was well aware of the revisions of the BCP that had been undertaken by Puritan writers such as Richard Baxter (1615-1691), as well as the liturgical revisions of William Whiston (1667-1752) and Thomas Deacon (1697-1753), both of whom he met while a student at Oxford. Non-Jurors like Deacon reached back to the Apostolic Constitutions (c. 380) to revive primitive Christianity (as they understood it) and this appealed to Wesley's idealisation of the early church period.[11]

In the 1940s, Frederick Hunter sought to identify the influence of Puritan ideas on Wesley's abridgment, particularly the 'Exceptions' given at the Savoy Conference of 1661, as recorded in Edmund Calamy's (1671-1732) *Abridgment of Mr. Baxter's History of His Life and Times* (1713) which Wesley had read in April 1754.[12] While many have followed this line of interpretation, Karen Westerfield Tucker is doubtful, seeing rather 'a general liturgical agenda, not necessarily identified with the Dissenting cause' and simply a reflection of 'the general tenor and trends extant in England in the late 18th century.'[13]

John Fletcher, an Anglican priest closely associated with Wesley and the Methodists, recommended revision in 1775, seeing the need for the 39 Articles to be 'rectified according to the purity of the gospel' and 'the most spiritual part of the Common Prayer' to be extracted, so that together with the Minutes of the Conference, these would form, next to the Bible, the authoritative canon of a Methodist church that was the daughter of its 'holy mother', the Church of England.[14] Wesley had a great deal of respect for Fletcher, whom he considered the holiest man in England and thus the best person to succeed him as leader of the Methodists. In 1775, Fletcher urged Wesley to use his influence to reform the church's liturgy.

> I love the Church of England, I hope, as much as you do. But I do not love her so as to take her blemishes for ornaments. You know, sir, that she is almost totally deficient in discipline, and she publicly owns it herself every Ash Wednesday. What are her spiritual courts in general, but a catch-penny? As for her doctrine,

although it is pure upon the whole, you know that some specks of Pelagian, Calvinian, and Popish dirt cleave to her articles, homilies, liturgy and rubricks. These specks could with care be taken off, and doing it in the circle of your influence might, sooner or later, provoke our superiors to godly jealousy and a complete reformation.[15]

All of this shows that when Wesley revised the Prayer Book in 1784, it was only the latest and most fully accomplished expression of a project he had been tinkering with for almost fifty years. Certain changes to the rituals for Baptism and Communion were made and there has been some debate over whether these were made by Wesley himself or by Thomas Coke.[16] Wesley conceded in a 1789 letter to Walter Churchey, 'Dr. Coke made two or three little alterations in the Prayer-Book without my knowledge. I took particular care throughout to alter nothing for altering' [sic] sake. In religion I am for as few innovations as possible. I love the old wine best.'[17] After the War of Independence, Anglicans in America also revised the Prayer Book beginning with drafts in 1786 and resulting in the 1789 *Book of Common Prayer of the Protestant Episcopal Church*. The compilers drew upon Wesley's earlier work and the changes are remarkably similar, including the deletion of the Athanasian Creed, as well as of the *Magnificat* and *Nunc dimittis* from the evening service.[18]

The *Sunday Service* in American Methodism

Though the 1784 abridgment is co-extensive with American Methodism, its fortunes were somewhat ill-fated. Frontier conditions in both America and Australia where literacy levels were often rudimentary at best made extemporaneous prayer a preferred option. This practical neglect of the Prayer Book was supplemented by the later rhetoric of revivalism with the rather mischievous conceit that extemporary prayer was more 'spiritual' than praying from a book. Let the dead letter Christians have their dead letter book while the Spirit-filled looked for a more Pentecostal outpouring upon their gatherings. The love feast on 1 January 1739 during which Wesley and over sixty of his Methodist colleagues had fallen to the ground in a swoon of religious ecstasy only to then stand and recite the opening lines of the *Te Deum* may be seen as a metaphorical ideal of a style of Methodist worship (enthusiasm mixed with formal liturgy) rarely arrived at.[19] The London edition of the Abridgement in 1786 was the last printed specifically for use in the American context.

Though a ritual section with services for the sacraments, marriage, burial, and ordination was provided for the American *Discipline*, the *Sunday Service* itself was set aside and almost forgotten until after the Civil War when it was again reissued under the influence of Thomas O. Summers.[20] Elements of the Sunday Service were incorporated into the Lord's Day services in the early part of the twentieth century but a more general appreciation for the American Methodist 'urtext' only occurred as a result of Methodist participation in the mid-twentieth-century Liturgical Movement. Even then, however, ecumenical resources were more determinative than the *Sunday Service* in shaping Methodist liturgical reforms.[21]

The twentieth century liturgical movement had a profoundly ecumenical outcome in that it saw different traditions rediscover elements of ancient liturgies and reinstate them into their own (for example epiclesis prayers and the eschatological aspects of the Great Thanksgiving). When I was at Asbury Theological Seminary in the late 1990s, there was little difference between the Methodist service of Holy Communion in Estes Chapel and the Catholic Mass in the Cathedral in Lexington. Back in Melbourne, when a concerned parishioner chided me for my use of 'Roman' elements in the Communion service, I pointed out that I was using the service of the *United Methodist Book of Worship*. Unconvinced, he saw this as no more than evidence that the American Methodists were 'going to Rome.' He was wrong, of course. What was really happening was that Catholics and Methodists had each revised their liturgies in a renewal movement, followed the developments in each other's churches, and found that they had arrived at a remarkable degree of convergence. Each had improved their own liturgies in a way that had led both to a renewal of their own traditions and to making an important contribution to ecumenism.

Following the 1939 union of the northern and southern Methodist Episcopal Churches (which had remained divided since 1845) along with the Methodist Protestant Church, the 1940 Conference of the newly-formed Methodist Church formed a Commission on Ritual and Orders of Worship to provide a new service book. *The Book of Worship for Church and Home* first appeared in 1945 with the caveat on its title page that it was 'for voluntary and optional use' and stated that 'Methodism has never been a liturgical church, but it always has had fixed forms to guide it in its recurrent acts of public worship.'[22] These fixed forms are traced from the early Methodists worshipping in their parish churches, supplementing participation in the BCP with the distinctive gatherings of the Societies. The 1784 urtext is, of course, recalled, though with the admission that it 'was never very widely used in America' and was 'supplanted in a few years' by the ritual sections of the Discipline appearing in 1792.[23] 'Methodism has thus a twofold tradition of worship – both liturgical and free. It is liturgical in conducting its recurrent stated services with reverence according to officially adopted forms; it is free in its ability to use extempore prayer, to bend each service to the glorifying of God and to the bringing of his saving grace unto men [sic].'[24]

The current *United Methodist Book of Worship* (1992) explicitly traces its origins to the 1784 *Sunday Service,* and acknowledges the Anglican liturgical heritage of American Methodism.[25] The twin concerns for both order and freedom are stated in its description of the basic pattern of Sunday worship. 'While the freedom and diversity of United Methodist worship are greater than can be represented by a single order of worship, United Methodists also affirm a heritage of order and the importance of the specific guidance and modelling that an order of worship provides.'[26] It has to be asked to what extent this is a statement of high theological principle and to what extent it is a pragmatic compromise between competing traditions, often at loggerheads with one another. My worship professor at Asbury Theological Seminary, Professor Donald Boyd told me that on one occasion in the Estes Chapel, when a United Methodist celebrant made the sign of the cross, the retired Wesleyan Methodist District Superintendent sitting beside him leaned across and muttered, 'Well, that was unnecessary!' Many a Methodist pastor has discovered that what she learned in worship class at seminary isn't received with as much enthusiasm in the rural churches of Ohio, Michigan, or Iowa.

American Wesleyan-Holiness churches showed an even greater dislike for formal liturgies though the larger groups all provided rituals which, though they were not mandatory, evidence their Methodist origins. The joint Wesleyan Church / Free Methodist Church hymn book *Hymns of Faith and Life* included the Holy Communion service of both denominations and the words of institution stand squarely in the BCP tradition. The Free Methodist service even retained the *Gloria Patri*. The book included eighty-six congregational readings designed to be read responsively, as antiphons, or in unison.[27]

The extent to which these were used in Wesleyan and Free Methodist congregations would be difficult to determine but it would be fair to say that a 'free' style of worship has always been the preferred mode in Holiness churches. Apart from the fact that Communion was only mandated quarterly and that even this level of frequency often went unmet, Wesleyan-Holiness pastors often preferred to make up their own service and were not well instructed in the proper use of the officially provided services, let alone their historical origins in the BCP.

It is frequently stated by Wesleyans that the 1968 merger between the Wesleyan Methodist Church and the Pilgrim Holiness Church had the effect of making the resultant Wesleyan Church less Methodist and more revivalist. This is a common sense observation, I suppose, though I am not aware of any research that has conclusively demonstrated it. African American Methodist churches have had their own distinctive style of worship but in liturgical resources have followed the pattern set in the United Methodist Church of pursuing the principle of ordered liberty. The 1984 *Book of Worship* of the African Methodist Episcopal Church drew on resources developed within the Consultation on Christian Union, and includes such elements as the Doxology (sung twice), the *Gloria Patri*, and the Lord's Prayer, designed to be embedded in what Vinton R. Anderson describes as 'an ordered spiritual journey.'[28]

The *Sunday Service* in British Methodism

The London edition of 1786 gained a new lease on life as *The Sunday Service of the Methodists in His Majesty's*

Dominions in that same year and then, in 1788, more simply (and less imperially) as *The Sunday Service of the Methodists*. The fact that it was reissued twenty-seven times between 1792 and 1882, averaging a new edition every three and half years, testifies to its wide use among nineteenth-century British Methodists. The 1795 Plan of Pacification forms a bridge between Methodism as a movement fully aligned with the Church of England and one that moved in a Dissenting direction. It granted sacramental privileges to its own preachers, though only under certain conditions, insisted that Methodist services should not clash with the parish church times and that either the *Book of Common Prayer* or Wesley's Abridgment should be used.

British Wesleyans used both throughout the nineteenth century, though less so in the smaller villages than in the cities and towns. In 1837, Thomas Jackson was even prepared to lay a wager that if anyone should attend a morning service in any Wesleyan setting and 'not find the liturgy or the lessons read, I will forfeit five pounds.'[29] In the Centenary celebrations of 1839, Jackson claimed that the 'incomparable Liturgy' was 'regularly used in many of the chapels in England and in all the Mission chapels of the West Indies. Translations of it have been made by Wesleyan missionaries into various languages for the use of their congregations, especially in the East. It is always used in the Lord's Supper at home and abroad.'[30]

Adam Clarke reverenced the BCP 'next to the Bible' as 'the depository of the true religion of Christ... Had it not been, under God, for this blessed book, the Liturgy of the English Church, I verily believe Methodism had never existed... I see plainly that, where we read these prayers, our congregations become better settled, better edified, and put farther out of the reach of false doctrine.' He then expressed a preface for the original over Wesley's Abridgment – 'Introduce the Church Service in God's name, not in any abridgment, but in the genuine original.'[31] Jabez Bunting also preferred the *Book of Common Prayer* over Wesley's abridgment and took strong exception to Wesley's abridgment of the Psalms as well as the reason given for the abridgment.[32] In 1812, Robert Newtown found the majority of Methodist chapels in the London West circuit to be using the BCP.[33] David Chapman comes to the conclusion that in nineteenth-century British Methodism, the *Book of Common Prayer* was given wider use than *The Sunday Service of the Methodists*, and 'that it was not until 1882 that they were both supplanted by *Public Prayers and Services*.'[34] This latter book was based directly on the 1662 Prayer Book, not Wesley's Abridgment, and included Morning Prayer, the Litany, and Holy Communion.

Love of the BCP was mostly found among the larger body of Wesleyan Methodists. Hugh Bourne, the founder of the Primitive Methodist Church, found it rather popish and left an Anglican service alarmed after the singing of the *Te Deum*.[35] None of the 'minor Methodists' ever prescribed the BCP or its abridgement. Nor did they provide their own (non-compulsory) service books, at least not until the 1860s, leaving the arrangement of the service entirely up to the minister.[36] The non-Wesleyan service books do not carry signs of a direct lineage to the BCP in the way that the Wesleyan book did. After the union of most British Methodists in 1932 (thirty years after union had taken place in Australia) the *Book of Offices* appeared in 1936.[37] It included a Communion service very dependent on the BCP tradition as well as a more simple service more like those of the non-Wesleyan precedent churches. The Litany from the 1882 book had entirely disappeared, though the Morning Prayer remained that of the BCP.

In 1975, *The Methodist Service Book* appeared and along with it the service of Morning Prayer had disappeared.[38] Borrowing the language of 1784 it offered a 'Sunday Service", though this was more a result of following the International Consultation on English Texts rather than John Wesley. It presupposed Holy Communion as a norm for Sunday Worship though a supplementary 'Service without the Lord's Supper' was also offered.[39] The current British *Methodist Worship Book* (1999) is described as 'the latest in a succession of Methodist service books which can be traced back to John Wesley's *The Sunday Service* (1784).'[40] It contains ten orders for 'Holy Communion', one each for Advent, Christmas and Epiphany, Lent and Passiontide, Easter (including Ascension), the Day of Pentecost and Times of Renewal in the Life of the Church, three for 'Ordinary Seasons', and a final one for 'in a Home or Hospital.'[41] While all of these successive books may be seen as constituting some kind of 'norm", A. Raymond George concedes that

'British Methodists have shown considerable freedom in varying from the norms.'[42]

The Sunday Service in Australia

Australian Methodism has its origins in a period of transition for Wesleyan Methodists as they moved from being a movement closely aligned to the Church of England to a church with a more Nonconformist identity (though 'Nonconformist' is something of a misnomer in a colonial setting where there was, at least officially, no Established Church). Most histories record the formation of class meetings by Thomas Bowden and John Hosking in 1812 as the beginning of Methodist work in New South Wales but this should be pushed back a little earlier to the work of Edward Eagar in the Windsor District from 1811. Eager, an ex-convict and converted forger, assisted the Anglican clergy in the reading of the Prayer Book service in outlying areas.[43]

The tensions between church and chapel Methodists played out in settler societies such as early NSW. The Rev. Samuel Leigh (1785-1852) fell out with all of his ministerial colleagues over his refusal to allow Methodist services at times that conflicted with Anglican Morning Prayer. This loyalty to the Anglican system was also reflected in the collegial relationship Leigh had with Anglican chaplain, the Rev William Cowper (1810-1902).[44]

The *Handbook of the Laws and Regulations of the Australasian Wesleyan Methodist Church* (1877) insisted on the use of either the BCP or Wesley's Abridgement. It then noted that this regulation was 're-enacted in 1839, so far as it respects England', the last clause perhaps suggesting that exceptions might be made in the Antipodes.[45] While extemporary prayer and a 'revival' style were very prominent among Methodists in nineteenth-century Australia, there were also instances where the more formal liturgy was utilised. Local Aboriginal people looked on no doubt with curiosity as Joseph Orton read 'the liturgy' at the home of early Melbourne pioneer John Batman on 24 April 1836 with responses led by 'James Simpson, Esq.'[46]

In 1877, the *Laws and Regulations* requested all chapels to 'be furnished with hassocks, or with kneeling-boards, so that every excuse may be taken away from those who persist in the irreverent and unscriptural custom of sitting while at prayer.'[47] D'Arcy Wood describes Australian Methodist worship as derived from the British pattern where the sacramental services followed the BCP tradition closely but non-sacramental services were left up to the individual preferences of local ministers and congregations.[48] The *Methodist Hymn Book of 1933* was quite high church in tone with its Psalms, ancient canticles and sung responses sitting alongside eighteenth and nineteenth-century hymns.[49]

The BCP tradition was certainly evident at Queen's College under the leadership of its first master, Edward H. Sugden. Even before a chapel was constructed in 1890 (in the Oxford college style), the students were led by the Master through the Morning Prayer service in the college hall via the 1882 *Public Prayers and Services,* a book very close in content to the 1662 Prayer Book.[50] The tradition was continued under the chaplaincy of Colin Williams from 1959-1962 using the 1936 *Book of Offices*. Robert Gribben remembers the heady atmosphere at Queen's in 1961 when under the influence of the liturgical movement 'the older, Wesleyan tradition' of Sugden was revived with Morning Prayer sung on Sundays, the neglected chants of the 1933 *Methodist Hymn Book* put to good use and a Latin anthem composed by Samuel Wesley (son of Charles) sung by a choir led by D'Arcy Wood. The ABC recorded a service during this period and even released an LP recording whose liner notes referred to Methodism's long-standing use of Anglican forms.[51]

The Prayer Book tradition in the Uniting Church in Australia is continued in *Uniting in Worship 2* (UiW2, the 2005 successor to the 1988 book).[52] As astute an Anglican observer as Stephen Burns has eulogised the value of UiW2 while Uniting Church ministers themselves all too often have no interest in using it.[53] Referring to the 1988 book, D'Arcy Wood observed in 1996 that only 20% of UCA congregations were using the *People's Book*, a disappointing number when the National Commission on Liturgy had modestly hoped for 50% of congregations to use it. More positively, however, he assumes that the influence of the book has been much greater than the sales figure might indicate.[54]

Most theological colleges of the Uniting Church still teach liturgy units but no longer employ full time teaching staff. United Theological College, Sydney, has benefited from the work of Graham Hughes, Anita Monro, Stephen Burns and Gerard Moore, all of whom made important contributions to liturgical theology there. Gary Deverell followed the respected liturgist Robert Gribben at Melbourne's Centre for Theology and Ministry in 2009 but was made redundant along with the role the following year. Stephen Burns' appointment to Pilgrim Theological College as Coordinator of Ministry Studies in July 2018 was a very welcome development as it placed an erudite liturgist in the centre of ministry formation for Uniting Church candidates of the VicTas Synod. Sean Gilbert is a PhD candidate and 'Lecturer in Ministry Practice' at Uniting College, Adelaide where he teaches a unit on 'Liturgy and Worship (in the Protestant Tradition)'. I could find no liturgist on the Trinity College, Brisbane website. This potted summary of the place of liturgical studies in Uniting Church ministerial training is admittedly somewhat anecdotal but it does not present a picture of a church fully embracing its own liturgical heritage drawn from Anglican, Wesleyan, and Reformed precedents.

 The study of liturgy can be thrown into a mix with the study of preaching or of ministry practice more broadly but when this is done, much of genuine liturgical value is lost. This is a perplexing development in ministerial training, especially when one considers that the leading of public worship is a week-in-week-out activity for Ministers of the Word. This neglect was itself something of an existing tradition among Methodists even before the Uniting Church was formed, as borne out by R.W.

Hartley's study of the almost complete neglect of liturgical training among NSW Methodists from 1902-1977.[55] The contemporary Charismatic pattern where 'worship' is mostly music followed by preaching can be learned easily enough through imitation. Deep reflection on the shape of the liturgy and the theologic embedded in the best worship patterns requires the kind of demanding, critical, creative and faithful response that is best learned in a formal context of study under skilled guides. Where this is not present, or where it is threatened, the future of the Prayer Book tradition in the UCA is rendered uncertain to say the least.

Endnotes

1. Quoted in John Bishop, *Methodist Worship in Relation to Free Church Worship* (London: Epworth, 1950), 98-99.
2. The concept of the *Sunday Service* as an 'urtext,' the original or earliest version of a text with which later versions are compared, is borrowed from Karen B. Westerfield Tucker, *American Methodist Worship* (Oxford: Oxford University Press, 2011), 4-8.
3. For an excellent collection of essays with a more global reach, see Karen B. Westerfield Tucker, ed. *The Sunday Service of the Methodists: Twentieth-Century Worship in Worldwide Methodism* (Nashville: Abingdon / Kingswood, 1996).
4. *Letters* (Telford) VII: 239. Note that in early American Methodism the term 'elder' referred to an ordained minister (presbyter).
5. *The Sunday Service of the Methodists in North America: With other Occasional Services (1784)*, preface.
6. 'If you have many possessions, make your gift from them in proportion; if few, do not be afraid to give according to the little you have. So you will be laying up a good treasure for yourself against the day of necessity.' (Tobit 4:8-9 NRSV)
7. Frederick Hunter, 'Note on Article on "Sources of Wesley's Abridgments of the Prayer Book, 1784-8",' with a reply from Rattenbury, *Proceedings of the Wesley Historical Society* (23:8), 173-75.

8 James White, *John Wesley's Prayer Book: The Sunday Service of the Methodists in North America* (Akron, OH: OSL Publications, 1995), 1.
9 Geordan Hammond, *John Wesley in America: Restoring Primitive Christianity* (Oxford: Oxford University Press, 2014), 108-109.
10 'Ought We to Separate from the Church of England?' *The Works of John Wesley, vol. 9 The Methodist Societies: History, Nature and Design*, ed. Rupert E. Davies (Nashville: Abingdon, 1989), 571-572.
11 Karen B. Westerfield-Tucker, 'John Wesley's Prayer Book Revision: The Text in Context,' *Methodist History* 34:4 (July 1996), 230-247.
12 Frederick Hunter, 'Sources of Wesley's Abridgment of the Prayer Book,' Proceedings of the Wesley Historical Society, vol. 23, no. 6 (1942): 123-133; See also An Abridgement of Mr. Baxter's History of his life and times: With an account of the ministers, &c. who were ejected after the restauration, of King Charles II ... and the continuation of their history, to the passing of the bill against occasional conformity, in 1711 https://archive.org/details/abridgementofmrb00cala accessed 6/8/2018
13 K.B. Westerfield-Tucker, 'John Wesley's Prayer Book Revision,' 246.
14 K.B. Westerfield-Tucker, 'John Wesley's Prayer Book Revision,' 232.
15 John Fletcher to John Wesley, 1 August 1775, Nehemiah Curnock, ed. *The Journal of the Rev. John Wesley*, vol. 8 (London: Charles H. Kelly, 1909), 331-32.
16 J. Hamby Barton, 'The Two Versions of the First Edition of John Wesley's 'The Sunday Service of the Methodists in North America,' *Methodist History* vol. 23, no. 3 (April 1985): 153-162.
17 John Wesley to Walter Churchey, 20 June 1789, John Telford, ed. *The Letters of the Rev John Wesley, A.M.*, vol. 8 (London: Epworth Press, 1931), 144-45.
18 Bryan D. Spinks, 'Anglicans and Dissenters,' in Geoffrey Wainwright and Karen B. Westerfield Tucker, eds, *The Oxford History of Christian Worship*. 492-553, 522; Karen B. Westerfield Tucker, 'North America,' in *The Oxford History of Christian Worship*, 586-632, 602-605. See Marion J. Hatchett, *The Making of the First American Book of Common Prayer, 1776-1789* (New York: Seabury, 1982).
19 John Wesley, *Works, vol. 19 Letters and Diaries II (1738-43)*, ed. W. Reginald Ward and Richard P. Heitzenrater (Nashville: Abingdon, 1990), 29.
20 Karen B. Westerfield Tucker, *American Methodist Worship* (Oxford: Oxford University Press, 2011), 273-274.
21 Hoyt L. Hickman, 'Word and table: the Process of Liturgical revision in the United Methodists Church, 1964-1992,' in K.B. Westerfield Tucker, *The Sunday Service*, 117-135.
22 Book of Worship, v.
23 Book of Worship, v.
24 *Book of Worship*, vi. In a recent study, R. Matthew Sigler has traced the way in which the liturgists Thomas O. Summers (1812-1882), Nolan B. Harmon (1892-1993), and James F. White (1932-2004), contributed to American Methodist liturgical reform and renewal through reliance upon the textual tradition inherited directly from Wesley's Sunday Service and the hymnody of Charles Wesley. R. Matthew Sigler, *Methodist Worship: Mediating the Wesleyan Liturgical Heritage* (London and New York: Routledge, 2018).

25 *The United Methodist Book of Worship* (Nashville: United Methodist Publishing House, 1992), Preface.
26 *United Methodist Book of Worship*, 16.
27 *Hymns of Faith and Life* (Winona Lake, IN: Light and Life Press and Marion, IN: Wesley Press, 1976).
28 *Book of Worship* (Nashville: AME Publishing House, 1984). Vinton R. Anderson, 'Under Our Own Vine and Fig Tree: Sunday Morning Worship in the African Methodist Episcopal Church,' in K.B. Westerfield Tucker, *Sunday Service*, 157-172, 170.
29 [Thomas Jackson], *The Wesleyans vindicated from the calumnies contained in a pamphlet entitled, "The Church of England compared with Wesleyan Methodism"*, *in a dialogue between a Churchman and a Methodist* (1837), 2nd edition (London: John Mason, 1837), 22 cited in Jérôme Grosclaude, 'The Book of Common Prayer in Methodism: a Cherished Heritage or a Corrupting Influence,' *Revue Française de Civilisation Britannique* (XXII-1, 2017): 5. Online since 02 May 2017, connection on 01 August 2018. http://journals.openedition.org/rfcb/1229; DOI: 10.4000/rfcb.12295.
30 Quoted in Bishop, *Methodist Worship*, 95. For a helpful survey of British Methodist worship see A. Raymond George, 'From The Sunday Service to the Sunday Service': Sunday Morning Worship in British Methodism,' in K.B. Westerfield-Tucker, *Sunday Service*, 31-52.
31 T.B. Bunting, *Life of Dr. Bunting*, vol. 1, p. 386, cited in Bishop, *Methodist Worship*, 92.
32 T.B. Bunting, *Life of Dr. Bunting*, vol. 1, p. 138, cited in Bishop, *Methodist Worship*, 94.
33 Thomas Jackson, *Life of Robert Newton*, p. 76, cited in Bishop, *Methodist Worship*, 94-95.
34 David M. Chapman, *Born in Song: Methodist Worship in Britain* (Warrington: Church in the Market Place Publications, 2006), 201.
35 John Walford, *Memoirs of the Life and Labours of the Late Venerable Hugh Bourne, By a Member of the Bourne Family (1854)* (Cambridge: Cambridge University Press, 2010), 145.
36 Primitive Methodists in 1860, United Methodist Free Church in 1865, and finally the Bible Christians and Methodist New Connexion in 1897.
37 The Book of Offices, being the Orders of Service authorized for Use in the Methodist Church, together with The Order for Morning Prayer (London: Methodist Publishing House, 1936).
38 *The Methodist Service Book* (London: Methodist Publishing House, 1975).
39 A. Raymond George, 'From *The Sunday Service* to 'The Sunday Service,' 40-46.
40 *The Methodist Worship Book*, Standard Edition PC230 (London: Methodist Publishing House, 1999), vii.
41 *Methodist Worship Book*, 114ff.
42 A. Raymond George, 'From The Sunday Service to 'The Sunday Service,' 51.
43 Glen O'Brien, 'Methodism in the Australian Colonies, 1811-1855,' in Glen O'Brien and Hilary M. Carey eds, *Methodism in Australia, A History*. (Farnham, Surrey and Burlington, VT: Ashgate, 2015), 15-27, 15.
44 Glen O'Brien, 'Not Radically a Dissenter: Samuel Leigh in the Colony of New South Wales,' *Wesley and Methodist Studies* 4 (2012): 51-69.
45 John C. Symons, *Handbook of the Laws and Regulations of the Australasian*

Wesleyan Methodist Church (Melbourne: Wesleyan Book Depot, 1877), 29.
46 W.L. Blamires and J.B. Smith, *The Early Story of the Wesleyan Methodist Church in Victoria* (Melbourne: Wesleyan Book Depot, 1886), 14.
47 Symons, *Handbook of Laws and Regulations*, 29-30.
48 D'Arcy Wood, 'Worship and Music in Australian Methodism,' in Glen O'Brien and Hilary M. Carey, eds, *Methodism in Australia: A History*. (Farnham, Surrey and Burlington, VT: Ashgate, 2015), 181-196, 182.
49 Andrew Pratt, *O For a Thousand Tongues: The 1933 Methodist Hymn Book in Context* (Peterborough: Epworth, 2004).
50 Robert W. Gribben, 'E.H. Sugden and His Chapels,' in Renate Howe, ed. *The Master: The Life and Work of Edward H. Sugden*. (Melbourne: Uniting Academic Press, 2009), 125-139, 125.
51 R.W. Gribben, 'E.H. Sugden and His Chapels,' 136.
52 Of course the BCP is only one of several liturgical texts that have shaped the Uniting Church's worship. Others would include the *Book of Common Order* (1562), the Westminster Assembly's 1664 *Directory of Public Worship*, and their many subsequent revisions. See Robert W. Gribben, 'The Uniting Church in Australia,' in *The Oxford History of Worship*, 541-44.; Robert W. Gribben, *'Uniting in Worship*: The Uniting Church in Australia,' in K.B. Westerfield Tucker, *The Sunday Service of Methodists*, 67-79; H. D'Arcy Wood, 'Text and Context in a Newly United Denomination: the Liturgical Experience in Australia,' in K.B. Westerfield Tucker, *The Sunday Service of Methodists*, 81-93. For other United Church liturgies see Eric J. Lott, 'Historic Tradition, Local Culture: Tensions and Fusions in the Liturgy of the Church of South India,' in K.B. Westerfield Tucker, *The Sunday Service of Methodists*, 53-66; Samson Prahakar, 'The Church of South India,' in *Oxford History of Christian Worship*, 534-44; Thomas Harding, 'Ordered Liberty: Sunday Worship in the United Church of Canada,' in K.B. Westerfield Tucker, *The Sunday Service of Methodists*, 95-116.
53 Stephen Burns, *Pilgrim People: An Invitation to Worship in the Uniting Church* (Adelaide: Mediacom, 2012).
54 *Uniting in Worship* (1988) consisted of a 674 page *Leader's Book* and an accompanying 362 page *People's Book*. H. D'Arcy Wood, 'Text and Context,' 81-83.
55 R.W. Hartley, 'The Eucharist in New South Wales Methodism from Methodist Union (1902) to the Uniting Church (1907),' *Church Heritage* 1:4 (1980): 305-34, 313.

4

Ecumenical Beauty: Evelyn Underhill's *Prayer Book*

Robyn Wrigley-Carr

The discovery

The recent discovery and publication of *Evelyn Underhill's Prayer Book* provides much to ponder. The up-take of this liturgical text, which was reprinted after only five months of publication, is interesting in and of itself. Why would there be so much interest in a text filled with historical prayers from the 3rd to 20th centuries from *all* branches of the historical, Christian church? Diverse individuals and groups in the worldwide, Christian (and secular) community seem to be interested in this collection of prayers, using it as an aid for both private and communal prayer. Could the ecumenical nature of the collection of prayers and the poetic beauty of both the prayers and the book itself, provide some pointers for the future of common prayer?

The story behind the discovery of *Evelyn Underhill's Prayer Book* is relayed only very briefly here. In 2016, while researching 'echoes of von Hügel in the writings of Evelyn Underhill', I spent time in a couple of UK University archives and was about to head to King's College London (the official home of the Evelyn Underhill archive), when at the last minute, as a complete afterthought, I chose to visit *The House of Retreat* at Pleshey (near Chelmsford, UK). This is the retreat house where Underhill led spiritual retreats between 1924 and 1938.

Within hours of my visit, I discovered a brown, leather-bound volume with bronze, engraved, Celtic clasps. It contained a collection of prayers and most pages had magnificent, red calligraphy headings. It suddenly dawned upon me that *this* was the book of prayers that Underhill had collected and hand-written to use when leading retreats. Several Underhill scholars had lamented the loss of this book, assuming it had vanished decades earlier. The letter accompanying the original prayer book indicated that the volume had been discovered many years earlier in an Oxfam shop by a Canadian-born priest, Father Bill Kirkpatrick and was posted to *The House of Retreat* in 2004. Apparently it was put in a suitcase for safe-keeping where it lay forgotten.

A few months later, I returned to *The House at Retreat* at Pleshey to check my copy with the original (often extremely illegible) text, and to my complete amazement, another Underhill prayer book with the identical red, calligraphy headings had also mysteriously emerged. This volume was hand-bound (probably by Evelyn) with a blue and yellow floral cover and faded, blue ribbon tie. Both prayer books had come to light in the 75th year of Underhill's death. I quickly copied that text as well and recognised it as the earlier of the two volumes, given the significantly larger and more legible hand writing. Repetitions between both prayer books were deleted, the language was modernised and the combined text of both prayer books along with an Introduction, Appendix, Author Biographies and Liturgical Sources and new Index was published by SPCK in January, 2018.

Historic ecumenism

One of the most striking aspects of *Evelyn Underhill's Prayer Book*[1] is its ecumenism. In her collection of prayers, Underhill enables the voices of women and men from all branches of the Christian church to be heard together. Charles Williams indicates that Underhill simply copied down 'prayers which specially delighted her. But each new prayer had to be on probation for some time before she admitted it to her collection.'[2] Those prayers that survived her test were from lovers of God who were Catholics, Orthodox or Protestants.

In addition to personal prayers, Underhill drew upon liturgies from all branches of the Christian church. She quoted from some of the oldest liturgical texts available such as the *Leonine Sacramentary* and the *Gelasian Sacramentary*, the second oldest Western liturgical book. Other Church liturgies she drew from include the *Roman Missal, Dawn Office Eastern Church, The Mozarabic Rite, Liturgy of Malabar, Monastic Breviary Matins*, the *Book of Common Prayer* and the *Revised Prayer Book* (1928) of the Church of England and *Veni Creator Spiritus*, a ninth century hymn sung in both Roman Catholic and Anglican churches.

In addition, Underhill chose prayers from theologians such as Augustine (third century), St Basil the Great and St John Chrysostom and Ambrose (fourth century), Pope Gregory VII (sixth century), Anselm (eleventh century), Aquinas (thirteenth century) and John Henry Newman and Edward Pusey (nineteenth century). Prayers from mystics include Richard Rolle and John of Ruysbroeck (thirteenth century), Thomas à Kempis (fourteenth century), Ignatius of Loyola and Nicolas of Cusa (fifteenth century), Teresa of Avila and Francis de Chantal (sixteenth century), Francois Fénelon (seventeenth century), Jean Nicolas Grou (eighteenth century) and Élisabeth Leseur (nineteenth century). Underhill also includes Anglican clergy such as William Law (seventeenth century) and Edward Keble Talbot, a contemporary of Underhill's who also led spiritual retreats at *The House of Retreat* at Pleshey. Underhill also selected prayers from poets such as John Donne (sixteenth century), Christina Rosetti (nineteenth century) and Margaret Cropper (twentieth century).

In addition to firmly established voices in the history of Christendom, Underhill includes prayers from some little-known writers. For example, the Hungarian, Roman Catholic, Ottakár Prohászka (nineteenth century), and early writers such as the monastic reformer, Æthelwold of Winchester (tenth century) and the scholar, Alcuin of

York (eighth century). True to her desire for a diversity of voices is Underhill's inclusion of a prayer from the British sea captain and politician Sir Francis Drake (sixteenth century). Perhaps the most intriguing ecumenical choice Underhill makes is the inclusion of a prayer from a female, Sufi mystic and poet, Rabia al-Basri (eight century).[3]

It is also noteworthy that Underhill selects many female writers. These include the well-known nun Gertrude More (sixteenth century) and the little-known nun, Janet Erskine Stuart (twentieth century). Underhill also includes women known for their letters of spiritual direction such as Frances de Chantal (sixteenth century). Further, we see the addition of prayers from some of Underhill's contemporary, female friends: the nun, Sorella Maria di Campello[4] and Marjorie Vernon, the woman who nursed her in her final years.

Underhill is ever aware of the communion of saints in her own prayers published in the prayer book and in her selected prayers. She deliberately brings together a variety of voices. We hear heart-felt prayers from educators, bishops, cardinals, Doctors of the Church, saints, mystics, clerics, poets and even a sea captain. In Underhill's own prayers, this sense of joining in with other voices is often present. For example, 'grant some part and fellowship with Your holy Apostles, Martyrs, Saints and Lovers, into whose company, not weighing our merits but pardoning our offences, we ask You to admit us, through Christ our Lord'.[5] For Underhill, this joining with the communion of saints means she has no choice but to be ecumenical. The ecumenical spirit is one of the most striking aspects of her *Prayer Book* and organically emerges from her own ecumenical spirit.

Underhill's ecumenical spirit

Though Underhill remained an Anglican her entire life, from early on, she also worshipped in Catholic churches.[6] As Charles Williams concedes, she may 'sometimes have said with a smile or a sigh the equivalent of: 'They order these things better in Rome'. But her submission was to the Catholicity of the English Church, and beyond that to the Union of Christendom.'[7] In her later years, her worship went beyond Catholic to Orthodox churches. In 1935, Underhill attended her first Orthodox Fellowship conference and a year later wrote about Eastern Orthodox liturgy and prayer in her final book, *Worship*. She subsequently joined the Fellowship of St Alban and St Sergius.[8] In 1938, she describes her experience of the Anglo-Russian Conference as 'thrilling and the Orthodox services quite unimaginably lovely.'[9]

The British Anglican priest, A. M. Allchin, argues that though Underhill only joined the Orthodox Fellowship late in life, she seemed to possess a 'long familiarity' with Orthodox worship.[10] Allchin goes as far as arguing that her meeting with Father Bulgakov

> had been a kind of crown on her lifetime's search for the fullness and simplicity of Christian truth. It is the combination of

symbolic richness with inner simplicity which seems above all to have struck her.[11]

Perhaps indicating his own position as much as anything, Allchin argues that Underhill became 'so convinced an Anglican... because she saw Anglicanism not as complete in itself, but as part of a greater whole... "a respectable suburb in the city of God",' in Underhill's own words.[12] Allchin argues that by 'her life and by her teaching, Evelyn Underhill opened out the Church which she had entered, and made it much easier for Anglicans to be at home with areas of the Christian traditions which before had been foreign to them.'[13]

Underhill writes that her spiritual director, Friedrich von Hügel, ('I owe him my whole spiritual life')[14] had told Underhill not to convert to Catholicism unless God compelled her to do so. Perhaps less well known is the influence on Underhill of von Hügel's spiritual director, the Catholic priest, Abbé Henri Huvelin. The Abbé stated to the Baron, 'There is no more profound and dangerous enemy of Christianity than everything which makes it narrow or petty.'[15] Underhill, a pioneer of ecumenism, appears to take this 'Saying' to heart, writing sympathetically about all the major traditions of Christian prayer and worship in her final work, *Worship*.

Her close friend, Lucy Menzies describes Underhill as 'truly ecumenical. Exclusiveness in religion was intolerable to her who was to exclaim, "Oh! That dreadful limiting of salvation! We are all too narrow for God!"'[16] In her book *Worship*, Underhill tried to 'get inside' and highlight key aspects of worship in the Jewish, Catholic, Reformed, Free Church and Anglican traditions.[17] As Lucy Menzies states, God showed Underhill her work in 'wide-spreading love to all in communion in the one indivisible church of Christ.'[18]

Underhill's letters to the writer and ecumenist, Maisie Spens, provide further insight into her ecumenism. Underhill engaged with 'Orthodox Liturgy' and 'Roman Mass' but as an Anglican, she was unable to be a 'communicant', which she believed, 'creates a barrier to real unity'. She continues,

> I am sure it is good sometimes to join in the worship of other Churches, but this alone won't lead us very far. The basis of reunion must be interior, secret, out of the reach of all ecclesiastical controversies... you have had a wonderful inspiration in basing it on Our Lord's own prayer, which as you say includes and over-passes the sacramental, and indeed all else... a Praying Church as the actual Body of the Lord.[19]

So for Underhill, prayer was the essential element in ecumenism. In a later letter to Spens, Underhill writes,

> For the development of Unity in and through the Praying Christ:- I do agree that... a widespread group of praying souls, Orders and

individuals, is essential. Still more that these should belong to all Christian Communions.[20]

So we see Underhill viewing prayer as essential to effective ecumenism. Rather than enter into theological arguments concerning unity, she believes in the power of prayer. Her own *Prayer Book* embodies this argument made to Spens in 1937, though she had collected the prayers between 1924 and 1938.

The purpose of prayer at retreats

So who is Underhill's intended audience for this collection of prayers? Retreatants at *The House of Retreat* at Pleshey. Underhill's two books of collected prayers were her private resource for leading small groups of motley women and men between 1924 and 1938 on weekend spiritual retreats. I am assuming that after Underhill stopped leading retreats in 1938 due to ill-health, the prayer books were circulated around other retreat leaders until somehow, the leather-bound, later *Prayer Book* was mistakenly donated by some deceased retreat conductor's family to an Oxfam shop. The earlier, flowery-covered *Prayer Book* somehow ended up in the hands of Underhill's main biographer.[21] I want to write briefly about Underhill's convictions concerning the purpose of spiritual retreats in order to shed light on her choice of prayers for *Evelyn Underhill's Prayer Book*.

We enter into Retreat, argues Underhill, 'to seek the opportunity of being alone with God and attending to God... for spiritual food and air - to wait on the Lord...'[22] Similarly, she states that 'the object of our Retreat: it is a time when we can listen to the secret whisper of the Spirit and look at Christ again, for the contemplation of Christ is the first part of Christianity.'[23] In yet another Retreat talk, Underhill makes it clear that 'The motto for your Retreat is *God Only*, God in Himself, sought for Himself alone.'[24] It is worth considering Underhill's aims for retreats and how they do or don't relate to prayer in corporate Church settings. Underhill repeatedly states some convictions concerning prayer at her retreats, which are the guiding principles in Underhill's selection of prayers and deeply relevant to 'the future of common prayer.'

From self-focus to God-focus

In our contemporary context, where spirituality has often broadened out to a worship of the self, Underhill calls us to adore God, who is Other. Underhill described von Hügel's 'constant death to self' and 'self-abandonment' as his 'crowning virtue' and was deeply influenced by his example and teaching.[25] We catch a glimpse of this crucial emphasis in Underhill's reflections after a retreat in 1923, 'The more vivid the vision of Christ grows... the more one can escape... from the maze of self-occupation.'[26]

This emphasis upon God-focus, not self-focus, is further outlined in her broadcast talks, published in 1936. Underhill states that people who think of the spiritual life as

> something which is for themselves and about themselves... need a larger horizon... Any spiritual view which focuses attention on ourselves, and puts the human creature with its small ideas and adventures in the centre foreground, is dangerous till we recognise its absurdity.[27]

Underhill's prayers are not self-grounded – finding 'god' in myself – but have a clear sense of a 'Reality', a God who is so much greater and larger than our own experiences and worthy of our adoration.

So Underhill invites her pray-ers to journey beyond themselves 'To dwell quietly and without self-occupation in the atmosphere of God.'[28] She encourages them in the prayer, 'Help us utterly to forget ourselves and to give ourselves utterly to You...'[29] Similarly, Underhill prays, 'Let us ask for closer communion with our Lord – therefore a greater forgetting of ourselves.'[30] The essential presupposition behind this emphasis is Underhill's conviction of the gap between Creator and creature.

The gap between creator and creature

In a letter to *The Spectator*, Underhill describes 'the fundamental distinction between Creator and creature' and the necessity to hold a philosophy of religion that is not 'pantheism' which she describes as 'an immanentism so extreme that both prayer and worship become meaningless.'[31] The necessity for this distinction between God and humanity is repeatedly stated by von Hügel. He highlighted the 'Otherness' of God, stating that to place humanity and God 'on a strict parity' is blasphemy!'[32] He writes, 'The creature is not the Creator, either in quantity or quality.'[33] This influence was clearly adopted by Underhill and I would argue is absolutely essential to the future of common prayer. In *Evelyn Underhill's Prayer Book*, we repeatedly see the gap between God and humanity through her humble posture. This gap presupposes we be caught up in adoration of God.

Prayer as adoration

Von Hügel stated that 'Religion without adoration is like a triangle with one side left out.'[34] Underhill clearly absorbed the Baron's stance that 'a soul must adore if it is to grow.'[35] Lucy Menzies, Underhill's close friend and Warden of Pleshey, argues that 'God' is the 'heart' of Underhill's teaching: 'Adoration was for her the essential. When that had been practised, there was not much time for anything else, certainly not for self.'[36] In

Evelyn Underhill's Prayer Book we see repeated prayers of adoration to God. For example, 'For to You belong all glory and honour and adoration, Father, Son and Holy Spirit, now and ever, world without end, Amen.'[37] Inclusion of quotes from the Psalms also keeps adoration at the forefront of many of the prayers.[38] Underhill's prayers can be incredibly passionate. For example,

> Let our lives run to Your embrace... and breathe the breath of Eternity. O God Supreme! Most secret and most present, most beautiful and strong. Constant yet Incomprehensible, changeless yet changing all! What can I say, my God, my Life, my Holy Joy... You are the only reality...[39]

Continuing on this passionate adoration of God, Underhill declares in a final public lecture in October 1937:

> In the days that are coming, I am sure that Christianity will have to move out from the churches and chapels, or rather spread out far beyond the devotional focus of its life... telling the truth about God and [hu]man[ity], and casing its transfiguring radiance on the whole of that world in which [hu]man[ity] has to live... Only those who have learned to look at the Eternal with the disinterested loving gaze, the objective unpossessive delight of worship, who do see the stuff of common life

with the light shining through it, will be able to do that.⁴⁰

This lengthy quote illustrates Underhill's passion for the most compelling, corporate witness that exists: the loving gaze of adoration. It reminds us of the importance of the Christian community at prayer, not simply the individual mystic in the prayer cell.

Prayer as corporate

In our individualised, contemporary world, Underhill reminds us of the importance of corporate prayer. Underhill writes

> remember how Dante says that directly a soul ceases to say Mine, and says Ours, it makes the transition from the narrow, constricted, individual life to the truly free, truly personal, truly creative spiritual life; in which all are linked together in one single response to the Father of all spirits, God. Here, all interpenetrate, and all, however humble and obscure their lives may seem, can and do affect each other.⁴¹

And part of that 'interpenetration' is the voice of the Church rising in adoration of the beauty of God, an aspect that is repeatedly emphasised in the prayers selected for *Evelyn Underhill's Prayer Book*.

Prayer as beauty

God as beauty

Worship of the perfect beauty of God is found in the prayers throughout *Evelyn Underhill's Prayer Book*. Underhill herself declares 'You are beauty,'[42] 'the vision of Your beauty,'[43] the 'splendour and beauty of God.'[44] And she chooses prayers from ancient and contemporary voices who echo this theme: the 'honour and beauty of Your holy name'[45] (à Kempis); 'beauty of eternal peace'[46] (Mozarabic Rite) and 'You are not only beautiful but beauty'[47] (Cropper). Underhill expresses her desire to 'never mistake the beauty' of God's works for God – 'the perfect beauty.'[48] And she speaks of 'the beauty of Your house' on two occasions.[49] Spiritual formation is repeatedly described as reflecting some of God's beauty: 'fashioned to a truer beauty by Your hand;'[50] 'changed into the likeness of His beauty;'[51] 'filled with that... beauty which only comes from You.'[52]

Given Underhill's repeated emphasis on God's beauty, it is hardly surprising that Underhill's two original *Prayer Books* are presented with beauty. The identifying red, calligraphy headings on most pages of both books, the hand bound, floral cover and blue, marker ribbon in the earlier *Prayer Book* and the leather and Celtic clasps of the latter *Prayer Book*. I asked SPCK to try to match the 'flowery covered' prayer book that Underhill had hand bound. They ended up selecting a 1902 furnishing fabric by the designer, Harry Napper (1860-1930) from the Victoria and Albert Museum in London. Not only is the cover attractive and authentically Edwardian, the feel of the cover, and the compact size of the volume (small enough for a handbag or satchel) also made the text perfect in terms of beautiful presentation. Aesthetics mattered to Underhill and is important in the presentation of any prayers published.

The importance of aesthetics

Underhill was the quintessential Edwardian lady. Her parents on both sides had been 'collectors of silver, glass and china'[53] so she was surrounded by beautiful objects, throughout her life. But more importantly, she appreciated the beauty of creation. As a gardener, she had a passion for flowers and birds. It is hardly surprising that we hear in her letters about botany, the light on European buildings and mountain vistas. Menzies writes that Underhill loved 'drifting up creeks silently in the dinghy to watch wading-birds' and 'landing to explore Cornish Churches.'[54] Alongside churches and cathedrals, Underhill had a deep appreciation for Italian, religious art.

As a young woman, it was her love of the Italian paintings in Florence that led to what she described as 'a sort of gradual unconscious growing into an understanding of things.'[55] The Italian painters invited her into the religion behind the art. Perhaps it is no surprise that in her early novel, *The Grey World*, the effect of European paintings on the protagonist leads him to experience the transcendent. But Underhill did not simply appreciate beauty of creation and art, but also the beauty of language.

Beauty through language

Underhill wrote poetry and novels before branching into religious writings. Poetic language was always important to her and it is no mistake that she include poets in the authors of prayers for her *Prayer Book*: John Donne (sixteenth century), Christina Rossetti (nineteenth century) and Margaret Cropper (twentieth century). Underhill also selected theologians and clerics who wrote poetry such as John Scotus Eriugena (ninth century) and Jeremy Taylor (seventeenth century).

In her own prayers in *Evelyn Underhill's Prayer Book* we constantly see poetic language. Here are a few snippets: For example, 'For beyond us are the hills of God, the snowfields of the Spirit, the other kingdom.'[56] 'Within Your wounds hide me'[57] 'stayed on the rock of Your faithfulness, through storm and stress, we may abide in You.'[58]

The beauty of authenticity

Perhaps the real beauty in the prayers that Underhill chooses and writes in *Evelyn Underhill's Prayer Book* are those that are obviously prayed, and authentically lived and embodied, the language of lovers – heartfelt and candid – rather than detached prayers. Many of the prayers Underhill provides offer a glimpse of her passionate heart and humble posture. Given the prayers that Underhill selected had to be on probation as she prayed them, for some time, it means that her *Prayer Book* contains prayers that are 'earthy' and have grit and depth and are actually worth praying, in Underhill's opinion. It is no wonder that Charles Williams gave Underhill the title, 'Motherhood of souls.'[59]

The beauty of flexibility

Underhill's *Prayer Books* were handwritten and working documents. In an age of apps, with more reading and writing migrating to screens, the question remains how to provide choices and flexibility in the use of *Prayer Books* for different events.

We see examples of Underhill's *Prayer Book* as working documents through the constant crossing out of words, inserted words, different fountain pens adapting earlier versions and at times up to three choices of an individual word in a particular prayer are provided. The most obvious examples of changes to individual words appear to be to make prayers more directly relevant to the theme of a retreat. For example, in the originals of Underhill's two *Prayer Books*, we see constant crossing out of words as prayers are modified for different retreats, different fountain pens and pencils. One obvious example is, for example, a prayer where 'true joys' is changed to 'peace' and the heading 'patience' is added, presumably to adapt the existing prayer to Underhill's retreat 'The Fruit of the Spirit' in 1936.[60] Similarly, an example of an adaptation for her retreat, *Light of Christ*, may be revealed through changing 'shine most sweetly' to 'shine most brightly.'[61]

Secondly, we see instances where Underhill provides two options for an individual word. For example, in one prayer Underhill originally writes the word 'their' then later, includes herself more explicitly in the corporate prayer and places the word 'our' above 'their' and has a vertical, squiggly line linking both words, indicating either word can be used.[62] At other points she originally wrote 'God' then changed it to 'Christ.'[63] In another example, Underhill changes the term 'walk' to 'sojourn' to 'companion' with the same vertical squiggly line, indicating the retreat conductor choose which word to use. So the latest version is 'Lord! who did companion with Your disciples...'[64] This raises the question of whether the 'future of common prayer' might gain from a flexible liturgy with options. Another obvious point is the inclusion of prayers related to her historical setting. For example, her prayer in 1940 for evacuated children during World War Two.[65] Perhaps having space for prayer leaders to put in specific prayers related to current issues is beneficial to ensure prayers are current and heartfelt.

Coda: ecumenical beauty

Evelyn Underhill's Prayer Book raises several questions concerning the 'future of common prayer.' First, we see Underhill's ecumenical spirit pulsing through the selection of prayers included in her two books of prayers. As an ecumenist, I strongly believe that our future lies in Christians coming together, praying together. In Eternity, we shall be an ecumenical community. Denominational allegiance and affiliations will have no significance. We shall declare with one voice - 'Holy, holy, holy is the Lord God Almighty...'[66] The challenge before us is how to become a more unified body of Christ *now*, with a common purpose in our corporate prayer.

Underhill provides some essential emphases for that common purpose: the necessity of God-focus, not self-focus; humble recognition of the gap between the Creator and the creature, and the subsequent adoration of the God who is beauty. And *Evelyn Underhill's Prayer Book* also reminds us of the importance of aesthetics – the beauty of language and the beauty of flexibility. As Underhill states, 'The Church will win the world for Christ when – and when only – she works through living spirits steeped in prayer.'[67] Considering the 'future of common prayer' is an essential and crucial task. Underhill herself declares that 'the regular, steady, docile practice of corporate worship is of the utmost importance for the building-up of your spiritual life.'[68] Perhaps *ecumenical beauty* may be an essential element for the future of Christian prayer.

Endnotes
1   Robyn Wrigley-Carr, ed., *Evelyn Underhill's Prayer Book* (London: SPCK, 2018).
2   Charles Williams, ed., *The Letters of Evelyn Underhill*, 2nd edn (London: Longman, Green and Co, 1944), 333.
3   Perhaps this is not surprising as in her early work, *Mysticism*, Sufi mystics featured in several places. Further, she spent time with Rabindranath Tagore translating his poems in 1914. However, Allchin states that Underhill never tended towards 'a superficial syncretism, her deep spiritual intuition and the influence of von Hügel held her back.' However, Underhill 'could make contact across frontiers and was recognised by all kinds of people as a person who spoke with the authority of experience as well as of learning.' (A. M. Allchin, *The Kingdom of Love and Knowledge: The Encounter Between Orthodoxy and the West* [London: DLT, 1979]189). In 1936, Underhill writes a letter describing a Muslim Professor confessing his need for 'experience of God.' (Williams, ed., *The Letters of Evelyn Underhill*, 250).
4   Sorella Maria was Sister Superior of an ecumenical community of sisters in a Franciscan hermitage at Campello, Umbria, Italy. In the original of *Evelyn Underhill's Prayer Book*, Maria has written her prayers in Italian.
5   Wrigley-Carr, ed., *Evelyn Underhill's Prayer Book*, 113.
6   Underhill was confirmed into the Anglican Church at boarding school and nearly converted to Catholicism in 1907 but the Catholic Modernist crisis and opposition from her fiancé halted that decision. However, it wasn't until 1921 that Underhill became a practising member of the Anglican church, under the influence of her Catholic spiritual director, Baron Friedrich von Hügel.
7   Charles Williams, ed., 'Introduction', *The Letters of Evelyn Underhill*, 2nd edn (London: Longmans, Green & Co, 1944), 42.
8   Charles Williams, ed., 'Introduction', *The Letters of Evelyn Underhill*, 2nd edn (London: Longmans, Green & Co, 1944), 42.
9   Charles Williams, ed., *The Letters of Evelyn Underhill*, 2nd edn (London: Longmans, Green & Co, 1944), 267.
10 Allchin, *The Kingdom of Love and Knowledge*, 193. Allchin was also a member of the Order of St Alban and St Sergius and advised the Archbishop of Canterbury on Orthodox-Anglican relations.
11 A. M. Allchin, *The Kingdom of Love and Knowledge* (New York: The Seabury Press, 1982), 193.
12 Allchin, *The Kingdom of Love and Knowledge*, 188.
13 Allchin, *The Kingdom of Love and Knowledge*, 188.
14 Charles Williams, ed., *The Letters of Evelyn Underhill*, 2nd edn (London: Longmans, Green and Co, 1944), 196.
15 Translation by A. M. Allchin. The original Huvelin saying is XXVI: *'Il n'y*

When We Pray

    a pas d'ennemi plus profound et plus dangereux du Christianisme que tout ce qui le rapetisse et le rend étroit.' In *Baron Friedrich von Hügel Selected Letters*, Bernard Holland, ed., (London: J.M.Dent & Sons, 1926), 61.
16 Lucy Menzies, unpublished biography of Evelyn Underhill, House of Retreat, Pleshey archive.
17 See chapters 10-15 of Evelyn Underhill, *Worship* (London: Nisbet & Co, 1941).
18 Menzies, Unpublished biography, 79.
19 Charles Williams, ed., *The Letters of Evelyn Underhill*, 2nd edn (London: Longmans, Green & Co, 1944), 256-7.
20 Charles Williams, ed., *The Letters of Evelyn Underhill*, 2nd edn(London: Longmans, Green & Co, 1944), 257.
21 The earlier, flowery-covered prayer book was donated to Pleshey by Revd. Dr Christopher J.R. Armstrong, author of the most theologically rich of all biographies about Underhill: *Evelyn Underhill* (London: Mowbray, 1975).
22 Evelyn Underhill, *The Fruits of the Spirit* (London: Longmans, 1960), 1.
23 Evelyn Underhill, *Light of Christ* (London: Longmans, 1960), 26.
24 Underhill, *The Fruits of the Spirit*, 2.
25 Evelyn Underhill, 1933, 231-2.
26 Dana Greene, ed., *Fragments from an Inner Life* (Harrisburg, PA: Morehouse Publishing, 1993), 40.
27 Evelyn Underhill, *The Spiritual Life* (Homebush: C.C.S. Publications, 1976), 25-26.
28 Evelyn Underhill, *Light of Christ* (London: Longmans, 1960), 105.
29 Wrigley-Carr, ed., *Evelyn Underhill's Prayer Book*, 96.
30 Wrigley-Carr, ed., *Evelyn Underhill's Prayer Book*, 76.
31 Quoted in LumsdenBarkway& Lucy Menzies, eds., 'Introduction' to *An Anthology of the Love of God* (London: A.R. Mowbray & Co, 1961), 22-23.
32 Gwen Greene, ed., *Letters from Baron von Hügel to a Niece* (London: J. M. Dent & Sons), 112.
33 Bernard Holland, ed., *Selected Letters of Baron Friedrich von Hügel 1896-1924* (London: Dent & Sons, 1926), 93-4.
34 Gwen Greene, ed., *Letters from Baron von Hügel to a Niece* (London: J. M. Dent & Sons), xx.
35 Douglas V. Steere, *Spiritual Counsels and Letters of Baron Friedrich von Hügel*, (London: DLT, 1964), 6.
36 Lucy Menzies, 'Memoir' in Evelyn Underhill, *The Fruits of the Spirit, Light of Christ, Abba* (London: Longmans, Green & Co, 1960), 15.
37 Wrigley-Carr, ed., *Evelyn Underhill's Prayer Book*, 68. See also page 85.
38 See Wrigley-Carr, ed., *Evelyn Underhill's Prayer Book*, 126-129.
39 Wrigley-Carr, ed., *Evelyn Underhill's Prayer Book*, 55.
40 Allchin, *The Kingdom of Love andKnowledge*, 190.
41 Evelyn Underhill, *The Spiritual Life* (Manly: Centre for Christian Spirituality, 1976), 33-34.
42 Wrigley-Carr, ed., *Evelyn Underhill's Prayer Book*, 62.
43 Wrigley-Carr, ed., *Evelyn Underhill's Prayer Book*, 114.
44 Wrigley-Carr, ed., *Evelyn Underhill's Prayer Book*, 48.
45 Wrigley-Carr, ed., *Evelyn Underhill's Prayer Book*, 26 (Imitation IV.3).
46 Wrigley-Carr, ed., *Evelyn Underhill's Prayer Book*, 38.
47 Wrigley-Carr, ed., *Evelyn Underhill's Prayer Book*, 49.
48 Wrigley-Carr, ed., *Evelyn Underhill's Prayer Book*, 21.

49 Wrigley-Carr, ed., *Evelyn Underhill's Prayer Book*, 29, 68.
50 Wrigley-Carr, ed., *Evelyn Underhill's Prayer Book*, 78.
51 Wrigley-Carr, ed., *Evelyn Underhill's Prayer Book*, 78.
52 Wrigley-Carr, ed., *Evelyn Underhill's Prayer Book*, 97.
53 Menzies, Unpublished Biography, 46.
54 Menzies, Unpublished Biography, 9.
55 Charles Williams, ed., 'Introduction', *The Letters of Evelyn Underhill*, 2nd edn (London: Longmans, Green & Co, 1944), 8.
56 Wrigley-Carr, ed., *Evelyn Underhill's Prayer Book*, 77.
57 Wrigley-Carr, ed., *Evelyn Underhill's Prayer Book*, 81.
58 Wrigley-Carr, ed., *Evelyn Underhill's Prayer Book*, 82.
59 Williams, ed., *The Letters of Evelyn Underhill*, 26.
60 Wrigley-Carr, ed., *Evelyn Underhill's Prayer Book*, 73.
61 Wrigley-Carr, ed., *Evelyn Underhill's Prayer Book*, 78.
62 Wrigley-Carr, ed., *Evelyn Underhill's Prayer Book*, 70.
63 Wrigley-Carr, ed., *Evelyn Underhill's Prayer Book*, 102.
64 Wrigley-Carr, ed., *Evelyn Underhill's Prayer Book*, 63.
65 Wrigley-Carr, ed., *Evelyn Underhill's Prayer Book*, 101.
66 Revelation 4:8, *NIV*.
67 Evelyn Underhill, *The Light of Christ* (London: Longmans, Green & Co, 1944), 107.
68 Williams, ed., *The Letters of Evelyn Underhill*, 260.

5

The 'Prayer Book Tradition': Back to the Liturgical Future

Charles Sherlock

Without liturgy the Christian gospel is not sustained – the health of both is inseparable. In this chapter, I wonder what the 'future of the Prayer Book tradition' might look like against this claim.

1 The 'Prayer Book tradition': its English origins

A distinctively 'Anglican' feature of the Christian tradition is that for four centuries from 1549, it took the form of successive 'prayer books'. Until the 1970s, Australian Anglican ordinands prepared liturgically by taking the subject 'Prayer Book' and experiencing *BCP* daily, with its 'thees' and 'doths', royal imagery and minimal variation.[1] This was my own experience as a theological student, and in my initial years teaching theology and liturgy. It is hard for Anglicans under 45 to realise how different is the 'worship world' of today.

Reflecting on the predominance of *BCP* is a foundational task in considering the future of this tradition. At least three interweaving factors were involved:

a) England is the major part of an island nation, distinct from the Continent: that its language would spread over the globe was completely unforeseen in the sixteenth century. French might then have been the language of the court, and Latin of scholarship and church life, but English was coming to the fore. With the Wars of the Roses past, the Tudors had a major stake in seeing the nation consolidated: England was becoming a more homogenous society. Pressures toward reform gave opportunity for Henry VIII, fixated about the royal succession, to claim independence from Rome. When occasion arose under Edward VI for a transition to English in church, it made social, cultural and political sense to do so in a *Book of Common Prayer,* a development which Elizabeth used to advantage.[2] It is not always realised that the book was produced for a particular, small and isolated national church – not for a global communion.

b) But such a prayer book could not have been made without technological developments, notably (increasingly cheap) printing, along with better ink and paper. Only a generation or so before 1549, all texts were written by hand. It is often said that the spread of Reformation ideas was enabled by printing: so also was the making of an English Prayer Book. Placing a Bible and *BCP* in every parish church would have been impracticable in 1509 when Henry VIII took the throne.

c) Yet without the impact of Reformation ideas initially, and ongoing doctrinal concerns reflected in the successive editions of *BCP*, there would not have been the energy to undertake the mammoth task of gathering the wealth of existing rites and ceremonies into a single book. It was Cranmer's genius to bring contemporary theological scholarship to bear on rendering age-old forms of prayer into English, and in ways that were memorable for a minimally literate population.[3]

By the end of the sixteenth century, the *Book of Common Prayer*, with the Geneva Bible and Shakespeare's plays, epitomised 'Englishness'. The established nature of the Church of England meant that, most Roman Catholics excepted, at least under Elizabeth and James all citizens were included in the national church. Despite the hiatus of the Commonwealth period, for centuries following, the 'prayer book' tradition sustained the heritage of 'common prayer' in England, and later its colonies, Empire and Commonwealth. This is its greatness. Its weakness, however, was the accompanying 'principle of uniformity' – of which more later.

2 The 'Prayer Book tradition': enduring foundations

The enduring worth of the 'Prayer Book tradition' can be crystallised in three key features. The contention of this chapter is that they continue to serve the mission of God. They represent much more than a narrowly 'Anglican' perspective: the demise of 'uniformity' means that a good claim can be made for their ecumenical significance. I believe that we neglect them to our spiritual peril.

a) Grounded in the scriptures: lectionary and more

Modern Anglican prayer books typically begin with service texts, e.g. Morning and Evening Prayer in *AAPB* and *APBA*. But *BCP* begins with 'Lessons Proper for Sundays and Holy Days', followed by 'The Calendar, with the Table of Lessons' for every day of the year. The First Testament (less some genealogies and cultic regulations) is read once, the New Testament (except Revelation 9, 13 and 17) twice, and the Psalms recited a dozen times! All the Reformers thought of the scriptures as having *formal* authority (rather than Church Councils or the Pope). In the 'prayer book tradition', however, it is the pastoral *use* of the scriptures, their *material* authority, which matters. That their public reading forms the substance of 'common prayer' can readily be seen by using *BCP* Morning or Evening Prayer for a few days. Some 50% of the time involves hearing the scriptures; 15% reciting psalms, 15%

scriptural songs. A mere 20% is left for liturgical texts, themselves woven from a tissue of scriptural allusions.

This practical centrality of the scriptures, and the transition to English, is the focus of 'Concerning the Service of the Church', the introduction to the first *BCP* (1549), included in successive editions. Its main section concludes by claiming that in the new book

> nothing is ordained to be read, but the very pure Word of God, the holy Scriptures, or that which is agreeable to the same; and that in such a language and order as is most easy and plain for the understanding both of the readers and hearers.

The Homilies likewise begin,

> Unto a Christian man, there can be nothing either more necessary or profitable, than the knowledge of Holy Scripture; forasmuch as in it is contained God's true word, setting forth his glory, and also man's duty ... And as drink is pleasant to them that be dry, and meat to them that be hungry; so is the reading, hearing, searching, and studying of Holy Scripture, to them that be desirous to know God, or themselves, and to do his will.[4]

Both texts, drafted by Archbishop Cranmer, reflect an ethos of being immersed in the scriptures, so as to engage

God's people with the whole drama of God's dealings and so Christian worship in liturgy and life. Further, this sense of 'immersion' extended beyond the lectionary to the liturgical text of *BCP*, notably the Exhortations, short litanies (largely drawn from the Psalter) and collects.

A first thesis of this paper is thus this: we are called to go 'back to the future' by engaging with the whole range of the scriptures, following Cranmer's lead in employing the tools of contemporary theological scholarship to see them permeate worship, not only in lectionaries but in the texts of written prayer.

I believe the *Three-Year Lectionary* (derived from the Roman Catholic *Ordo*, and used in *AAPB*), and even more, the *Revised Common Lectionary* (derived from ecumenical reflection on the *Ordo*, and used in *APBA*) go a fair way to meeting this call – but it is not always observed in congregational life, not least in those whose clergy and leaders identify as 'Bible-based'. Further, the modern tendency is to shape written prayers around themes or metaphors, or employ *ex tempore* prayer whose nature is experiential or conversational: in either case, biblical imagery, citations or allusions are much less frequent than *BCP*.

b) Liturgy made public, accessible and life-related

Gathering all that is needed for public worship into one volume arose in a particular political context. Though it would lead to an oppressive 'uniformity', it expressed a further foundational principle of the 'prayer book tradition': making the key resources of the Christian tradition accessible to all. Placing a copy of the Bible and *BCP* in each church building, and using them daily, encouraged a climate of openness among all the baptised, and excluded spiritual secrecy. This was cognate with the abolition of compulsory auricular confession, while the transition to English saw the end of the priest's 'silent' prayers in the eucharistic canon.

A further consequence of having everything in one public book was that it constituted an implicit 'covenant' between clergy and people, which set 'boundaries' to both clerical power and local idiosyncrasies. This continues today, as the declaration Australian Anglican clergy make on being licensed indicates:

> I, NN, in public prayer and administration of the sacraments, will use the form prescribed in the *Book of Common Prayer* or a form authorised by lawful authority and none other.[5]

I am well aware that some clergy take this lightly, but it liberates more than restricts: alongside *BCP*, which retains its standing as a doctrine norm,[6] *AAPB* and/or *APBA* are 'a form authorised'. This declaration relieves from the pressures of 'making it up' each Sunday, and offers the heritage of a scripturally-grounded, doctrinally secure and pastorally sensitive resource for 'common prayer'. The point is to foster trust among all the faithful that what is experienced in church is spiritually sound and 'safe' (in compliance terms). When an incumbency is vacant, not a few parishioners will pray hard that the new rector will listen rather than inflict on them his/her liturgical fads! They rightly expect clergy to honour the 'prayer book tradition' in its local form (a principle protected under the Constitution of the Anglican Church of Australia).[7]

Also, the lectionary in *BCP* is all of a piece with the Calendar, which mixes Christian feasts with (northern hemisphere) seasonal days, and the sovereign's accession: a similar blend of Christian and civil commemorations continues in *AAPB*, and more richly in *APBA*.[8] This interweaving of eternal matters within the context of a particular age expresses a catholic outlook on the wide range of creaturely existence. As in Israel of old, the 'prayer book tradition' holds together the drama of salvation with the realities of human life and the cycles of nature.

A second thesis of this paper is thus: we are called to go 'back to the future' by keeping what matters accessible to all and sustaining a covenant relationship between clergy and people, so fostering a context-sensitive approach that weaves together matters temporal and eternal.

c) Sustaining graced truth

The men who drew up *BCP* refused to start from scratch, as other Reformers wanted. They were shaped by Reformation ideals and Renaissance scholarship, but respected the heritage of the past. Sarum was both received and reformed – rubrics and Collects at the level of detail, the 'hours' services re-gathered into Morning and Evening Prayer, etc. The change to English may have been dramatic, but (with a few exceptions of doctrinal sensitivity) the new rites sought to retain the 'feel' of the past familiar to ordinary folk. The Calendar was purged of excesses, but continued to hold the rhythms of Christian memory and time. It is noteworthy that five feasts associated with the Blessed Virgin Mary continue: not only those with scriptural grounding (Presentation, Annunciation, Visitation), but also her conception and birth (but not August 15).

The wealth of the patristic and medieval heritage (East and West) was thus both taken up and sifted: the number of new compositions in *BCP* is minimal – the 'prayer of humble access' and exhortations in holy communion (1549); the exhortation in Morning & Evening Prayer (1552); and the General Thanksgiving (1662) are examples. The aim was to foster spiritual health, both personal and communal, not doctrine alone: the scholastic separation of theology and spirituality was redeemed so that divine truth might grace heart and mind alike. The language of *BCP* 'rang bells' in English hearts, shaping public spiritual life well into the twentieth century: consider the work of Sayers, Chesterton, Tolkien, Christie and the like. Even so, the shift in our day away from 'thee', 'hath' and frequent royal imagery was unavoidable, especially after television began to change people's awareness of relevant public communication. Within the churches, the proliferation of English translations of the Bible and increasing diversity in liturgical life has seen a loss of 'heart familiarity' with the text. When words are varied and new, few 'stick'.

It is essential at this point to note that while 'language' is a crucial factor in liturgy, it cannot be isolated from 'trans-textual' aspects: what is seen, how furniture is placed, body-language, dress, music and the like all affect what is communicated about divine truth. *BCP* addresses some of these matters in rubrics, but minimally, a factor that lead to sharp debates in earlier times.[9] It should also be noted that, beyond the Psalter (sung by chants or metrically) and Gloria, *BCP* makes little provision for singing. The inclusion of hymns as we know them only came about generally in the nineteenth century. The assessment of the suitability of their lyrics and melodies is a matter for local clergy and congregations rather than ecclesial authorities, especially since electronic communication has spread: the 'worship wars' of recent decades have revolved around music rather than liturgical text.[10]

But debate about liturgical text dominated intra-Anglican debate for the century before modern prayer book revision, especially around the relation of doctrine and text in eucharistic theology. The Liturgical Commissions appointed to prepare *AAPB* and *APBA* both proceeded under the principle that, if full agreement on a text could not be found, then the wording of *BCP* was to be used. The intention was not to diminish poetic or contemporary ways of expressing Christian theology, but to ensure that all Australian Anglicans could use the book in good conscience. In *AAPB*, *BCP* was reverted to only once, in the prayer over the water in Holy Baptism. The draft of *APBA* presented to General Synod was fully agreed by the Commission, but the Third Thanksgiving Prayer in Holy Communion (Second Order) was replaced on the floor of Synod. The change led to the Synod of the Diocese of Sydney refusing to pass a Canon to authorise *APBA*, though it moved a resolution to allow parishes to apply to the Archbishop for permission to use it.

This unhappy development came about at the behest of the Bishop of Ballarat, David Silk, newly arrived from the Church of England, where he was known as a liturgist in the 'Anglo-Catholic' tradition. The resulting shift in policy around liturgical authorisation also led to some loss of trust between dioceses, and loss of interest in the work of the Liturgical Commission. Bishop Silk had approached the General Synod discussion of *APBA* assuming that it worked along the lines of the Church of England. That Church, in its process of liturgical revision, chose not to follow the Australian principle, but to permit the use of wording that is doctrinally ambiguous – a step backward. The reality of living together 'in communion' is not sustained by 'rules' of themselves, however. The trust between clergy and people expressed in the implicit 'covenant' behind *BCP* deepens only as differences in doctrine are faced openly – and new ones keep emerging as contexts change, a notable example being issues around gendered imagery.

A third thesis of this paper is thus: we are called to go 'back to the future' by attending to how graced truth – in its doctrinal, affective and aesthetic dimensions – sustains reverent reality in public prayer.[11]

3 Beyond the 'principle of uniformity'

a) An unhappy inheritance
'Concerning the Service of the Church' (*BCP* 1549) concludes (with hope) that 'now from henceforth all the whole Realm shall have but one Use'. Elizabeth came to the throne in a fraught situation, with the imminent danger of civil unrest. In her first year, the 'Act for the Uniformity of Common Prayer' was issued, imposing imprisonment for deliberate flouting of its provisions – and it remains printed at the front of *BCP*.[12] While understandable in the context of 1559, it brought about the persecution of faithful English Christians, not least by my royal namesakes.

The 'principle of uniformity' is all of a piece with the nature of the Church of England as the established church of that nation. As noted earlier, under Elizabeth and James, it could be interpreted as encouraging an 'inclusive' ethos: a national church cannot not avoid the particularities of diverse places, and must put up with citizens' foibles (especially those squires, colleges and associations who hold the 'living' of each parish). Suspicion of 'conventicles' began under Elizabeth, but did not lead to suppression, provided the Act was not overtly challenged.

The main group affected was Roman Catholics, for whom strict obedience to papal directives meant treason: the Gunpowder Plot at the beginning of James' reign would see popular revulsion arise at anything 'Roman'.

Under Charles I and Archbishop of Canterbury William Laud, however, the 'Star Chamber' became the means by which the Church of England persecuted other Christians – now labelled 'dissenters' or 'non-conformists'. If under the Westminster Commonwealth the boot was on the other foot for 'Anglicans', Cromwell at least did not press the law and allowed some toleration. Charles II promised religious liberty before the Restoration in 1661, but hundreds of ministers ended up being ejected, and others imprisoned (notably John Bunyan).[13] The Preface of *BCP* (1662) – a most unfortunate addition – reads as if its author is looking down the nose at anyone who dares to question it in any way, and could well be described as 'snobbish'.

England, as part of the British Isles, was necessarily a sea-faring nation. The seventeenth century saw colonies emerge overseas, some arising from desire for liberty from the established church (notably in what is now the USA), others taking opportunities for trade (notably slaves, especially in the West Indies). In England, it would not be until 1831 that Christians who did not belong to established Church could live without the burdens imposed by 'uniformity'. As the British Empire spread, the churches which followed may not have been 'established' officially, but this ethos came with them, including to the Australian colonies. Many

Anglicans continued to look down on other Christians, and restrict their practice, not only in England but across the developing Empire. The first Bishop of Australia, William Broughton, for example, used his influence to limit the ministry of Roman Catholics and non-Anglican Protestants, and later bishops would follow his example.

b) *'Inclusiveness': a new Anglican marker?*

As the Anglican Communion of Provinces emerged, 'the prayer book tradition' had become a 'prayer *books*' one by the 1960s. The divisive debates over 'churchmanship' in the preceding century arose in large part due to the 'uniformity' assumption that exactly the same rites must be used by everyone. Thus responses to the Royal Commission of 1906-20 saw a variety of whole prayer books proposed – grey, orange, black, etc. The 1927/28 'crisis' in large part issued from the inability of any party to think beyond 'uniformity'.[14] It led, however, to an increasing acceptance of a diversity of rites: the English bishops agreed not to prosecute clergy who varied from *BCP* within the constraints of the 1928 'Deposited Book', but these limits were widely ignored.

Intra-Anglican divisions began to ease as modern English was introduced in the 1970s, but new forms of difference emerged from increased attention to inculturation in the Provinces of the Anglican Communion.[15] The welcome flexibility of the new services and books saw diversity at the level of local congregations increase, furthered since 2000 by data projection. But these are all matters of internal church life. Of greater concern has been the reality that in the West, churches and society have steadily pulled apart, especially since the 1960s. As a consequence, rural settings aside, many congregations – whether parishioners are locals or from afar – are 'gathered': they naturally want to have liturgy reflect their preferences, whether doctrinal, aesthetic or in lifestyle.

The 'principle of uniformity', whose ethos was still largely in place in the sixties, has been overturned. Many Anglicans now view their part of the Christian tradition as 'inclusive' at heart – a sharp reversal of the historic position! An ethos of 'inclusiveness' applies not only around diverse approaches to gender (notably over the ordination of women) and sexuality (notably around attitudes to divorce and same-sex relations), but also to contested governance, and diversity in liturgical practice. Positively, this shift has been furthered by less exclusive ecumenical relationships,[16] growing awareness of the universal scope of God's grace, and an ethos of hospitality gradually displacing one of superiority. Yet it has also tended towards extremes of practice. In congregations self-identified as 'catholic', services are conducted in an esoteric style, tending towards the congregational being an audience to clerical gymnastics. In stark contrast, 'lowest common denominator' approaches to liturgy are taken elsewhere, ironically, in some places self-identified as 'evangelical' or ' Bible-based', little public reading of the scriptures takes place, and few if any intercessions for the wider world are offered. Singing and (long) sermons predominate, even over Bible reading – and both are clergy-controlled as much as among 'catholic' liturgical fundamentalists. With all this goes a lack of knowledge, critical awareness and even interest in pre-*AAPB* Anglican history and liturgy.

The 'principle of uniformity' may have died among Anglicans, though in different guise there are pressures to extend it in the Roman Catholic Church.[17] But what is to take its place?

c) Common prayer shaped by the mission of God

Sustaining 'common prayer' remains crucial. Without this, congregations grow apart unwittingly, and the door is open for consumerist ideology to dominate church life ('church shopping' is no laughing matter). Anglicans tend to think of 'common prayer' as the contents of *BCP*, but the concept is wider. It is an ethos, a sense of corporate prayer that crosses boundaries of place, culture and language. More than an Anglican phenomenon, 'common prayer' ideally embraces the spiritual life of all who own the name of Christ. But how is this sustained in the post-modern air we breathe today?

Having the words of a service the same across congregations made sense in ages past: until the 1960s, Anglicans (and other Protestant Christians) had a shared vocabulary and experience of worship, heightened by the *King James Bible* being the only English version in use, and a 'canon' of well-known hymns. Today such an idea belongs to history. But sharing key words matters: someone who participates regularly in church should after a few months be able to join along with others in saying the Lord's Prayer, confessing sin and faith, sing some songs with familiarity, and make congregational responses. Beyond this minimal level, creative work has seen widespread ecumenical agreement on common *structure* as sustaining common prayer.

Classically, two shapes for Christian liturgy emerged: the 'office' shape, consisting of psalms and songs framing readings from scripture, together with intercessions; and the 'eucharistic' shape of two 'tables' of the Word proclaimed (*synaxis*) and enacted (the Lord's Supper) – *verbum audibile et visibile*.[18] The rubrics of *BCP* saw both parts brought together in the standard Sunday service, as Morning Prayer, Litany and Holy Communion, though these became separated in the nineteenth century. Liturgical revision in the Anglican world has seen them brought back together,[19] restructured into an overall five-fold shape derived from ecumenical scholarship: *gather, listen, pray, do, go*. Alongside this, the continued use of classical 'shapes' for particular elements (intercessions and the Lord's Supper) assists common prayer at a more detailed level.

The shape of God's mission

Significantly, this overall structure corresponds to the 'shape' of the mission of God. Israel of old was *gathered* by

God at Sinai to *listen* to the covenant, to offer the three-dimensional *prayer sacrifices* of dedication, thanksgiving, well-being and humility,[20] to *celebrate* the covenant and *live it out* in justice and peace. A similar 'shape' undergirds the New Covenant/Testament. Jesus Christ called people to *gather* around him as disciples, to *listen* to his teaching, and to follow his example of *sacrificial prayer* and holy living. He assured them of his living presence as they obeyed his commend to '*do this* for my remembrance', and commissioned them to *go out* into all the world. This shape – gather, listen, pray, do, go – thus begins with God's call, attends to God's word, responds in prayer and action and issues in being sent out to perform the gospel. It is the shape of God's mission, epitomised in the following graphic.[21]

Being gathered by God	**Gather**	
	Listen	Listening to the words of the covenant
Responding in prayer	**Pray**	
	Do	To celebrate the covenant
Perform the gospel in daily living	**Go**	

This represents a major part of the 'theory' behind *APBA*: its main Sunday services each follow this shape.[22] It is not the only structure possible for Christian use: a 'pilgrimage' shape is more appropriate for 'rites of passage' such as funerals (as in *APBA*). But a Sunday service lacking rites of gathering, listening, praying, doing and being sent out is significantly impoverished. Each occasion calls for varying emphases in the parts of the common structure. At a baptism, for example, the gathering can include the introduction of the candidate; the prayers may be minimal, and the sermon crafted with visitors in mind, but the 'doing' (baptising) will form a natural focus and climax. An image that captures this flexibility is playing an accordion: the breath which makes it work comes from it being expanded and contracted. And so it is in Christian life: the ever-blowing Spirit breathes the mission of God.

Classical shapes

This structure by itself looks rather thin. It is assisted by strong lectionary provision, good preaching, and employing classical 'shapes' for intercessions and celebrating the Lord's Supper. As regards intercessions, a responsive Litany form, using topics from *BCP*'s 'Prayer for the Church Militant' (said by the priest alone) – world, church, community, those in need, the communion of saints – was taken up in *AAPB* as a flexible way of enabling a congregation to pray beyond its immediate interests.[23] It allows for a variety of voices, congregational participation through responses, and so enables 'common prayers'.[24] The 'collect' form is a classical shape for a particular prayer. In full, it has five parts, each closely related to scriptural teaching: divine address, divine attribute or action, petition arising from this, outcome of the petition, and its grounding in Christ.[25] This sets 'common prayer' in the context of *God's* being and act, and looks to where our prayer will lead, thus avoiding starting with just our situation, or praying without reflecting on what will happen when God responds! Not every part has to be used – this shape is an aid, not a regulation. But once internalised, it is a significant help in shaping our *ex tempore* praying.

A significant classical 'shape' is that for the Lord's Supper. At the Last Supper, Jesus did seven actions: took bread, gave thanks, broke and shared it, then after the meal took wine, gave thanks and shared it. All early accounts of the Lord's Supper, however, omit the meal and consolidate the actions into four: taking bread and wine, offering thanks, breaking the bread, and sharing the bread and wine.[26] The meal formed the *context* of the Last Supper, but is not essential for the Lord's Supper, whose meaning is expressed in these four actions. This 'four-fold' shape became confused over the centuries, especially around debates over the meaning of Christ's presence and action in the eucharist.[27] One of the gains of the Liturgical Movement has been to remove this resulting 'clutter' and get us back to the core. Where there is a deliberate 'taking' (table-setting), offering of thanksgiving focused around 'proclaiming the Lord's death until he come', breaking of the bread and sharing it and the wine, authentic eucharistic common prayer is offered.[28]

Conclusion

To foster 'common prayer' for the future, the rigidity of the 'principle of uniformity' will not do – but neither will 'anything goes'. Adopting a 'common structure' and 'classical shapes' approach carries forward the intention behind uniformity, replacing it with the harmony of a heritage-consistent, mission-shaped flexibility.

This paper has argued that three features of the 'prayer book tradition' remain vital for participating in the mission of God: the scriptures permeating liturgy; keeping what matters accessible to all, so people and clergy worship as covenant partners; and having liturgy support graced, reverent truth. Going 'back to the future' for these aspects of the 'prayer book tradition' is an enduring and ecumenical calling.

On the other hand, common prayer is hindered by the 'principle of uniformity' – a former cornerstone of the 'prayer book tradition' now thankfully abandoned. A better way for the future of this, and every Christian tradition facing post-modernity, is to approach Christian liturgy through a common structure that reflects the shape of the mission of God, employing classical shapes and is sensitive to shifts in culture and context.

Endnotes

1. 'Prayer Book' covered the origins, history and detailed commentary on BCP, with a brief section on 1927-28 and the Liturgical Movement. A year-long subject, it was examined by one three-hour unseen examination.
2. As Bryan Spinks rightly notes, despite the usual focus among Anglicans on the differences between 1549 and 1552, both were short-lived. It was Elizabeth's book which 'settled in' and became familiar to the English

people: this changed little in its 1604 Jacobean and 1662 Restoration versions (beyond a new Preface). Bryan Spinks, *The Rise and Fall of the Incomparable Liturgy. The Book of Common Prayer 1559-1906*. Alcuin Club 92. (London: SPCK, 2017). See also Judith Maltby, *Prayer Book and People in Elizabethan and Early Stuart England*. Cambridge Studies in Early Modern British History (Cambridge: CUP, 2000).

3   See Charles Sherlock, "The Food of the Soul. Thomas Cranmer and Holy Scripture", *Australian Journal of Liturgy* 2/3 (1990) 134–141; Colin Buchanan, *What did Cranmer think he was doing?* Grove Liturgy 7 (Bramcote: Grove, 1976).

4   Homily I, *Exhortation to the Reading and Knowledge of Holy Scripture* Available at http://churchsociety.org/issues_new/ doctrine/homilies/iss_ doctrine_homilies_01.asp.

5   *Oaths Affirmations Declarations And Assents Canon 1992*, available at https://www.anglican.org.au/ data/canons/Oaths_Affirmations_ Declarations_and_Assents_Canon_1992.pdf.

6   As the Constitution Section 4, part of the 'permanent' provisions, states, Provided, and it is hereby further declared, that the above-named *Book of Common Prayer*, together with the Thirty-nine Articles, be regarded as the authorised standard of worship and doctrine in this Church, and no alteration in or permitted variations from the services or Articles therein contained shall contravene any principle of doctrine or worship laid down in such standard.

Provided further that until other order be taken by canon made in accordance with this Constitution, a bishop of a diocese may, at his discretion, permit such deviations from the existing order of service, not contravening any principle of doctrine or worship as aforesaid.

7   Section 4 continues by requiring a parish meeting before changes are made to the regular liturgy. This was widely observed in the 'trial use' rites period leading up to *AAPB* and *APBA*, but in the time since would not seem to be as well known or applied. Yet appealing to the 'rules' is rarely the best way of change!

8   Charles Sherlock, *Australian Anglicans Remember* (Mulgrave: Broughton, 2015) provides information, readings, sentences and prayers for each Australasian event or person in the *APBA* Calendar.

9   For discussion of these and similar factors, see Charles Sherlock, *Performing the Gospel in Liturgy and Life* (Mulgrave: Broughton, 2017), and Juliette Day & Benjamin Gordon-Taylor (eds), *The Study of Liturgy and Worship*. An Alcuin Guide (London: SPCK, 2013), especially 'Foundations' and 'Elements'.

10   See *Performing the Gospel*, Chapter Six.

11   It is often said that Anglican theological reflection revolves around scripture, tradition and reason. The difficulty with this (nineteenth century innovation) is that it is like comparing a recipe, cooking and eating: the scriptures are a thing, tradition is a process, and reason is an instrument of logic. A better approach is found in ARCIC II, *The Gift of Authority*, #14-23.

12   The 'Reformation Settlement' of Elizabeth has personal relevance, since Ridley faculty are required by the College's Articles of Association to affirm its 'constructive and evangelical principles'.

13   Geoffrey Robertson, *The Tyrannicide Brief* (London: Vintage, 2006) and Charles Spencer, *Killers of the King* (London: Bloomsbury, 2014). These

two books, by lawyers rather than church historians, trace the careers of the legal figures (themselves practising Christians) who took part in drawing up the Bill for the execution of Charles I. Contrary to Charles II's promise, after the Restoration they were hunted down; several were hung, drawn and quartered.

14 See Donald Gray, *The 1927-28 Prayer Book Crisis*. Alcuin / GROW Joint Liturgical Studies 60, 61 (Norwich: SCM, 2005, 2006).

15 See David Holeton (ed.), *Liturgical Inculturation in the Anglican Communion*. Grove Liturgy Studies 18 (Bramcote Notts: Grove, 1991).

16 An important example was the adoption in 1973 by General Synod of the 'Admission to Communion Canon', which allowed 'communicant members of a Christian tradition that holds the apostolic faith' to receive holy communion in Australian Anglican churches. Prior to this, only Anglicans were admitted. As a young adult, I vividly remember kneeling at the communion rail next to my devout Presbyterian, and so 'unconfirmed', uncle. The priest administered holy communion to me, but passed my uncle by, shocking me into wanting this to change. We had both been present at my grandfather's funeral a day or two earlier, in the same Anglican church with the same priest.

17 See for example Gerald O'Collinss sj and John Wilkins, *Lost in Translation. The English Language and the Catholic Mass* (Collegville MN: Liturgical Press, 2017).

18 'Lord's Supper' is used here to refer to the second part of the full service that *BCP* describes as 'Holy Communion'. Roman Catholics helpfully employ such usage to distinguish this from the full service, which they describe as the 'Mass' or 'Eucharist'.

19 *Prayer Book Revision in Australia* (Sydney: General Synod Standing Committee, 1969) was the turning-point for Australian Anglicans. If you see a copy of this book (it has a distinctive purple / blue cover), take and read it!

20 This description seeks to convey the meaning of the various sacrifices, none of which dealt with intentional sin (that was the distinctive function of *yom kippur*, the Day of Atonement. See Charles Sherlock, *Words and the Word. Case Studies in Scripture* (Melbourne: Mosaic / Morningstar, 2013) chapter 7.

21 My thanks to Sarah Crutch, Editor, *The Spirit* (Anglican Diocese of Bendigo) for this graphic.

22 Holy Communion Outline Order (*APBA* page 813) shows this structure on a single page. First Order Morning & Evening Prayer (*APBA* pages 3ff) are modern translations of the respective *Book of Common Prayer* services, in 'office' shape. The only heading is 'Introduction', to clarify what is to be used on Sundays.

23 This list is itself drawn from scriptural directions for intercessions, for example 1 Timothy 2.1-5. It has been well said that when the *BCP* Litany has been offered, prayer has been made on the basis of, and with supplication for, every ground and topic mentioned in the Bible.

24 See *APBA* Holy Communion (Third Order), 172-3, and 'Prayers for Sunday Services', 184-187.

25 Examples include the Collect for Purity which opens Holy Communion (#4 on pages 101, 119, #2 on 168), the Prayer of St John Chrysostom (in two forms at #23 on page 27) as well as the Prayers for the Week and Day. The

evening collect 'Lighten our darkness ... ' (*APBA* page 14 #19) is an example of the form being reshaped.

26 This analysis arose from the painstaking research of Dom Gregory Dix, whose *The Shape of the Liturgy* (London: Dacre Press, Adam and Charles Black, 2nd Edition, 1945) remains a classic. He argues that this 'shape' is what is in common across the earliest Christian churches, rather than common words or doctrine. His thesis has been qualified, but remains a basic strategy of modern liturgical revision.

27 As regards the 'action' of the eucharistic, the Protestant Reformers, reacting against views of the Mass as 'repeating' Christ's sacrifice, tended to see the Holy Communion as 'repeating' the Last Supper (thus primarily looking back - *mimesis*), rather than as celebrating the Lord's Supper (which looks forward and upward as well as 'back' – *anamnesis*). This further confused what it means to obey Christ's command to 'do this.'

28 Much more could be said: the work of *ARCIC* is to my mind helpful in sorting out what matters about eucharistic doctrine and practice – *The Final Report* (1981) as well as the awkward but necessary *Clarifications* (1994), of which I was a signatory. For documents, see https://iarccum.org/org/?o=6

6

The LORD's Song in a Foreign Land

Bosco Peters

Common Prayer is like learning a new language

Go back about five decades, and wherever you went in the English-speaking world, from Aotearoa to Zimbabwe, Anglicans essentially recited the same sonorous Cranmerian words. Anglicans followed a *Book of Common Prayer* (BCP). Let me stress the title: *common prayer*.

It was the same for Roman Catholics. The Roman Catholic Mass was in Latin, and worldwide, Roman Catholics had a common prayer. The ritual may have varied – from humble to grand – but, the words everywhere were identical. There was one Eucharistic Prayer, one set of agreed readings, ubiquitously.

I serve as a priest in the Anglican Church in Aotearoa, New Zealand and Polynesia (ACANZP). I will draw my reflection from that context. This Anglican province has moved from this uniform common recitation of the same words to where, when visiting an unfamiliar Anglican church, one cannot predict what you will encounter. The pendulum has swung from one side to the other. I hope that it is helpful for Anglicans (and others) to be able to locate themselves somewhere on this continuum (from uniformity to diversity) and to reflect on the benefits and disservice of where they stand. A pendulum can swing back the other way, or it can keep going in the same direction and go out of control. I confess to being unable to predict which way the liturgical pendulum of common prayer will progress in my own province, but in this paper I will propose a different model of common prayer which gives more attention to action than to the recitation of identical words.

For Anglicans in Aotearoa New Zealand using *A New Zealand Prayer Book He Karakia Mihinare o Aotearoa (NZPB/HKMA)*, there are different eucharistic rites with intentionally different responses – even to similar cues. The aim was to have these rites feel different, one from the other. When, in a rite's evolution, it had the same response as in another rite, that was changed towards the conclusion of this Prayer Book's development so that there would be a greater sense of variety. So for Anglicans here, it is not until one reaches the biblical readings that responses are found to be the same across the different NZPB/HKMA rites. Those, and the people's response to the Dismissal, are the only parts where the words are the same for all rites. Alongside that, the 1662 BCP (or its slight, 1928 variants) is another alternative. And, when it comes to the biblical readings, different sets of readings are authorised for New Zealand's Anglicans (the Three Year Series, its revision, the Revised Common Lectionary, a home-grown Two Year Series, and the readings in the BCP).

From the mid twentieth century, the Parish Communion movement had impacted New Zealand so that its aim of 'gathering the Lord's people around the Lord's table on the Lord's day' has now mostly become the norm here. Alongside this common prayer of the Eucharist as the jewel in our worship's crown there was daily prayer. As elsewhere, New Zealand Anglicanism had a requirement of its clergy to pray Morning and Evening Prayer from the BCP. Although that book had some options in the sequence of psalms and readings, again, let us note, people had a real sense of praying the same words – whether one was praying alone or together. And with all contained in one prayer book, lay people easily joined clergy in this praying, or they could pray this at home. Daily prayer, in this sense, formed the crown in which the jewel was set. Together, Eucharist and daily prayer constituted the core of the sense of common prayer.

Beginning in the 1960s, New Zealand Anglicans produced different revisions of the Eucharist that were bound together in NZPB/HKMA as described above. Revisions of Daily Prayer for NZPB/HKMA also began in the 1960s. Many felt the agreement requiring clergy to pray daily prayer was more honoured in the breach than in the observance, and so, rather than uphold the rule as an aspirational requirement, in the 1980s, Anglicans in New Zealand's General Synod went through the complex process of removing this obligation that clergy pray daily common prayer. Such a change to the formularies (the agreed teaching and practice of the Church) means assenting to the change by majority in all three Houses (laity, clergy, bishops), followed by agreement from a majority of diocesan synods, followed by two thirds majority in all three Houses (all three orders) of a newly elected General Synod, after which a year ensues in which anyone may raise an appeal on the basis that the change contradicts foundational doctrine. The only discipline the ordained promises to have in his or her prayer life is now to wait upon God daily, a notably individualised intention, underscoring the move away from common prayer that this survey is describing.

The Bishop says to each candidate in turn

N, will you then give glory to God,
the holy and blessed Trinity?

Each candidate responds

Glory to God on high, God of power and might.
You are my God.
I can neither add to your glory
nor take away from your power.
Yet will I wait upon you daily in prayer and praise.

I have described the flexibility, alternatives, and exemption from use provided in the 1980s by ANZPB/HKMA. Soon, this was not seen as being sufficient. The new Prayer Book had *A Form for Ordering the Eucharist* (pages 511-514). This was obviously based on The Episcopal Church (TEC)'s 1979 *Book of Common Prayer* (pages 400-405) *An*

Order for Celebrating the Holy Eucharist. This TEC rite is clear that it 'is not intended for use at the principal Sunday or weekly celebration of the Holy Eucharist' (page 400). And the NZPB/HKMA version, similarly, had the second rubric on page 511 which read, '*It is intended for particular occasions and not for the regular Sunday Celebration of the Eucharist.*'

New Zealand's *A Form for Ordering the Eucharist* has a simple list of headings of sections in a eucharistic service ('Gather in the Lord's Name; Proclaim and respond to the Word of God;…') and a framework for a Eucharistic Prayer, with some fixed wording and some places where the text was flexible.

In 1996, General Synod Te Hinota Whanui (GSTHW) passed that 'it is desirable to alter the rubrics which constitute part of the Formulary "A Form for Ordering the Eucharist" to enable more regular use of that form of service.' And it did this 'by deleting the second rubric'. This change to the formularies was confirmed at GSTHW 1998, and came into effect in 1999.

After this, for the Eucharist (including the regular Sunday Celebration of the Eucharist) you could use lots of different responses, borrow them from other countries or places, even make them up, or not use responses at all. But there was still a minimum of responses and agreed words for the Great Thanksgiving (the Eucharistic Prayer).

This was considered still not flexible enough. In 2004, GSTHW passed *An Alternative Form for Ordering the Eucharist* which not only now allowed the borrowing and creation of any responses and texts (and removing any requirement to use local material) but expanded the previous provision by allowing any Eucharistic Prayer authorised by the equivalent to General Synod in any member church of the Anglican Communion. It received sufficient approval at diocesan and hui amorangi levels, was confirmed at GSTHW 2006 and, hence, came into effect in 2007.

At the same time as authorising *An Alternative Form for Ordering the Eucharist*, GSTHW authorised *A Form for Ordering A Service of the Word*. This provides for a flexible framework for non-eucharistic services not covered by the two Forms for Ordering the Eucharist.

Also at the 2004 GSTHW, *A Template for Anglican Worship* was passed (having been presented in 2002) and made a Liturgical Standing Resolution of this Church. This Template asserts, 'The prayer book is the foundation of the template and provides the principal content for its use. However new understandings may happen from the process of rethinking familiar services; in some cases to provide additional insights and in others to discover completely new possibilities.'

The Template is a framework of three movements. In 'Gathering, we establish the community of faith'. In 'Story, a new community is formed and nurtured' (Liturgical components, in no special order, could include: Scripture read or enacted; responses through sermon, meditation, prayer; non-verbal, symbolic actions involving candles, images, greenery, water, etc; sacramental actions such as a blessing and breaking bread, anointing, blessing of places, baptising, making and renewing of vows, hurakohatu, tuku and last rites). In 'Going out, a new community is launched'.

Perhaps a hint of concern may be seen in the Judicial Commission in 2006 adding a rider to the Template's Standing Resolution that

> when conducting services for which there are prayer book forms, they must still follow the specific instructions given there for each service, concerning the order of service and the forms of prayer, etc, which must be used. This template does not contradict any of those requirements.

By now, readers previously unfamiliar with New Zealand's Anglican means for altering agreed teaching and practice will be beginning to follow the procedure to change such 'formularies'. The 'twice round' process, as it is affectionately termed, (of GSTHW, dioceses and hui amorangi, back to GSTHW, and waiting a year in case there is any appeal), comes from a 1928 Act of Parliament.

Alongside the ever increasing liturgical flexibility, a 'Canon of Alternative Services' (dating from at least 1976) had three different schedules listing authorised services, experimental services, and services that could be used upon certain conditions being fulfilled. But, at the 2014 GSTHW, our Church finally acknowledged that it has been acting inconsistently with the 1928 Act and in a way that these schedules of experimental services lacked fundamental authorisation in the first place.

At that same 2014 GSTHW, the process began to enable bishops to authorise services in the episcopal unit over which she or he has oversight. That has come into effect now. It is surrounded by qualifications (including, surprisingly, that what the bishop authorises 'must conform to *A Form for Ordering a Service of the Word* or *An Alternative Form for Ordering The Eucharist*').

In 1914, the Rev. H. T. Purchas wrote in *A History of the English Church in New Zealand* (page 231) that 'The conduct of public worship in New Zealand presents no special features in contrast with that of the mother Church.' Leaving to one side this colonial oversimplification which neglected to observe the unique Maori pattern of worship, the statement points to the liturgically conservative nature of this particular Anglican province which continued like this until about half a century ago. I hope what has been made clear in this brief survey is that this province has become one of the most audacious.

Alongside this growing elasticity of the province's liturgical agreements, we find other developments:

Increasingly, those responsible for worship do not know what our agreements consist of – there is not one place where one can easily find what we have actually agreed to. And even when those agreements are found, there is disagreement and confusion about what they mean. Take, for example, the latest change – a bishop being allowed to authorise a rite within her or his jurisdiction. Disagreement about what this means extends all the way to the House of Bishops.

Can a bishop authorise and use a way of ordaining different to the agreed rite of ordination? Bishops have, contrary to NZPB/HKMA, ordained priests and deacons (and even licensed lay ministries) within the single ordination prayer (called the 'prayer of consecration' in NZPB/HKMA page 896). Bishops have changed presider within that prayer, changed language part way through the prayer (with the translation not translating what the agreed English text says), moved at which point in the prayer hands are laid on heads (and even, I am told, omitted the laying on of hands).

Some say that bishops can authorise whatever they like, except that they cannot change the ordinal as that goes against the Canon of Standards Required of a Bishop (which defines as misconduct 'Refusal or neglect to use authorised Ordination Liturgies', Title D, Canon II, 4.3). Others say that the bishops can only authorise rites for which there is no formulary. These claim that if there's a formulary for it, that's what has to be used. And then there are those who claim that bishops now can authorise anything whatsoever – they cannot, by definition, 'neglect to use authorised Ordination Liturgies' because a bishop who ordains in a certain way has, by the very fact of doing that, authorised it.

In 2011, confusion got to the point where the ACANZP was preparing to print a new copy of NZPB/HKMA, replacing about a fifth of it without having followed the agreed process for altering its content. Furthermore, there are some who see the Church's legislation referring to NZPB/HKMA as meaning anything liturgical authorised beyond the BCP, whilst others see NZPB/HKMA as referring solely to the (different editions of the) physically bound book.

Alongside it being difficult to ascertain what we have actually agreed to, there is a paucity of liturgical study, training, and formation. Liturgy has an image problem. And people have the impression that studying liturgy is about arguing about things like should the priest's thumb and forefinger be joined together at certain points in the service, and if so, when?

Finally, even when agreements are crystal clear, there are significantly large numbers of clergy and communities that flaunt their defiance of our agreements. Obeying the agreements we have vowed and signed up to is seen by some as a pharisaical obsession with rules, a disregard of our missional context, and straining out a gnat while swallowing a camel.

Before proceeding, let's summarise where this chapter has reached thus far. New Zealand Anglicanism is a good example, possibly the best example, of a province that has over the last half decade moved from a common prayer where everyone recited identical words to a new situation where our liturgical agreements are so flexible, confused, and confusing that 'reciting identical words' cannot be used as a descriptor of contemporary 'common prayer'. Even when agreements are clear, that is no assurance that these agreements will be followed.

In the previous paragraph, I used the word 'example' to indicate that our evolving flexibility is also found, to varying degrees, in other Anglican provinces. The Church of England has moved from a single book to a series of volumes of *Common Worship*. The Episcopal Church complements its 1979 *Book of Common Prayer* with a variety of other resources. And ignoring agreements is not something found in New Zealand alone!

Furthermore, such flexibility is not limited to Anglicanism. Since the Second Vatican Council, Roman Catholics have variants within their English language eucharistic rite. Nowadays, after the Sign of the Cross, there are four possible different greetings, followed by a plethora of options for the Penitential Act, and later a choice may be made from a number of Eucharistic Prayers. Yes, responses to the readings are fixed, the conclusion to the Offertory is also, as is the Communion Rite. What I have described, in relation to English language services, means that on the same day, in the same city in New Zealand, Roman Catholics can end up participating at different Masses where most of the words are *not* the same. Furthermore, what I have just described is the 'Ordinary Form'. For at least the last decade, the 'Extraordinary Form of the Roman Rite' (the Latin Missal issued by Pope John XXIII in 1962) is used in places alongside the vernacular. This has different readings, and the Extraordinary Form is not simply some Latin version of the Ordinary Form. So, Roman Catholic faithful can be at Mass on the same day now, and not even have the same biblical readings.

Alongside this variety in the Eucharist, Roman Catholics have The Divine Office – the daily prayer of psalms, readings, and prayers. This has a stronger sense of common prayer as being recitation of identical words. The Divine Office binds all to pray the same psalms at the same time of day. And translations are determined so that all within the jurisdiction of a Bishops Conference are using the same translation. But all is not as tight as might first appear. Roman Catholic monasteries, for example, may have their own, quite different, sequence of psalms, let alone a different translation.

So the pendulum has been swinging from one side, reciting identical words, to the other, where all of us act according to our own desires (Deuteronomy 12:8), and all the people do what is right in their own eyes (Judges 17:6; 21:25). I cannot judge whether this pendulum of verbal homogeneity will swing back. Or will it lurch wildly further, detach from its pivot, and lose its anchor point?

The most recent meeting of GSTHW began with a Eucharist in which the Eucharistic Prayer was not one approved by our province – it was a translation into English of a Te Reo Maori one. The irony was not lost on people: GSTHW was meeting primarily to debate intensely on a particular liturgical agreement (the formularies around marriage and the place that committed same-sex couples have within that agreement). Some objected that a non-authorised Eucharistic Prayer was being used. Others disputed the quality or appropriateness of the translation. And there are those who disagreed with the theology of the text. In any case, all this was part of the energy that led to GSTHW 2018 beginning the process of removing the right to use Eucharistic Prayers authorised beyond this province (the heart of *An Alternative Form for Ordering the Eucharist*). This debate now heads to the dioceses and hui amorangi. Whether removing this right this will be accomplished, and whether this is the beginning of returning to a more common verbal prayer may take some decades to ascertain. I do not think that getting this reciting-identical-words toothpaste back into a liturgical practice tube is a realistic, even-medium-term goal. As I indicated at the beginning of this paper, I think a more fruitful approach is viewing common prayer differently, alongside a more moderate aspiration of shared wording.

Before we turn to that model, let's take a final look at some of the advantages and drivers of flexibility as well as the possible disservices that it brings.

The *Book of Common Prayer*, of course, was made possible, from the sixteenth century onwards, by originally relatively new technology: the printing press. The variety and flexibility of words that I have been describing has also been made possible by new technology: computers, printers, photocopiers, projectors and screens.

We arrive at the service with little idea of what lies ahead and are presented with a newly-printed booklet for that service and that service alone. In many places, only when the slide is projected onto the screen do you know what you are about to pray, profess or sing.

Rather than declaring in church that life is about worship, about edification, this approach embodies the belief of much of our surrounding culture that life is basically about entertainment, and entertainment is about things constantly being different.

Rather than being common prayer – owned by the laity as much as the clergy – the power has shifted to the leadership of that particular service.

Words that our liturgical tradition understands as being addressed to each other are now directed to the screen or to the booklet in our hands. For example, at The Peace, when we should be addressing each other, in the NZPB/HKMA, the responses to 'The peace of Christ be always with you' (page 419), or 'The peace of God be with you all' (page 466), or 'The peace of God be always with you' (page 485) are completely different in each case. And, I remind you, that is if the leader is not being 'creative' and providing us with words beyond these three options.

Yes, our attention at worship is being held by the ever-changing words, but our attention is not being drawn to God or each other; our attention is on the screen or the sheet. There is little encouragement to worship 'by heart'

A concomitant reality is that there is inordinate time and energy expended in preparing creative, diverting services. Surprisingly, Cranmer's Preface to the 1549 edition of the Book of Common Prayer becomes challengingly relevant. He describes the pre-Reformation, inherited pattern of services where more time was taken to find what needs to be read than actually to read it once it was found: 'Moreover the number and hardness of the rules called the *pie*, and the manifold changings of the service, was the cause, that to turn the book only, was so hard and intricate a matter, that many times, there was more business to find out what should be read, than to read it when it was found out.'

The model of common prayer that I have been writing about thus far focuses on words, the praying of identical words. Those who contributed most to NZPB/HKMA were quality wordsmiths. Instructions, the rubrics (from the Latin *rubrica*, red), for actions and gestures were kept to a minimum. In the catch cry, 'say the black; do the red', this essay has put saying the black first. And I have demonstrated that uniformity in saying the black has been swinging towards disparity.

But there is also a language of gestures and actions. Jesus said, 'Do this in memory of me', not 'Read these pages, recite these power-point texts, in memory of me.' So, rather than seeing gestures and actions as interpretive embellishment of the all-important words, let's put the red first: what happens when we start focusing on gestures and actions and seeing the words as interpreting the actions?

In what follows, I want to draw on this understanding of a language of symbols, gestures and actions. This non-verbal dimension has its own grammar. I need to emphasise, because of our focus on the verbal, and liturgical renewal's strong emphasis on getting the words right, that I now want to use the valuable understandings we have from grammar and apply this to the non-verbal, this non-verbal language in liturgy.

Let us first clarify how language and its grammar works. If you are a good, native speaker and writer, you take certain things for granted. For example, it is 'the book' not 'book the'. Such a foundational norm, that the article comes before the noun, makes English, for example, the language that it is. You only disregard this rule if you are tired or distracted. Breaking such a rule of English would make a sentence cease to be clear language. 'The article comes before the noun' is a rule that describes how the language works. It is descriptive. But, if you are teaching people the English language, and English is new to them, then this rule appears prescriptive.

Rubrics in a prayer book describe the way that Christians worship. Just as in English grammar, there are different categories of grammatical rules. A preeminent tier consists of foundational norms of actions, signs, and gestures that make what we do Christian worship. Breaking one of these foundational-norm rules of liturgy would make these actions, signs, gestures, (and words) cease to be Christian worship.

There is a second group of rules in grammar that, again, native English writers and speakers will follow naturally. This second group of rules are conscious of context. The way we write formally for an academic journal will be different to the way we speak in a conversation in a café. Well-formed, native speakers follow these rules as naturally as they observe the foundational norms. They think about them only when they notice others contravening them.

Using water to baptise, for example, is a foundational norm. But what to wear presiding at the Eucharist, I suggest, belongs to the second category I have described.

Problematically, standard grammar books do not always distinguish between foundational norms and the social norms of context that the second group refers to. And the same is often true for rubrics, although rubrics can attempt to distinguish different levels of obligation: 'does', 'should do', 'appropriately does', 'may do'.

NZPB/HKMA (page 515), for example, says, 'The presiding priest at the Eucharist should wear a cassock and surplice with stole or scarf, or an alb with the customary vestments.' What the presider wears at the Eucharist does not affect whether the worship is Christian liturgy or not. I suggest that wearing jeans and a T-Shirt in Canterbury Cathedral for Christmas Midnight Mass would be inappropriate. Similarly, I suggest that, in a small house-group or hospital-bedside Eucharist, fully vesting in alb and chasuble could be inappropriate.

I am sure we are all clear: in writing in English, good, native speakers and writers take certain things for granted. Grammar rules, then, are descriptive. But for someone newer to the English language, these same rules are prescriptive – they indicate how one should speak and write English. The same is true in worship. The more one is immersed in the Christian tradition of liturgy, the more the rules are descriptive, not merely prescriptive.

There is a third group of rules of grammar which are essentially invented 'rules': don't split infinitives; don't end a sentence with a preposition; don't use 'hopefully' for 'I hope'; and so on. There are, of course, grammarians who do not distinguish these three categories, treating them all as of equal status. In liturgy, I think most of us who worship intelligently can recognise what would fit into this third category of invented 'rules': increasing numbers of swings of the thurible towards clergy as compared to laity; never taking the consecrated bread and wine from the front of the altar; always having an ordained person administer the consecrated bread; and so on.

The story of the abbot's cat helps. Each afternoon, at 3pm, the abbot would address the monks and any visitors. The cat would wander around and distract people from the abbot's talk. So the monks decided that at 2:55pm, they would tie the cat to a tree near its bowl. Each day, at 2:55pm, tie up the cat before the abbot speaks. Some years passed, the abbot died, and a new abbot was appointed. Each day, at 2:55pm, tie up the cat before the abbot speaks. Time passed. That abbot died. A new abbot was appointed. Each day, at 2:55pm, tie up the cat before the abbot speaks. Finally, the cat died. Now, remember, the rule is, 'Each day, at 2:55pm, tie up the cat before the abbot speaks.' So, they had to get a new cat in order that the rule be obeyed.

For Anglicans particularly, the dearth of rubrics might be intended to allow for intelligent adaptation to a particular context, but that assumes quality liturgical formation. Instead, usages that may have been appropriate in one context are transferred without critique into another. An example is that the burse and veil were seemly when the priest presided *ad orientem* (facing East), but they end up as clutter between priest and people for the Ministry of the Word when the priest presides facing the people *versus populum* (for which I have coined *in circuitu altaris*, around the altar; *in circuitu mensae*, around the table). For Roman Catholics, The General Instruction for the Roman Missal (118) has clear instructions that the burse and veil, if used, are not on the altar. Many Anglicans, however, lacking rubrics about this, continue to place the burse and veil on the altar during the Ministry of the Word. This forms just one example of an 'abbot's cat'.

Liturgical practices, then, accrue over time. Uncritically, people often imitate and continue practices they admire, from people and communities they esteem. Actions end up being forced onto a rite – they have no intrinsic connection to it but are imported into it. Rather than being self-explanatory, as most good actions are, they normally need considerable explanation and are often allegorical in nature.

I contrast to poor practices, symbols need to be large and obvious – we use a lot of water, not droplets. Gestures need to be simple, clear and expansive. A Christian priest is not involved in esoteric, arcane gestures – liturgy is the work done by the whole the Christian community, it is not the work done by the priest for the Christian community. That is the distinction between liturgy and magic. Simple, ample, clear, and understandable – these are the sort of focuses in liturgical study, training and formation. Just as one cuts back on the clutter of passives and prepositions if we are forming people to write well in English.

Ecumenical agreements have leaped over misunderstood conflicts from the Reformation period. Rites across denominations now regularly have the same shape. This is a common prayer in the form of action and with a shared underlying grammar that we can build on by more intentionally shared study, training and formation.

In September 2017, Pope Francis issued a motu proprio, *Magnum Principium* (The Great Principle). This changes Canon 838 on translating liturgy into the vernacular. It returned the authority over liturgical translations to the conferences of bishops, and changed canon law. Canon 838.3 now reads, 'It pertains to the conferences of bishops to prepare and publish, after the prior review of the Holy See, translations of liturgical books in vernacular languages, adapted appropriately within the limits defined in the liturgical books themselves.' This is quite a leap forward from *Liturgiam authenticam*, promulgated by the Vatican in 2001. It had a very strict word-for-word translation rule and resulted in an English-language translation of the Roman Missal from Latin into English which abandoned ecumenically-agreed texts, and hence also lost musical traditions which were shared ecumenically.

Anglicans, Roman Catholics, and others who stand within the liturgical tradition have a shared lectionary, a shared grammar of actions, symbols, and gestures, and a shared shape and dynamic of rites and prayers. With a stronger attention to liturgical study, training, and formation (and I am challenging my own Church most forcibly), we could have a new form of common prayer at a deeper level and even, possibly, sharing texts across denominations in our local, country context.

Common prayer begins the moment two or three gather to pray in Christ's name, and even when one person prays alone, conscious that others also pray. Liturgy is like a language. While liturgical grammar is descriptive of the way well-formed Christians pray, it can appear more prescriptive for those growing into the Christ life. In the end, common prayer is individuals being drawn and immersed into Christ, and, by the power of the Holy Spirit, being raised up to the divine life of Christ. That is the action of common prayer.

7

Liturgical Authorisation in Australian Anglicanism: Who still cares?

Elizabeth J. Smith

An important part of prayer book tradition is the high level at which books have historically been authorised. In the past 100 years, in a trend which has accelerated in the past 20 years, the level at which liturgical material is authorised in Anglicanism has dropped significantly. Now a dispersed process of authorisation has been added to the mix.

The first lowering of the level at which liturgical resources are authorised came when the British Parliament ceased being asked to approve Prayer Books. The British Parliament had been the originating authoriser of the *Book of Common Prayer of 1662*, the Prayer Book of colonial Australia. After Parliament's failure to approve the proposed BCP of 1928, secular authority was not sought again for subsequent Church of England liturgical material. Classically, since then, around the Anglican world and in Australia, agreed texts are signed off not by a parliament but by a national Church, through its synod. There is only one place where Australian Anglican liturgical provisions still intersect with secular law. Anglican clergy celebrating marriages are required to use authorised Anglican rites. Otherwise, the State has no interest in how Anglicans worship.

Authorisation by General Synod

For Australians, the General Synod road to authorisation became possible after the 1960s, when local Anglicans shed their 'Church of England' label. In the 1970s, the Anglican Church of Australia set about producing its own Prayer Book. It managed to navigate its own synodical authorisation process so that in 1978 *An Australian Prayer Book* (AAPB)[1] was published. AAPB was a first-wave revision of the BCP, with attendant clunkiness and gaps. It had some conservative revisions – those called 'First Order' – that were almost pure BCP minus the thees and thous. They kept the Cranmerian sequencing of elements but used 20th century vocabulary and slightly simplified syntax. AAPB had other material –usually headed 'Second Order' – that drew on the liturgical scholarship and ecumenical convergence of the previous two decades. In this category were Second Order Holy Communion, Daily Prayer, Marriage, Funerals, Baptism in Holy Communion and more.

Generally, the Cranmerian-sequenced orders appealed to the more Evangelical and conservative areas of the Australian Church, while the new, ecumenically-influenced orders appealed to more Catholic and progressive Australian Anglicans. New body-language was important, too, as north-end or eastward-facing priests and kneeling congregations learned, sometimes reluctantly, to face each other, to stand rather than kneel for many prayers, and to make eye contact and even hand contact at the Greeting of Peace. Lay people took new roles in helping the priest to lead services, preparing intercessions and assisting with the distribution of Holy Communion. Congregations grew accustomed to participating in scripted dialogues with the priest.

During these years, bishops were often the liturgical innovators, urging conservative clergy and reluctant laity to embrace the changes. AAPB took its place alongside renewed liturgies in many other provinces, whose new Prayer Books and other resources began to appear on clergy bookshelves. Interesting comparisons were drawn.

The second wave of revision from the mid 1980s to the mid 90s was harder. New issues, especially the ordination of women, had polarised Australian Anglicans. 'Inclusive' language was called for, so that it would no longer be 'for us men and our salvation' that Christ was 'made man'. Sisters needed to be named along with brothers, and addresses to God needed to be diversified from the purely patriarchal to a more expansive biblical vocabulary. Through these years, non-liturgical Australian English was also changing away from 'sexist' language a little more slowly than in the USA and considerably faster than in the UK. More work had been done on the Ordinal, with women already ordained as deacons and priests by 1992. The Marriage service needed to reflect big social changes. Funeral orders expanded to provide resources for the tragic death of young children and of babies around the time of birth.

Work towards *A Prayer Book for Australia* (APBA)[2] also reflected the fact that ecumenical liturgical renewal had continued apace through the late 1970s and into the 1980s. The English Language Liturgical Consultation (ELLC) produced internationally agreed texts for key liturgical elements such as the Creeds, canticles, the Lord's Prayer and eucharistic responses. The International Anglican Liturgical Consultation (IALC) began meeting biennially to share new scholarship and resources from around the Communion, with provinces enthusiastically borrowing and adapting each other's new texts. The three-year Sunday eucharistic lectionary, a paradigm-shifting innovation from Rome found almost unchanged in AAPB, continued to evolve ecumenically towards the Revised Common Lectionary. The renewal of rites of Baptism, Confirmation, Reception and Reaffirmation was important in this period. Roman Catholics developed their influential Rite of Christian Initiation of Adults (RCIA), drawing on historical sources. Many denominations rediscovered the Catechumenate in a Western world where rates of infant baptism were dropping and adult converts needed careful preparation for an integrated rite of Baptism, Confirmation and Holy Communion. These developments added an ecumenical dimension to Anglican authorisation processes.

APBA also showed evidence of a maturing Australian accent in local liturgical writing, in the occasional prayers and pastoral prayers in services for funerals, weddings, and ministry with the sick. The Australian Anglican liturgical accent is characterised by simplicity of vocabulary and syntax and directness and accessibility of meaning. It cannot be accused of being 'flowery'. It has sometimes been criticised for its lack of poetic resonance. The proposed new Prayer Book offered the fruits of all these trends as trialled by many congregations, and as argued over by liturgical scholars representing both catholic and evangelical Australian Anglicans.

Whatever the accent, conformity with the doctrine of the BCP still had to be demonstrated for every innovation and variation, however historically based and ecumenically acclaimed. There is no Cranmerian precedent for material common in most other renewed liturgies around the Communion, such as the solemn Good Friday liturgy or the Great Vigil of Easter, Palm Sunday processions, ashes on Ash Wednesday, and so on. Anointing with oil of chrism and the lighting of a candle after baptism are found only in the notes to Holy Baptism in APBA, not in the order itself. Cranmer had nothing to say about all these matters, and APBA would therefore also be silent on them.

When the 1995 General Synod met to discuss the draft of APBA, the debates were to some extent a proxy for other Anglican tensions, such as the ordination of women and lay administration of Holy Communion. Most of the Cranmerian purists had already abandoned both the BCP and AABP for all but the early morning Holy Communion service, in favour of locally published orders for preaching and prayer. But they used General Synod first to remove from APBA anything too objectionable to Reformed sensibilities, and then to reduce the status of APBA from a Prayer Book 'for use together with the BCP' to something less iconic: 'liturgical resources authorised by General Synod'.

APBA was nevertheless embraced with enthusiasm in most Australian dioceses. Some of it still clunked. Compromises had been made. APBA did not provide – no Prayer Book could – for every local liturgical need. Yet the culture around the church was increasingly hungry for innovation and quickly bored with repetition. APBA had many permissive rubrics, encouraging the use of 'these or other suitable words,' but the capacity of local communities and clergy to generate those words was limited. Over many attempts at local creativity hovered the shadow of fear that using non-APBA words might be illegal, uncanonical, heretical, and likely to attract the wrath of the bishop. Others blithely shed all textual, lectionary and rubrical constraints along with clerical robes and traditional hymnody, in the supposed interests of cultural relevance or missional effectiveness.

Authorisation by Episcopal and Ministerial Discretion

Behind many of these anxieties hovered Section 4 of the *Constitution* of the Anglican Church of Australia. Whether bishops were cautious or extravagant in their local embrace of non-BCP, non-AAPB, non-APBA liturgical resources, they had limited grounds for authorising such material. In section 4 of the Constitution, the relevant paragraphs read:

> ... it is hereby further declared, that the above-named Book of Common Prayer, together with the Thirty-Nine Articles, be regarded as the authorised standard of worship and doctrine in this Church, and no alteration in or permitted variations from the services or Articles therein contained shall contravene any principle of doctrine or worship laid down in such standard.
>
> Provided further that until other order be taken by canon made in accordance with this Constitution, a bishop of diocese may, at his discretion, permit such deviations from the existing order of service, not contravening any principle of doctrine or worship as aforesaid, as shall be submitted to him by the incumbent and churchwardens of a parish.
>
> Provided also that no such request shall be preferred to the bishop of a diocese until the incumbent and a majority of the parishioners present and voting at a meeting of parishioners, duly convened for the purpose, shall signify assent to such proposed deviations. Such meeting shall be duly convened by writing,

placed in a prominent position at each entrance to the church and by announcement at the morning and evening services, or at the service if only one, at least two Sundays before such meeting, stating the time and place of such meeting, and giving full particulars of the nature of the proposed deviation.[3]

The phrase 'until other order be taken by canon' is sometimes referred to as the 'trial use' provision. It was intended to allow the testing of preparatory drafts for new Prayer Books. Around Australia, based on this provision, countless 'deviations' from the BCP, AAPB and APBA were officially authorised or quietly permitted. This represents a process of authorisation that rests with the discretion of the bishop of a diocese rather than with the General Synod. But questions arise. Do these authorised deviations have an expiry date? Did all of them arise at the request of an incumbent and a majority of parishioners present and voting at a meeting (the Constitutional wording suggests a grassroots source, or at least a grassroots request, for the introduction of deviations). Or did many of them arise because a General Synod, a diocesan Synod, a Standing Committee or a Liturgy Commission offered them in good faith, in a more top-down movement?

Another way of permitting 'variations' (less sinister-sounding than the earlier 'deviations') was legislated in the *Canon Concerning Services 1992*. Section 5 of the Canon Concerning Services provides that

(1) The minister may make and use variations which are not of substantial importance in any form of service authorised by section 4 according to particular circumstances.

(2) Subject to any regulation made from time to time by the Synod of a diocese, a minister of that diocese may on occasions for which no provision is made use forms of service considered suitable by the minister for those occasions.

(3) All variations in forms of service and all forms of service used must be reverent and edifying and must not be contrary to or a departure from the doctrine of this Church.

(4) A question concerning the observance of the provisions of sub-section 5(3) may be determined by the bishop of the diocese.[4]

It is noteworthy that in this canon the 'minister' rather than the 'bishop' has the discretion to make and use variations. Permission is granted either because the proposed variation is 'not of substantial importance' or that it is for an occasion 'for which no provision is made'. The reference to 'particular circumstance' may hint at a growing desire to adapt liturgical materials to mission contexts. It places quite a responsibility of discernment on the shoulders of a 'minister', who must determine both the variation's importance – or lack of it – and also its doctrinal conformity.

This permission points to the next emerging source of authority, which was triggered in the 1990s and has expanded exponentially since. APBA was slowly, expensively and with daunting complexity, made available in digital form. The revolution of the internet, desktop publishing and data projection opened up new ways to use, avoid using, and supplement APBA. Online, other Anglican Prayer Books and non-Anglican resources were easily plundered for fresh-sounding text. Infinitely more variety is made possible by new technologies of desktop publishing for booklets and data-projected material. The range of possible bending, stretching, warping, supplementing and omitting of authorised texts has been greatly increased as the internet brings international, ecumenical and completely idiosyncratic liturgical resources of high and low quality to within a few mouse-clicks of every worship planner.

Meanwhile, although most Anglicans continued to value a degree of predictability in the texts and structure of their liturgical worship, many, especially younger worshippers and new converts, had a much lower tolerance for repetition than previous generations of worshippers. APBA, despite its permissive rubrics, seemed stifling to some. In some places, the main Sunday eucharistic service may now change on a weekly basis. Even seasonal or monthly variations represent much more frequent changes than anyone would have predicted even 20 years ago. Event-based, evangelistic or Fresh Expressions liturgies will vary even more frequently, often being generated on a service-by-service basis, each (we may hope) from good principles of liturgical design. Worship planners certainly do not give two weeks' notice of parish meetings to approve proposed variations for each special event, and bishops will hardly wish to have to evaluate and authorise each one-off service as it is produced.

The material in Sydney's *Common Prayer: Resources for Gospel-shaped Gatherings*[5] presumably sits under section 4 of the Constitution or the Canon Concerning Services. So do the Liturgy Commission's supplementary Eucharistic orders, occasional prayer texts, Lent, Holy Week and Easter resources, and many other diocesan resources and wider borrowings.

Authorisation by small-group consensus, national non-objection and digital distribution

In the wake of the authorisation by General Synod of APBA as 'Liturgical Resources', the Liturgy Commission of General Synod continued to meet. Its membership and leadership gradually underwent a generational change. Its early task was to produce material for the great fasts and feasts of Lent, Holy Week and Easter. Coming from late 20th century ecumenical liturgical experience, these orders would never have made it through General Synod, but could be offered on a diocese-by-diocese base with a lower level of authorisation. They were first presented to the Standing Committee of General Synod and then to diocesan Bishops. Section 4 of the *Constitution* has that reference to liturgical deviations at a bishop's discretion 'until other order be taken by canon'. This 'trial use' provision, originally intended to allow consultation ahead of Prayer Book revision, together with the *Canon*

Concerning Services, became the slightly wonky platform on which post-APBA national liturgical resources were posted. Not all bishops trusted the platform, and some declined to authorise the material posted on it.

Liturgy Commission members are appointed by the General Synod Standing Committee, and have always included voices representing the dioceses espousing Cranmerian purity as well as those with liturgical sensibilities more historically Anglo-Catholic or more ecumenically progressive. When the Commission promotes a text, it has already been through several very fine filters. Does it avoid creating unpleasant 'vibrations' (as the former Dean of Sydney, the late Boak Jobbins used to say) for adherents of chaste Cranmerian orthodoxy? Can a moderately feminist Anglican woman or man pray it without choking? Does it add something to the basic fare in APBA? Does it have something of an Australian accent? How accessible is it for worshippers from the many cultures of today's Australia?

This is liturgical authorisation by small-group consensus followed by national non-objection (rather than national acceptance). It has produced orders for Ash Wednesday, Palm Sunday, Maundy Thursday, Good Friday and the Easter Vigil, which have since been included with the digital and online versions of APBA. Digitally packaging these with APBA lends them an aura of respectability they technically do not have. Yet they represent the same 'borrow, improve, contextualise' approach to liturgy that fuelled all the new Prayer Books around the Anglican Communion from the 1970s to the 1990s. They are a distillation and local adaptation of Anglican and other mainstream liturgical traditions around the English-speaking world, with only a few locally-written texts.

The Liturgy Commission has since produced texts and orders that are not just adaptations of other provinces' Prayer Books. There are a couple of new Great Thanksgivings and two simple Orders for the Eucharist. Communion resources are mostly in the family of APBA's Second Order Holy Communion but with language in a slightly lower register: simpler syntax, less polysyllabic vocabulary. There are suites of prayers on various themes requested by General Synod and others, including environmental issues and violence against women. Prayers for many occasions, some in high and some in lower registers, have been offered for wider use. Most of these texts originate with one prolific Commission member before they go through the necessary filters ahead of national distribution. Some have been taken up around the Anglican Communion.[6]

These supplementary resources produced at Liturgy Commission level have been generally, if occasionally reluctantly, approved for 'trial use' at the level of General Synod Standing Committee. They are posted on the General Synod website, where they may be found by a diligent searcher. It is then up to a diocesan bishop to allow or refuse permission for clergy in that diocese to make use of the material. Most bishops have been fairly relaxed about granting permission. Some, however, think that in the absence of plans for a new Prayer Book, the 'trial use' provision is not valid, or that any potentially theologically fraught material, including eucharistic material, cannot not be authorised indefinitely under Section 4 of the *Constitution* or the *Canon Concerning Services*.

A dispersed authorisation process

At the 2017 General Synod, in an effort to allay these concerns, an amendment to the *Canon Concerning Services* was promoted, although not by the Liturgy Commission. It also responded to the message from the Liturgy Commission that neither a new Prayer Book nor even a revision of APBA was on the table. The *Canon Concerning Services* now includes what could be described as a dispersed authorisation process. Instead of all the interested parties gathering on the floor of General Synod to debate, amend and eventually authorise or dismiss a liturgical resource, the proposed resource will do the rounds. So the *Canon Concerning Services* now provides that liturgical material may be authorised by completing a four-part process:

- on the recommendation of the Liturgy Commission,
- with the concurrence of the Doctrine Commission,
- by a decision of at least two-thirds of the Diocesan Bishops including all of the Metropolitan bishops,

- and approved for use within that diocese by the diocesan council of that diocese.[7]

This is a high bar for liturgical resources to clear. The process spreads the stages of approval across time and into separate rooms inhabited by different groups with their differing expertise and interests. Unlike General Synod, there is very little scope for informed contributions by Anglican lay people. A 'no' at any stage of the process means the material can go no further. General Synod Commissions are lucky to meet twice a year. The bishops meet only once a year. If discussion and decision-making happen only in face-to-face meetings, rather than by, for example, circular resolutions approved by email, it could be a very long time indeed between moments of authorisation.

Will the 'national non-objection' climate of the past 15 years continue under this new provision? The process outlined in the amended *Canon Concerning Services* is beginning to be tested. The Liturgical Commission has sent its Lent, Holy Week and Easter material to the Doctrine Commission for the first step of this new approval process, with a covering letter to the effect that the resources were prepared with the intention that they be acceptable to the widest possible range of Australian Anglicans, and that the resources are already in wide use in many dioceses around the country. The Diocese of Sydney has referred its *Common Prayer: Resources for Gospel-shaped Gatherings* to the Liturgy Commission with a request that it be authorised through the new process.

It should be noted that unlike the General Synod process, the 2017 dispersed process includes no mechanism by which the Doctrine Commission or the bishops may send back the proposed liturgical material to the Liturgy Commission for a re-think, a re-write or a re-submission. It is a process for authorisation without amendment.

Who still cares about authorisation?

We await with interest the answers to many questions:

Will there be sufficient trust, on the part of the Doctrine Commission and the bishops, in the theological integrity and competence of the Liturgy Commission as a group, to take the Commission's proposals as likely, rather than unlikely, to be widely acceptable?

When material already in diocesan use, such as Sydney's *Common Prayer* is presented for consideration, what criteria will the Liturgy Commission use to evaluate whether it can recommend that the material proceed to the Doctrine Commission in the next stage of the process?

Will the ordained members of the Doctrine Commission and the House of Bishops, who are not passive observers of liturgy but leaders of it in their own context, with their own acquired habits and preferences, be willing to focus on the material before them, rather than what might have been presented had they themselves been preparing it?

How well has the Liturgy Commission, over the past 25 years since the publication of APBA, been reading the liturgical and theological climate of the national Church, in order to offer resources that are actually wanted, and that will in fact fill gaps in the existing provisions?

How will liturgical resources that survive this dispersed authorisation process be made available for users in dioceses that embrace them? Print runs of small parcels of text are unlikely. Digital provision, preferably free to the user, is more or less expected, but who will pay for the formatting and the digital platform? Gone are the days when profits from Prayer Book printing supplemented the General Synod budget to the tune of tens of thousands of dollars a year. Liturgical resource publication is a cost, now, not a cash cow.

Will resources that may be authorised under by the 2017 process be distinctive enough to add to the Australian Anglican liturgical accent that was first heard in AAPB and was developed in APBA? Or will they be swallowed up in the cloud of English-language material that swirls around the world-wide web, generated in a handful of countries and consumed, perhaps uncritically, in a hundred? Will the new resources be new enough to inspire more local writers to produce, first for their own community and then perhaps for wider consideration, new liturgical material that is theologically substantial and culturally relevant?

What will be the effect of the decline of liturgical education on the ability of bishops, clergy and laity to make the decisions that are increasingly devolved dispersed and subtle? Fewer and fewer clergy have known, let alone used, the BCP. Pre-ordination training skimps on liturgical education about the rationale for the reforms of the past 50 years. Missionally-oriented though some services are intended to be, there is a risk of that structure and doctrine will be diminished as respect for authorised text evaporates.

What role will authorised liturgy play as the mission field in Australia continues to change? The surrounding culture grows more and more secular. The percentage of nominal Anglicans continues to decrease. Good liturgy is not going to be the magic bullet that will bring the lapsed back to church, though dreary liturgy will probably put off any who happen along hoping for something to engage body, mind and spirit. What local liturgical changes will be more than window-dressing in Fresh Expressions of church that aim to reach the unchurched?

How will local liturgical creativity and authorisation be funded, as Australian Anglicans make reparations to survivors of institutional child sexual abuse and face the other challenges of 21st century mission? The changing workload of liturgically minded clergy and lay leaders may squeeze out genuine creativity in favour of a quick internet search for something someone else has written that roughly fits. Some dioceses have the scholarly, creative and financial resources to generate and publish their own new texts. Most simply do not have the capacity to do so, and may resort to borrowing, if not from Australian sources, then from other Anglican provinces.

And the perennial question: if the words, the text, the Order or the Rite make up only a modest fraction of what qualifies as good liturgy, how will the new resources, if authorised, promote the better embodiment, performance, enactment of common prayer without a common Prayer Book? Fresh Expressions of Church, pioneer ministries, supplementary non-Sunday-morning congregations in a mixed economy of parish worship opportunities – these rely hugely on the constructive use of space, symbols, actions, music, and on skilled, responsive presiding. Many Sunday morning worshippers have resisted being moved far from their APBA groove almost as strongly as they have continued to resist the reordering of their buildings for 21st century worship. Notoriously, the non-textual elements of liturgy are possible to model, difficult to teach, and impossible to bestow by an authorisation process that is still focused firmly on texts.

More recently-ordained clergy may be less patient with the geological speed and unpredictable outcomes of national authorisation processes. Bishops, whatever their levels of liturgical authorisation anxiety, have other problems on their minds in the wake of the Royal Commission and amid post-Christendom culture.

So lay woman pioneer minister Annabelle may just lift her material unapologetically from Messy Church publications and other material on the internet.

Mid-career priest Ben will continue to rely for his meditation services on text he typed into his computer a decade ago from the Celtic spirituality collection on his shelves.

Activist preacher and pastor Christine will despair of ever getting an Australian Anglican text to pray over the married same-sex couples in her congregation, and will use something from another province without bothering the bishop with it.

Donna and David, recruited from the Church of England, will keep using *Common Worship* online just as they did before they emigrated.

Elizabeth will continue to find it much quicker and more interesting to write a new prayer text than to find someone else's and fix it up. She will make sure her bishop has a copy of anything eucharistic, baptismal or which is otherwise likely to have the blood of past liturgical battles on its pages. You may see her contributions float past you on Facebook, that completely unauthorised distribution channel, and you will make up your own mind about what level of authorisation it needs or deserves.

Endnotes

1. The Standing Committee of the General Synod of The Church of England in Australia, *An Australian Prayer Book, for use together with the Book of Common Prayer, 1662* (Sydney: AIO Press, 1978).
2. The Anglican Church of Australia Trust Corporation, *A Prayer Book for Australia, for use together with The Book of Common Prayer (1662) and An Australian Prayer Book (1978) Liturgical Resources authorised by the General Synod* (Sydney: Broughton Books, 1995).
3. The Standing Committee of the General Synod of the Anglican Church of Australia, *The Constitution, Canons and Rules of the Anglican Church of Australia 2017* (Sydney, 2018), 3
4. *Constitution, Canons and Rules*, 127.
5. Archbishop of Sydney's Liturgical Panel, *Common Prayer: Resources for Gospel-Shaped Gatherings* (Sydney: Anglican Press Australia, 2012).
6. Anglican Communion Environment Network, http://acen.anglicancommunion.org/resources/liturgical-resources.aspx; International Anglican Women's Network, http://iawn.anglicancommunion.org/resources/gender-based-violence.aspx
7. *Constitution, Canons and Rules*, 126.

8

Beyond *Common Worship*: Imperatives and Hindrances for the Church of England

Mark Earey

Introduction – *Common Worship*: success or failure?

Common Worship has now been the Church of England's authorised alternative to the *Book of Common Prayer* for over 20 years. It is often thought of as the millennial liturgy because the notional deadline for its introduction was the year 2000, when the authorisation of the *Alternative Service Book 1980* ran out. Indeed, in the period before the name 'Common Worship' was coined, the whole revision project was often referred to as 'Liturgy 2000'.[1] However, the *first* parts of it actually began to appear from 1997 onwards, meaning that those parts have now been in use for longer than the 20-year period of authorisation of the ASB 1980.[2]

The messiness of the arrival of *Common Worship* (CW) is matched by the confusion and misunderstanding that still exists about its very nature. Ordinands, in essays, can still be found referring innocently to '*The Book of Common Worship*' as if it were a single volume in direct succession to the Prayer Book and the *Alternative Service Book*, rather than (as it is) a library of resources, published in books, booklets and online – more a project than a product. This is probably due to the fact that many ordinands, like most other worshippers in the pew, have either only come across the *Common Worship* main volume, or have only encountered the liturgy through locally produced service booklets or via liturgical text on screens. In the case of those who experience *Common Worship* through local booklets or on screen, I suspect that they therefore imagine that behind the scenes there is one book that their local clergy and lay worship leaders are mining for the material that is used locally. Whatever is the case, it demonstrates something of the hold that a 'prayer book tradition' can have on a Church that for 20 years has not had one book as an alternative to its default prayer book.

'Has *Common Worship* worked, do you think?' somebody asked me the other day. It's a question that is difficult to answer, because in the Church of England today it depends hugely on who you ask. The Archbishop of Canterbury, in a preface to a recent book to honour the work of the late Michael Perham (a key figure in the Liturgical Commission that produced *Common Worship*), described *Common Worship* as 'a liturgy which has found a very broad acceptance and is a rich resource.'[3] Until fairly recently I think that this would have been a fair comment, and in relation to some parts of *Common Worship*, it remains true. The *Common Worship* funeral and wedding provision, for instance, is not often commented on negatively. The initiation material, on the other hand, has been through two lots of alterations – the first was fairly soon after initial publication, when the rubrics were loosened to make more texts optional, and the second was in 2015 when extra alternative texts in 'accessible language' were provided alongside the existing material.[4] The *Common Worship* collects received a savaging in some quarters fairly early on, and alternatives were produced.[5] In practice the most significant thing is that the *Common Worship* services of Holy Communion (and particularly Order One, which is the most commonly used), have 'found a very broad acceptance'. For a large proportion of the Church of England, Holy Communion Order One has become the default Sunday morning service, or at least the standard eucharistic service, even if that is only once or twice a month. Like every other form of liturgy in the Church of England, what it looks like 'in performance' will vary from parish to parish depending on the tradition of the church and the accompanying ceremonial (or lack of it) and musical repertoire, but on the whole an Order One Eucharist will be fairly recognisable wherever you encounter it.

So, as a rule of thumb we might say that *Common Worship* has found 'broad acceptance' for 80% of the Church of England. However, that 80% rule of thumb is now beginning to change, and this is for two key reasons.

The evangelical factor

One factor is the growth of evangelical influence in the Church of England. A dominance of evangelicals among ordinands is producing a growing proportion of evangelicals among serving clergy, which means that some churches that might have considered themselves 'eucharistic' in spirituality and worship are becoming less so. Some evangelical clergy – especially if their own roots are in less liturgical Christian traditions – do not value regular eucharistic worship themselves, and are therefore bolder in encouraging their congregations to be less focused on it. When this is combined with a desire to make worship more 'accessible' to the unchurched, coupled with an assumption that the eucharist is 'exclusive' (and therefore *not* accessible), you can see how there is a *gradual* shift to a less eucharistically dominated pattern of Sunday worship across the parishes of the Church of England. This means that the 'broad acceptance' of *Common Worship* is becoming less visible, because what replaces eucharistic worship in parish churches is often something less visibly 'liturgical', less obviously 'Anglican', and not clearly from *Common Worship* (even though it might actually conform to the requirements of the *Common Worship* 'A Service of the Word' framework).

The 'Fresh Expressions' factor

A further significant factor is the growing number of 'fresh expressions of church' in the Church of England (or what is sometimes referred to as 'emerging church'). In these contexts, all of the factors noted above come to a particular focus. These pioneering approaches to church life and growth are increasingly reaching the stage where questions about corporate worship, liturgy and the sacraments are becoming pressing. Perhaps the most visible among these fresh expressions of church are Messy Church congregations. Because Messy Church is a Fresh Expression with a fairly standard and replicable formula, and an international support network and set of resources,[6] it has become the simplest way for many parishes to extend their reach in their community, and the form of Fresh Expression most 'visible' to the rest of the Church of England. In many parishes, this is where the growth is occurring, and where energy is being focused.

As Messy Church gatherings mature, one of the questions they naturally ask is about how to introduce the sacrament of Holy Communion to their life, as part of their journey to becoming 'church' in their own right, rather than an activity of 'proper church'. For Messy Church congregations in the Church of England this is a challenge, because the rules governing Holy Communion in that very informal context are the same as those that apply in any other context. There is flexibility within *Common Worship*, which can help, but whilst some of those involved in producing *Common Worship* might have been aware of those sorts of contexts, the rules were never written with Messy Church (or other Fresh Expressions) in mind as a regular context in which the rules needed to work – and it shows.

A really positive step in recent years has been the appointment of Lucy Moore (who heads up the international Messy Church team at Bible Reading Fellowship) to the Church of England Liturgical Commission. This has resulted in some important guidance notes being produced by the Commission to help Church of England Messy Church groups to find the best route through the *Common Worship* rules that has integrity both with what the rules are trying to protect and with what Messy Church has been all about.[7] It is a creative and exciting step forward – but it isn't necessarily where we might have started, given the choice. Messy Church is just one example of the tensions that are increasingly obvious within the Church of England around worship, identity, and the notion of 'common prayer'. It is a telling sign of a growing problem.

Contrasting perspectives on *Common Worship*

In May 2018, the diocese of Leicester held a day conference on the subject of Liturgy and Fresh Expressions. It was specifically called to help those who are 'pioneering' and working in fresh expressions of church and who are bumping up against the liturgical rules. The overwhelming mood among those present was one of frustration with the rules and a sense that they are not fit for purpose in Fresh Expression contexts. Many of those working in such contexts simply assume – from a common sense perspective – that there must be a loosening of the rules for Fresh Expressions, and that bishops can give them permission to be more experimental and creative. There is often shock and disbelief when they discover that there are no such concessions.

Just one month after the conference in Leicester diocese, a feature in the *Church Times* lamented the dominance of 'throwaway' liturgy sheets and called for a return to a simpler prayer book-type commonality.[8] The writer looked for this to be focused around a smaller range of shared forms of worship which could be more permanent and therefore known by heart, and thereby 'owned' by the worshippers more than the ephemeral and constantly changing creative liturgies provided on leaflets or screens. This is not an unusual perspective to encounter in the Church of England among those for whom the flexibility of *Common Worship* has made it feel anything but 'common'.

In these two examples, we see the growing problem for the Church of England. On the one hand, a growing number of pioneers frustrated with a perceived restrictions of *Common Worship* and its inability to flex to their needs; on the other, a frustration with a perceived 'no holds barred' irresponsible over-use of creativity and flexibility to the detriment of stability and familiarity in worship. What is interesting is that the desire for worship to be 'owned' by the worshippers is present in both these cases. In the first, by the assumption that worship is owned only when it emerges from the particular local context; in the second, that it is owned only when it is part of a regular repeated pattern shared more widely.

Both groups share the view that *Common Worship* has not worked, but for very different reasons. But it is not just at the 'edges' that there is frustration. Caught in the middle are the notional 80% where *Common Worship* has been working pretty well. Here, too, the mood is changing. This is primarily because the mission-shaped approach which is most obvious in Messy Church and other fresh expressions of church, is also increasingly part of more 'ordinary' parish life and worship. The parish that wants to introduce Holy Communion into their all age service (or to introduce an all age element into their regular Eucharist); the church that is running a Café Church as its main Sunday service once a month; the church with a monthly informal evening service which is experimenting with Taizé-style worship and now wants to include a Eucharist; and so on.

With 'growth' on the agenda everywhere, and pressure to show you are responding to it with 'Mission Action Plans' and the like, the 80% are increasingly also bumping up against the rules and asking how they can be flexed to fit their missional aspirations. Here they discover the other aspect of *Common Worship* which has been the cause of some criticism – its complexity. For those looking for a creative, but essentially parochially-focused, approach to liturgy, it is not so much the restrictions in the rules that is the problem as the sheer difficulty of finding out what the rules are. The number of volumes in the *Common Worship* suite of resources, plus the decision to put the Notes to the services at the end, rather than the beginning, means that many users – even experienced and liturgically aware clergy – have no idea where to find the rules or how to apply them. The dispersed nature of the material also means that sometimes those rules seem contradictory, or hard to reconcile with one another.[9]

Presumably then, a missionally-focused and liturgically-centred Church like the Church of England is responding centrally to this situation and urgently considering a way forward? No. So, *why* is this not happening?

Underlying assumptions about worship

The first thing to acknowledge is that below the presenting challenges of practice, there is a fundamental disjunction between Fresh Expression thinking about worship and the historical assumptions of the Church of England. The Church of England has tended to assume that even in 'mission-mode', worship comes first. This is obvious from the 19th and early 20th century pattern of establishing 'daughter churches' in newly expanding parts of parishes, right through to late 20th century church planting approaches which started churches in school halls or other 'neutral' premises. These approaches saw mission as establishing new places of worship, with the hope of drawing new worshippers to a place which was geographically nearer to where they lived (the daughter church approach) or closer to their cultural comfort zones (the idea that a school hall or pub function room – or even a church hall – might be less intimidating than a church building). The assumption in this approach is that having established a new worshipping congregation, Christian community will follow, along with the nurturing of new disciples, and then service to the wider community.

Fresh Expressions and pioneering thinking starts elsewhere, with the creation of community. That community is established on other foundations, such as a shared activity, a shared form of practical service, or shared experience, for instance. Only then does worship emerge, and the assumption is that it will grow organically from the context of that community, rather than being adopted in a form borrowed from elsewhere.[10] No wonder pioneers find *Common Worship* frustrating.

Historic assumptions

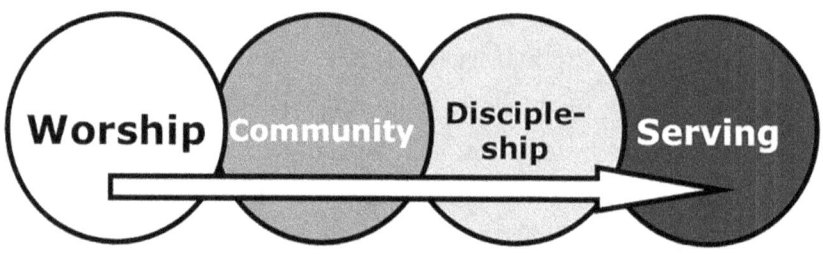

'Fresh Expressions' assumptions

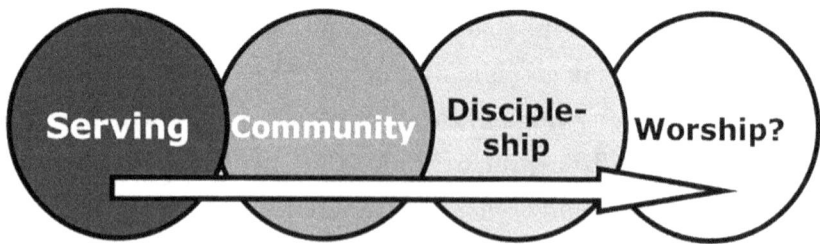

Fig. 1 – Different assumptions about the place of worship in mission

The Church of England has implicitly accepted this 'twin-track' approach to mission and church life, without addressing the implications for understandings of the place of worship and for practical liturgical outcomes.

A chronological accident

One of the reasons for this inability to address the liturgical implications of new mission thinking is the simple 'accident' of chronology. That accident involves the timing of *Common Worship* in relation to another key publication. In 2004, hot on the heels of *Common Worship,* came *Mission-Shaped Church* (MSC), the major Church of England report which has proved to be extremely significant – one might even say, game-changing – in relation to the fresh expressions thinking we have already discussed.[11] MSC signalled what is sometimes thought of as a shift in the Church from a maintenance perspective to a missional perspective. The report did not start this, but it reported it, made it okay to talk about it, and made it feel an 'official' Church of England stance. It was supported by the then Archbishop of Canterbury, Rowan Williams, and has since become so embedded in Church of England thinking that its assumptions are simply taken for granted in Church reports and General Synod debates. It ushered in significant changes to make cross-parish church planting possible (that is, officially possible) through the introduction of Bishop's Mission Orders (BMOs). More importantly, it changed the atmosphere and the mood. Suddenly it was 'mission-shaped' everything for the Church of England.[12]

The key chronological significance of all of this is that it came out just *after* the Church had been through its biggest liturgical revision process for decades. Even if people could see that there might be liturgical implications for all of this, no one was ready to face them. For instance, it is significant that in the legislation to allow for Bishop's Mission Orders, mentioned above, the only reference to worship is in the accompanying Code of Practice for church plants set up under a Bishop's Mission Order (BMO). In an appendix to the code of practice are a few pages addressing worship, the gist of which is that *Common Worship* should provide all the flexibility that will be necessary for a church plant to hold the balance between being contextually relevant and catholically connected in its worship.[13]

It is worth pondering how things might have turned out if *Common Worship* had come along ten years *after* MSC. It is possible, perhaps even likely, that *Common Worship* might have been conceived with a very different remit and designed to function in very different contexts. As it was, the advent of MSC, and all that went with it, suddenly made *Common Worship* seem strangely out of touch, out of date and unfit for purpose. Or, at least, it did for those whose energy and vision was focused on the new possibilities for fresh expressions of church and pioneering models of ministry. That chronological accident cannot be changed, but it is important to recognise it. It is unfair to criticise *Common Worship* (and those who produced it) for not addressing a situation which, at the time, looked more like a cloud on the horizon than the central feature of the landscape that it now appears to be. More importantly, the effect is that the Church of England has changed a key part of what was thought of as its essence (the parish system) but is still operating liturgically like a Church in which 'one size' can be made to 'fit all', albeit with a little bit of adjustment from skilled tailors.

The absence of a 'best before' date

Some of the issues addressed above might have been forced to the top of the Church's agenda, and found their way into the General Synod, if *Common Worship* had been treated like previous authorised alternatives to the *Book of Common Prayer*. Before *Common Worship*, these alternatives had been given limited periods of use. The first forms (Series 1, Series 2 and Series 3 services) were published in booklet form, which reinforced the sense that they were temporary and experimental, and for limited periods of use. The *Alternative Service Book 1980* marked a significant shift back into a bound volume to put alongside the Prayer Book, but the inclusion of the date in its title was meant to be a constant reminder that it was a book of its time, and would not last forever. It was given a ten-year authorisation which was extended in 1990 for another ten years, but at that point the parts that were wearing thin meant that a further blanket extension was not on the cards. General Synod was, therefore, forced to give it attention and the whole range of services was considered afresh.

Common Worship was treated differently. It was authorised 'until further resolution of the General Synod'.[14] Positively, this allowed parts that are working fine to be left alone, whilst still allowing for changes to parts that were seen to be less successful. More negatively, it means that there has been no incentive to consider the *whole package* and to ask whether it is still fit for purpose. The result has been the national equivalent of laminating a local service booklet – because the material doesn't wear out naturally, there is no automatic trigger to re-assess it.

From diagnosis to treatment

Although, as we have seen, there are some in the Church of England who are still lamenting the loss of commonality that 'Common Worship' has allowed, there are an increasing number of people who seem to accept the analysis of the problem, that the Church of England is left with liturgical rules – and to some extent, resources – which are no longer fit for purpose. But there is a big leap to make from accepting the diagnosis to developing and putting into practice a 'treatment plan'.

There are several factors which combine to make it hard to move from seeing the problem to planning to improve the situation.

People don't understand the mechanisms for change

If people do accept the analysis of the problem, and the need for change, they are often unaware of how the Church goes about making such changes. Sometimes people imagine, for instance, that the Church of England Liturgical Commission could simply change the rules or produce new material. Sometimes, they assume that this is already happening behind the scenes, and are waiting for it to be announced. They are often shocked to hear that nothing is happening, and then sometimes get quite cross with the Liturgical Commission, not realising that the Commission can only operate on instructions from the House of Bishops, usually as requested by the General Synod.

Mechanisms for change are themselves complex

Once the process for change is understood (that is, that General Synod needs to get involved, and that someone needs to start that process off), we hit another problem.

First, those with most to gain (e.g. the 'pioneers') are least inclined to get embroiled in the long synodical process involved in changing authorised liturgy or the Canons of the Church of England. The *process* of change itself is part of the perceived problem. It can feel like a case of: 'Let's change a series of arcane and complex rules using an arcane and complex process'. Those with an aversion to the rules are unlikely to be attracted to the bureaucratic process for changing them. They are too busy getting on with doing the mission-shaped stuff.

Unfortunately, many of those who are most familiar with (and engaged with) the synodical process are also those least inclined to want to spend time on further liturgical change. Because *Common Worship* emerged over a period of over a decade (for reasons elaborated above), it left a memory of a *lot* of synodical time taken up with liturgical business, business that some might consider to be 'liturgical minutiae'. The long and tortuous process of producing *Common Worship* has inoculated General Synod against enthusiasm for liturgical business.

There have been some changes to *Common Worship* already, of course, but this has used up any lingering goodwill or energy for more liturgical business. We had additional collects (as further alternatives); we had additional eucharistic prayers (for use as alternatives when lots of children are present); we had additional baptismal texts in accessible language (as further alternatives).[15] Note that they have all been *additions* of extra material, making *more* choices. Though this helps in some senses, it also adds to the vicious circle: more flexibility leads to even more perceived complexity. There has so far been no significant reduction in material or relaxation of rules.[16]

The 'all or nothing' myth

There is another problem, which is linked to the mentality of a 'prayer book' Church, in which the default is still assumed to be one liturgical pattern for the whole Church, enforced by law. This means that when flexibility is suggested, the assumption is that this will force a change on everyone, whether they like it or not. The clearest example of this is the debates about the change to the Canons on vesture. Canon B8 used to allow flexibility for vesture at a Service of the Word, but required robes of some form for eucharistic services.[17] When General Synod was presented with a motion to change the canon to allow more local decision-making about robes in services (including Holy Communion), some seemed nervous that this permission-giving change would inevitably lead to churches being somehow *forced* to abandon robes. When it is suggested that *Common Worship* needs an overhaul to allow for more local responsibility, the response from some is to suggest that doing so would inevitably lead to the end of any liturgical approach to worship in the Church of England and its replacement with a Free Church 'style' and a Congregationalist approach to determining worship at local level.

Conclusion: how could change happen?

For all the reasons outlined above, despite the pressures from some in the Church of England for there to be a change in the liturgical rules, that pressure has thus far produced no result. General Synod does not *have* to revise *Common Worship*; those that would want to are least likely to be part of the synodical government processes; even if they were, they are unlikely to have the political knowledge to know what to do; even were that to happen, there is still a resistance among some in General Synod to giving large amounts of time to further liturgical revision.

What is really needed is not so much a change in *Common Worship* itself, but a change in the canons that determine how *Common Worship* and the *Book of Common Prayer* have to be applied at local level. Canonical revision is also not an appealing prospect to many on General Synod, but if the canons were changed to give more responsibility to the local context along with systems of accountability to the wider Church, some relatively small changes could result in some relatively large possibilities.

The recent experience of the production and authorisation of the *Common Worship* Additional Baptismal texts probably gives us the most likely way for change to happen, which is for grass roots pressure to work its way up to the General Synod level. The new baptismal material began with a group of clergy in Liverpool diocese sharing a sense of frustration with the *Common Worship* initiation services, and in particular with the baptism service when used with families with little familiarity with church culture or language. Those clergy worked together to bring the issue to their Diocesan Synod. Discussion there resulted in a diocesan motion to General Synod. Discussion there resulted in a resolution asking the House of Bishops to instruct the Liturgical Commission to produce some material – and within a few years new texts were authorised.[18]

The timescale for more major revision is likely to be longer, but the process will be the key. In the short term it probably needs some key players in the Fresh Expressions world to step back from hands-on work in church planting and to give themselves and their energy to encouraging this synodical process. The recent change in the canons about vesture (noted above) gives a sign that Synod might just be ready for those kind of permission-giving changes to the canons, changes which take seriously the reality in the Church and seek to make possible what to many people feels like common sense.

Why does this need to happen? Because until it does, pioneering ministers will go on pioneering, churches will continue to be planted, fresh expressions will carry on being expressed, and no one will be able to ask for permission for what they want to do liturgically. And when no one can ask for permission, no one can be held accountable. The 'don't ask – don't tell' culture pushes liturgical innovation and contextually-shaped worship underground. That cannot be good for a Church that says its liturgy is central to its identity.

Endnotes

1 See, for instance, Michael Perham (ed.), *Towards Liturgy 2000: Preparing for the revision of the Alternative Service Book* (Alcuin Club Collections 69) (London: SPCK and Alcuin Club, 1989) and Michael Perham (ed.), *Liturgy for a New Century: Further essays in preparation for the revision of the Alternative Service Book* (London: SPCK and Alcuin Club, 1991).

2 *Calendar, Lectionary and Collects* came out in 1997; *Common Worship: Initiation Services* was first published in 1998. Other parts of the suite of resources came later: *Common Worship: Daily Prayer* did not come out in a definitive edition until 2005 (though there was provision before that time, as daily prayer was covered by the provisions of A Service of the Word, and a provisional version of the *Common Worship* material appeared earlier);

Common Worship: Times and Seasons came out in 2006; and Common Worship: Ordination Services was a late-comer, appearing in 2007.
3   Justin Welby, in the preface to Aidan Platten (ed.), *Grasping at the Heel of Heaven: Liturgy, leadership and ministry in today's church* (London: Canterbury Press, 2018), vii.
4   *Common Worship:Additional Baptismal Texts in Accessible Language* (London: Church House Publishing, 2015). These texts are also available online via the Church of England website: https://www.churchofengland.org/prayer-and-worship/worship-texts-and-resources/common-worship/christian-initiation#na and click on 'Holy Baptism (Accessible Language)'.
5   *Common Worship: Additional Collects* (London: Church House Publishing, 2005). The Additional Collects can now be found online, alongside the original collects for each Sunday of the year (https://www.churchofengland.org/prayer-and-worship/worship-texts-and-resources/common-worship/common-material/collects-post-communions).
6   Messy Church is a ministry of Bible Reading Fellowship, and has full-time staff there who support it, along with web resources too: https://www.messychurch.org.uk
7   The guidance can be found online here: https://www.messychurch.org.uk/resource/holy-communion-messy-church
8   Philip Welsh, 'Time to Retreat from Throwaway Liturgy', *Church Times*, 15 June 2018, 14 and 17.
9   For an example of rules that don't easily work together, see Mark Earey, *Beyond Common Worship: Anglican Identity and Liturgical Diversity* (London: SCM Press, 2013), 14-16
10 For a clear explanation of this essential difference between a 'worship-first' and a 'serving first' approach, see Michael Moynagh, *Church for Every Context: An Introduction to Theology and Practice* (London: SCM Press, 2012), 206-10.
11 Church of England, *Mission-Shaped Church: Church Planting and Fresh Expressions of Church in a Changing Context* (GS 1523) (London: Church House Publishing, 2004).
12 Here are just some examples: Paul Bayes and Tim Sledge, *Mission-Shaped Parish: Traditional church in a changing context* (London: Church House Publishing, 2006); Steven Croft (ed.), *Mission-Shaped Questions: Defining Issues for Today's Church* (London: Church House Publishing, 2008); Michael Collyer, Claire Dalpra, Alison Johnson and James Woodward, *A Mission-Shaped Church for Older People?: Practical suggestions for local churches* (Solihull: Leveson Centre, 2008); Steve Hollinghurst, *Mission-Shaped Evangelism: The Gospel in Contemporary Culture* (Norwich: Canterbury Press, 2013); Harvey C. Kwiyani, *Mission-Shaped Church in a Multicultural World* (Grove Mission & Evangelism Series 118) (Cambridge: Grove Books, 2017).
13 *Dioceses, Pastoral and Mission Measure*, Code of Practice to Part V, Appendix 3, section 1.2.5. For more on this, see Mark Earey, *Beyond Common Worship: Anglican Identityand Liturgical Diversity* (London: SCM Press, 2013), 54-56.
14 See the authorisation page in the *Common Worship* main volume: *Common Worship: Services and Prayers for the Church of England* (London: Church House Publishing, 2000), vii.

15 *Common Worship: Additional Collects* (London: Church House Publishing, 2005); *Common Worship: Additional Eucharistic Prayers - with Guidance on Celebrating the Eucharist with Children* (London: Church House Publishing, 2012); *Common Worship: Christian Initiation - Additional Baptism Texts in Accessible Language* (London: Church House Publishing, 2015).
16 The one exception to this was the relaxation of some of the rubrics of the original *Common Worship* initiation services to make parts of the baptism service optional and to provide more alternative forms. This went through General Synod in February 2000, in time for the changes to make it into the basic form of baptism service included in the *Common Worship* main volume when it was published later that year, as well as the full Christian Initiation volume in 2006.
17 For an argument in favour of making a change to the canon, see Andrew Atherstone, *Clergy Robes and Mission Priorities* (Grove Worship Series 197) (Cambridge: Grove Books, 2008).
18 For more on the background to the new resources and commentary on the texts themselves, see Tim Stratford, *Accessible Baptisms: A Commentary on the Alternative Common Worship Texts* (Grove Worship Series 226) (Cambridge: Grove Books, 2016).

Part B:
Liturgical Themes and Foci

9

Creation is also our Prayer Book

Carmel Pilcher

> '...*everything has a right to be recognised and revered. Trees have tree rights, insects have insect rights, rivers have river rights, and mountains have mountain rights*'.[1]

We live in a time where scientists are making new discoveries about our planet that were not possible before the advent of sophisticated technology. Nuclear physicists and astrologists are discovering new ways to delve into the vastness and beauty of our cosmos that invites us into the mystery of time and an ever-expanding notion of space and planetary systems. Theologians, such as Denis Edwards, remind us that these discoveries add to the mystery of the creative process that is ongoing through the divine power of the Creator.

Those same scholars signal that the future of planet Earth is in crisis, largely due to human factors. Denis Edwards warns that 'the human community has never had to face anything like the crisis of life that is already upon us in this twenty-first century'.[2] Many agree that human intervention is largely responsible for this current ecological crisis. They cite evidence of climate change;

pollution in waterways; the extinction of many plants and animals. The disruption of whole biological systems was preventable, had not humanity stripped away forests, created waste that litters our earth and toxic materials that pollute our waterways.

This chapter will reflect on worship and creation. Founded in the ancient Judeo-Christian tradition contemporary prayer books are rich with liturgical texts, song and ritual that invite us to join with creation in praise of God's gracious gift. In my own land of Australia, we are grateful to Aboriginal and Torres Strait Islanders who have a relationship to the land that they sustained and nurtured continuously until the settlement of Europeans some 200 years ago. Their 'prayer book' is creation itself, that they express in song, ceremony, ritual and art. We believe that by inculturating our liturgy with aspects of indigenous culture, our Christian worship could urge us to take our rightful place as co-creators with God in protecting our planet.

Contemporary Christian prayer texts and rituals

For many people, an encounter with nature can be a profound experience. Observing a sunrise or sunset, a majestic tree, the sight of a powerful lion or interacting with a gentle domestic pet, feeling a warm sunny day, or life-giving rain can lift people to another plane. Those who are religious might describe this experience as an encounter with the sacred creator God: 'The universe unfolds in God, who fills it completely. Hence, there is a mystical meaning to be found in a leaf, in a mountain trail, in a dewdrop, in a poor person's face'.[3] In official church worship, our prayer texts, songs and ritual also invite us to acknowledge the God of creation:

> By your word,
> Lord God,
> we and all your creatures
> are formed, sustained, and fed.
> Teach us to live in peace
> with the world your hands have made,
> that, as faithful stewards of your good earth,
> we may reverence you in the works of your creation.
> We make our prayer through our Lord Jesus Christ your Son.[4]

This prayer not only reminds us that God creates but that we are called to live in harmony with all and to act as faithful stewards reverencing all God has made. Words of acknowledgment and praise to the Creator of all of life are found in many prayer texts. The Roman Missal echoes Jewish table prayer in its gifts dedication: 'Blessed are you, Lord God of all creation.' Eucharistic Prayers use poetic words to offer gifts back to the God who created them, acknowledging: 'You are indeed Holy, O Lord, and all you have created rightly gives you praise.'[5] In the Anglican tradition a thanksgiving prayer for Australia speaks to the God of creation:

> God of holy dreaming, Great Creator Spirit
> from the dawn of creation you have given your
>   children
> the good things of Mother Earth.
> You spoke and the gum tree grew.
> In the vast desert and dense forest,
> and in the cities at the water's edge,
> creation sings your praise.[6]

Christian traditions, including the prayers of the Roman Missal also have prayers for nature's catastrophes, including drought, cyclones and bushfires.

The Psalms that are part of our tradition and often prayed in the context of worship, repeatedly invite praise for the majesty of God and God's gracious and generous gift of creation:

> Your steadfast love, O Lord,
> extends to the heavens,
> your faithfulness to the clouds
> your righteousness is like the mighty
>   mountains,
> your judgements are like the great deep;
> you save humans and animals alike, O Lord.
>   (Psalm 36:5-7)

Hymns also reflect the gift of God's creation and its unending song of praise.

> All living things upon the earth,
> green fertile hills and mountains,
> sing to the God who gave you birth,
> Be joyful, springs and fountains.
> Lithe waterlife, bright airborne birds,
> wild roving beasts, tame flocks and herds:
> exalt the God who made you.[7]

In ritual celebrations, water is poured, oil is smeared, the new fire brings warmth while candles give light. Bread and wine are taken, blessed, broken, poured and shared. The church's worship is rich with liturgical texts and ritual that remind us of the abundance of God's graciousness evident in all of creation, that calls for our response.

Creation as gift from God: Judeo-Christian tradition

Our ancient Judeo-Christian tradition recognised that creation was God's gift and it was the responsibility of the followers of Christ to provide for its care. The Israelites recognised their utter dependence on the God who called them out of Egypt, but also acknowledged their role to steward the earth. Remembering God's faithfulness led them to be in covenant-relationship, not only with God but with each other and all of creation. Deuteronomy records that relationship to the earth extended to those in need:

> When you reap your harvest in the field and forget a sheaf in the field, you shall not go back to get it; it shall be left for the alien, the orphan, and the widow so that the Lord your God may bless you in all your undertakings. When you beat your olive trees ... When you gather the grapes of your vineyard ... (what is left) shall be for the alien, the orphan and the widow. Remember that you were a slave in the land of Egypt; therefore I am commanding you to do this. (Deuteronomy 24:19-22)

God provides the earth, the seed and the water. Humans co-operate with God in planting, nurturing and harvesting. But this food is gift, so not only the sower or reaper but also the poor person is entitled to share this gift. Praise and thanksgiving to God for creation is reflected in Jewish rituals, in the offering of first fruits at harvest time and other festivals. Earthly symbols such as bread and wine that symbolised their story were used in temple or domestic services weekly to mark the Sabbath, culminating each year in Passover feast of the lamb.

Throughout the gospels, reference is made to nature, the wheat fields, fish, birds of the air, and the many table meals where bread and wine is shared. Christians have always brought the gifts of the earth to the eucharistic table to offer back to God, the bounteous giver. The notion of the offering of first fruits finds its culmination in the memorial of the life, death and resurrection of Christ, the 'first born of all creation.'

The Fathers of the Church recognised that the right use of the things of the earth in ritual led worshippers to a sacramental encounter with the bounteous God and an acknowledgment of their dependence on the divine. Things of the earth are gifts of God the creator and are to be used ritually. In *The Apostolic Tradition,* besides bread and wine brought by the community for eucharist, milk and honey were included in the ritual of initiation as a reminder of God's promise to the Israelites. Oil, cheese and olives were blessed during the doxology, linking gifts of the faithful to praise of the God who created them.[8] Irenaeus of Lyons reminded his community that they offered the first fruits of bread and wine 'from God's own creatures,' so that they themselves 'may be neither unfruitful or ungrateful'.[9]

The Early Fathers reinforced the sacramental character of creation in Christian worship through mystagogical catechesis. Cyprian of Carthage spoke of unity in a fragmented community by appealing to the elements of bread and wine:

> For when the Lord calls bread His own body – and bread is a conglomerate of many individual grains, made into one – He signifies that we, the people whom He bore, are united in one. Similarly, when He calls wine His own blood – and wine is pressed from a great many clusters of individual grapes squeezed into

one juice – he again indicates that we, His flock, being a multitude gathered together, are mingled and joined into one.[10]

In his preaching to the neophytes, Augustine explained the mystery of becoming the body of Christ, of bread and wine that they had just shared. He reminds them of the process that wheat undergoes to become bread and compares this to the journey of initiation where the neophytes are likewise moulded through water and the fire of the Holy Spirit to become the sacrament of the Body of Christ.[11] John Chrysostom asked his assembly: 'For what is the bread? The body of Christ. And what do they become who partake of it? The body of Christ.'[12] Gift giving back to God what God had already given has always been a strong element of Christian worship. Central to this teaching was the gift of Christ, the new creation, 'the mediation of the Word in redemption in itself (who) exalts and restores creation'.[13]

Early Christians brought produce from home to offer at Eucharist. Some of the bread, wine and perhaps oil would be used in the ceremony and the rest given to those who depended upon the community for food. In this tangible bringing of earthly things to the celebration, the early Christians were not only reminded of the connection between creation and Christ's redemption, but also saw themselves as essential actors, as participants of the eucharist, offering to God the gifts God had first given them to become one with Christ's sacrifice. In the words of Alexander Schmemann, 'the Eucharistic memorial for early Christians was not something altogether new, discontinued from the old, but rather Christ was the 'new creation', the fulfillment and actualisation of the new covenant'.[14] To recognise the sacramental character of creation in Christ is to recognise, as did the early church, that sacraments are always understood within the context of liturgical celebrations.[15]

These few examples illustrate the rich tradition of an acknowledgment of God as creator and reverence for all that God has made, finding its fulfilment in Christ, remembered not only through instruction but ritually expressed in worship.

Loss of connection with creation as gift

Coming from such a rich heritage, how did Christians over time come to view creation, not as gratuitous divine gift, but as objects provided simply for our own use and convenience?

Orthodox theologian John D. Zizioulas would argue that an evolving understanding of humanity as *lord* and *proprietor* of creation comes from two major sources in Western societies: the anthropology of the Enlightenment that understood humankind to be the master and controller of nature; and Christianity, that took literally the directive to 'subdue and have dominion over the earth' (Genesis 1:28).[16] Pope Francis concurs that 'dominion' occurred when 'the harmony between the Creator, humanity and creation as a whole was disrupted by our presuming to take the place of God and refusing to acknowledge our creaturely limitations'.[17]

Yet another factor to be considered is the ritual use of things of the earth. In the Roman tradition as the Mass became distanced from the people so a disconnect happened between the liturgy and the peoples' domestic gifts presented in the eucharist. Not only did they not bring gifts but eventually the faithful did not even receive holy communion. They no longer ate and drank at the table of the Lord, and the notion of the Eucharist as meal lost any ritual meaning.

Roman liturgy has restored symbols of the earth, but in our own time the elements themselves have become so contrived that they are barely recognisable. Thin discs of wafers bear little resemblance to the bread of the domestic table. Water is so sparingly used in the baptismal ritual or the *Asperses* rite that it no longer inspires the assembly to imagine its life giving or destructive power. Oil is dabbed onto the body of a new initiate or an ordinand so minimally that its healing or strengthening properties cannot be experienced or its fragrance touch the senses. The assembly is often denied the wine of the sacrifice, so that the fulness of the sign of eating and drinking is denied.[18] Consequently, the power of these symbols has been diminished. One wonders why ministerial priests are not more attentive to the power of ritual and symbol through the elements of creation?

However, the late David Power is of the opinion that at a time when there is an impoverishment in the sacramental elements and the sacramental action, symbols of the earth such as Lourdes or Easter water, and in some cultures blessed oil, continue to spark devotion in popular imagination.[19] He is convinced that 'imaginative and symbolic language becomes more important in such a flux, for beyond the rational mind it has ways of expressing awareness and feeling and faith that remains alive and lively'.[20] We are basically people of word, ritual and symbol.

In her book, *From the Beginning to Baptism: Scientific and Sacred Stories of Water, Oil, and Fire,* Linda Gibler makes an important contribution to our subject by exploring new scientific discoveries of each of the three elements of creation that are the key ritual symbols of Christian initiation.[21] Gibler explores in some depth the scientific origins, billions of years ago, of water, fire and oil. She then reflects on their sacred significance in the Christian tradition, appealing to biblical, patristic and liturgical texts. In his foreword to this work, David Power commends the author's attentiveness to 'divine presence through things of Earth' at a critical time, not just as a reminder to Christians of their dependence on God for creation, but also the urgent call to 'eco-justice'.[22]

An Indigenous 'Prayer Book'

For more than 65,000 years,[23] Aboriginal and Torres Strait Islander people sustained and nurtured our vast continent. Scholars have determined that over time these first peoples developed an extraordinarily complex system of land management that used fire and the cycle of the seasons to protect and ensure wildlife and natural vegetation for food and the future.[24] Bruce Pascoe provides us with an insightful study, using the written and visual observations of the first European settlers, to describe what life was like 200 years ago. Their evidence paints a picture of communities who had learned to live in harmony with the land, often in harsh conditions of climate and terrain.[25] But this care for the earth has deeper foundations. Indigenous people lived in relationship: to country, to kin and to all of life, passed down from generation to generation through ceremony, story, song, dance and art.

Three examples illustrate this connection. The first comes from Warmun, a community in the Eastern Kimberley that formed in the 1970s when Aboriginal people were no longer employed on large stations after the government required them to be remunerated with the same wage as non-Aboriginal people. The school is the centre of the community and is built around a tree – a tree where many local people were whipped by their station 'owners' to 'teach them white ways'. School children who play around the tree are constantly reminded of their sad history. Beside the river bed, a rusted refrigerator is lodged in the branches of a tall gum tree – a sombre reminder of the last major flood that destroyed the town. Visual objects ensure that major events can never be erased from the consciousness of the community.

Artists also capture their country and events that have shaped it. Mark Nodea (born 1970) describes his work:

(The original belongs now to Gerard Kelly at CIS)

> *This painting is about the 2011 Floods that wiped out Warmun. It was March 13th, 2011, a very memorable year for all people of Warmun Community, as this was when the flood disaster happened in Warmun. This*

> *was a time of fear and grief as the people from the community witnessed their houses being washed away as well as their beloved pets. All people had to be evacuated and flown to Kununurra on a helicopter, then after almost 4 months of living in Kununurra the Gija people of Warmun were allowed to finally go home to country and to their new houses. The black hill is the Warrarmany Eagle Dreaming or 'WarrmanWarraninj – Turkey Creek Eagle Dreaming'. It is a Ngarrangkarni (Dreaming) site close to Warmun Community... the story is about a Wedge-tailed Eagle looking for Kangaroo meat. He is Jaangari skin from the dreamtime.*[26]

Art and symbol become the 'prayer book' of Aboriginal people, as does dance. In 2010, a group of young Aboriginal people from remote and urban communities gathered in Darwin to prepare the procession of gifts during the Mass of thanksgiving for the canonisation of Mary MacKillop. They were invited to describe the new saint in their way. They instinctively connected her to a totem: a kangaroo who over many months cared for her joey (newly born) before it left her pouch; or perhaps an emu. They decided on a brolga, a large bird that treads gently on water lilies. This dance, with the brolga being shadowed by the spirit brolga, led the bringing of gifts to the table of the Basilica of St Paul's outside the Walls in Rome.

Yet another example of the ritual connection between the land and ritual is recounted by a former missionary from the Balgo community in the Eastern Kimberley desert:

> When I came to Balgo, Sunfly was a very respected man. He was an important law man for his people and was respected by the Kartiya (white people). He asked for Baptism for himself in 1981 and was very anxious that the old ones were baptised also. ... When Sunfly was baptised he requested baptism for the old pensioners down the camp. John Lee and Sunfly instructed those old people because they had no English and only spoke the old Kukatja language.
>
> Sunfly and others wanted special water for those old people's baptism. They collected living water from the water holes, down in the desert, from which those old people had drunk, when they were hunting and gathering years ago. When they brought the water back they danced around it and sang, 'This water kept those old people alive in the desert, now it will give them God's life'.[27]

Sunfly knew that the gift of living water that sustains life also nurtures life in Christ. Aboriginal people continue to live in accord with creation, finding ways to map its significance through art, song and ceremony.

Connection to the land – Aboriginal spirituality

Even before the Pentecost event or the Word of God became incarnate in Christ and dwelt amongst us, the Spirit was active amongst Aboriginal and Torres Strait Islanders who respected and lived in relationship with each other, the land and all of God's creation. In the words of Denis Edwards: 'The Spirit of God who graciously accompanies and celebrates the emergence of every form of life delights in the emergence of human creatures who can respond to the divine self-offering love in a personal way'.[28]

Patrick Dodson speaks of 'the deeply spirituality nature' of Aboriginal people, a continuity between the creative and life-giving forces of the past into the present:

> For Aboriginal people the creative and life-giving forces are still very much alive. The land is full of spirits, thoughts and deeds of the creative forces. The spirits of the ancestors of all human, plant and animal life are represented in the land forms. This extends to celestial forms such as the planets and the stars, the moon and the sun. There are stories and songs throughout the land which relate these things.[29]

This interconnectivity and understanding of time as continuous and evolving is made tangible by sacred sites and extends to the complexity of family kinship systems linking Aboriginal groups to certain stories: stories that not only remind them of their intimate connection to certain plants, sites and animals, but also their responsibility to nurture and care for them: 'It is from these life forces that Aboriginal people get their identity. Indeed, their whole lives revolve around these points of reference.'[30]

Graham Paulson, a Warlpiri man and Baptist minister, tells us that at some point in the dreaming spiritual beings who are responsible for shaping creation and animating all of life, emerged from their hidden worlds and shaped the world of today.[31] Every part of living creation is, in Paulson's words, 'vested with a spirit being that animates the real life of that part of creation, whether it be flora or fauna or any part of the landscape or sea.'[32]

Miriam-Rose Ungunmerr-Baumann[33] offers a further insight into the Aboriginal character that she calls 'Dadirri'. She speaks of 'Dadirri' as listening over and over to stories around the campfire, stories that are told by the elders and then passed on to the next generation to be retold. Miriam-Rose tells us that 'Dadirri' spreads over our whole lives. It renews us and brings us peace. It makes us feel whole again.'[34] Ceremony and corroboree play an important role in this listening. At the death of a relative, it is important to wait for the right time to 'own our grief and allow it to heal slowly'.[35]

Through ceremony, active remembering *(anamnesis)* in the form of dance, song and music on sacred land, Aboriginal people bring to consciousness the story of their origins and their continuing role in creating and nurturing the earth. As a group of Elders tells us:

Each Aboriginal group has a sacred place in the land and a sacred song about its land. At this sacred place we perform our ceremonies, singing our songs and dancing our dances. These ceremonies are part of our responsibility as custodians of the land: they ensure that we preserve our connections with the Creator Spirit, that we maintain the resources and life-forces of the land, and that we keep alive the law and culture given us by our ancestors.[36]

Ceremony has always been an essential component of Aboriginal life: 'In Aboriginal cosmology there is not this distinction between the sacred and the profane; the sacred, while being a paradigm for proper existence, is also present in the contemporary world. It is the thread of interconnectedness between the Dreaming, humans and the natural world'.[37] Dodson tells us that the integrity of Aboriginal life can be described as 'a beautifully worked out spirituality, complete with a full and coherent sacramental system.'[38]

Sunfly decided that the same living water that provided survival for his people in the desert should be used in the sacrament of baptism to offer new life in Christ. His own mother and grandmother and countless generations before them searched for living water for their families. Before setting out on their journey through the parched land of their country, they first sang to the spirits of their ancestors to help them find this life-giving source. At the same time, they were attentive to signs:

the presence of birds or other animals. When it seems to be the right place 'we dig for water. When we find it, we clear off the brackish water then first kneel and sprinkle ourselves with the water while singing. We gather the water in the coolamon and then drink it.'[39] This simple ritual of acknowledgment and gratitude has been adapted into the beginning of the Mass at Balgo and other parts of the Kimberley as a blessing and sprinkling rite.

Smoking is a significant ritual associated with the beginning of life. When babies are born 'we smoke them to invite the good spirits to make them strong.' The women dig a hole in the earth, and get leaves from a special tree, add water and then light a fire to produce the smoke. They then put the baby in the hole and ensure he/she is enveloped in smoke. Then the mother sits on top of the fire. This is to ensure she has enough milk to feed the baby.

Smoke is also used at the time of death. When a person dies, their home is smoked. Then special leaves are used to sweep every place where the dead person has walked so that the 'bad person' goes away. The immediate family of the person who died goes into 'sorry camp' where they fast from most food and paint their bodies with ochre from the earth. Many different rituals are performed by others who are less closely connected to the deceased, perhaps extended family. These take place over many months, and it is these people who determine when the funeral is to takes place. Again, only certain people can attend the funeral. After the burial, the mourners in sorry camp are notified and a feast begins.[40]

Other big ceremonies take place where groups of people travel long distances to attend. These can take many days. As Miriam-Rose Ungunmerr says:

> We wait for the right time for our ceremonies and our meetings. The right people must be present. Everything must be done in the proper way. Careful preparations must be made. We don't mind waiting, because we want things to be done with care. Sometimes many hours will be spent on painting the body before an important ceremony.[41]

A way forward

a) Truthful engagement with the liturgy

Christians can restore an understanding of right relationships in 'our common home' by truthfully engaging in the church's liturgy. It is in worship that creation-incarnation-resurrection finds its culmination in praise and thanksgiving for all of creation in Christ. In the richness of the Orthodox understanding: 'The entire universe is a liturgy, a cosmic liturgy that offers the whole of creation before the throne of God.'[42]

The liturgy is an action of the whole assembly, the work of Christ himself, the one sacrament, made visible in the assembly that is the Church. In the ritual use of things of the earth and works of human hands, Christians bring all of creation to the eucharistic memorial to unite with the saving action of Christ of the Paschal Mystery. The church has always brought earthly gifts of bread, wine and oil to eucharist. It has also brought the needs of the world. By 'bringing the world as it is with them, the faithful receive a foretaste of paradise, an eschatological glimpse of the world as it will be, and then are called again to "go in peace" back into the world.'[43] In recognising ourselves as liturgical beings we treat creation as a sacred gift, rather than something that we can exploit for our own use and self-interest.

Pope Francis reminds us that: 'Through our worship of God, we are invited to embrace the world on a different plane. Water, oil, fire and colours are taken up in all their symbolic power and incorporated in our act of praise.'[44] Bread that looks like bread will be blessed at eucharist to immediately connect us to domestic meal sharing. The wine of the sacrifice will always be offered so that the fulness of the sign of eating and drinking is realised.[45] Oil will be lavishly poured onto the body of a new initiate or an ordinand so that its healing and strengthening properties can be experienced and its fragrance fill the air. Water will be used so lavishly that we feel its life-giving force.

Alongside praise and thanksgiving must come lament. We have much to lament – the destruction of trees and plants to make way for mining and other industry; the disappearance of habitats that were once home to native animals, insects and birds to make way for buildings; the overfishing of streams and oceans endangering and destroying fish life; and the extinction of whole species of plants and animals in the interests of 'development'. We must lament that 'we can no longer hear the voice of the rivers, the mountains, or the sea. The trees and meadows are no longer intimate modes of spirit presence'.[46]We lament that we have silenced the ability of these to praise God. How can we continue to truthfully pray with the psalmist: 'All creation rightly gives you praise'?

b. Engagement with Indigenous people

The Indigenous worldview could well inform Western rational thinking that continues to give little value to the power of ritual and symbol. By carefully collaborating with Indigenous peoples some of their elements of ceremony might help bring us to the wonder and relationship we share with all of creation. These of course can only be performed in collaboration with Aboriginal people and often only by Aboriginal people. Smoking and water rituals are part of their long ceremonial tradition. These could be incorporated into rituals, both at Eucharist and Initiation. If Aboriginal Christians are present, we could be welcomed with smoke. In the introductory rites, an Asperges might be replaced by a water blessing. First fruits (still given to chiefs in some cultures) ritualise our connection to the land and mark the seasons, at harvest time and thanksgiving. Bringing home-grown produce to worship can sustain this tradition. Coolamons and conch shells are local objects used domestically in communities and these serve similar ritual functions in the church's liturgy.[47] With the permission of the Aboriginal person who might have carved it, the coolamon can be the vessel that holds water or the bread to be used in the eucharist.

Traditional musical instruments, dance, art and architecture immerse all our senses, earth us in a place, strengthen our identity, and invite an active response. In Australia, we have a practice of acknowledging the traditional carers of the land at the beginning of a liturgy or important event. A local story that reflects the occasion and the place might accompany this acknowledgment. Similarly, the local worshipping community could converse with and engage an Aboriginal artist to create an artwork or sculpture to adorn a church.

Conclusion

We are blessed by our theologians, scientists and new technology that invites us into an ever-evolving world of exploring the cosmos. A new 'prayer book' is needed in Australia. This would include ritual action and storytelling through art, music and dance in collaboration with indigenous people. It could well re-engage our Western rational consciousness so that we not only imagine but make real the call of Pope Francis to 'care for our common home.' But it requires us to take time to dialogue with our Aboriginal and Islander sisters and brothers to learn from their rich cultural heritage. This task is urgent – both for ecological sustainability but also to ensure the ongoing memory of indigenous language, symbol and ceremony.

Endnotes

1. Thomas Berry, 'The Great Work', in *The Great Work*, 5.
2. Denis Edwards, *Partaking of God: Trinity, Evolution and Ecology* (Collegeville, MN: Liturgical Press, 2014) 2.
3. Pope Francis, *Laudato Si': On Care for our Common Home*, 233.
4. Roman Missal, 1998.
5. Eucharistic Prayer II, Roman Missal 2002.
6. Anglican Church of Australia, *A Prayer Book for Australia* (Sydney: Broughton Books, 1995), 218-219.
7. Carl P. Drew: Let all Creation bless the Lord. https://hymnary.org/text/let_all_creation_bless_the_lord Accessed 31/7/2018. Words © 1989 Hope Publishing Company, 380 S Main Pl, Carol Stream, IL 60188
8. R.C.D. Jasper and G. J. Cuming, eds, *Prayers of the Eucharist: Early and Reformed* (Collegeville, MN: The Liturgical Press, 1990), 36-37.
9. *AdversusHaereses*, Trans. David N. Power, Irenaeus of Lyons on Baptism and Eucharist: Selected texts with Introduction, Translation and Annotation. Alcuin/GROW Liturgical Study 18, Grove Liturgical Study 65 (Bramcote Nottingham: Grove Books Ltd, 1991), 15.
10. Cyprian of Carthage Letter 69.5.2. Vol IV, trans by G.W. Clarke, Johannes Quasten, ed., *Ancient Christian Writings*, 47.
11. See especially Augustine Sermon 227, 272.
12. John Chrysostom, Homily on 1 Cor 24, trans. from Daniel J. Sheerin, *The Eucharist*, Vol. 7 Message of the Fathers of the Church, ed. Thomas Halton (Wilmington, DL: Michael Glazier, 1986), 210.
13. David N. Power, *The Eucharistic Mystery Revitalising the Tradition* (New York, NY: Crossroad, 1992), 93.
14. Alexander Schmemann, *For the Life of the World, Sacraments and Orthodoxy* (New York, NY: St Vladimir's Seminary Press, 1973), 143-144.
15. Schmemann, *Life of the World*, especially 135-151.
16. John D. Zizioulas, *The Eucharistic Communion and the World* (London: T & T Clark International, 2011), 133.
17. Pope Francis, *Laudato Si'*, 66
18. General Instruction of the Roman Missal 2002, No. 281.
19. See David N. Power, Foreword, Linda Gibler, *From the Beginning to Baptism. Scientific and Sacred Stories of Water, Oil, and Fire* (Collegeville, MN: Liturgical Press, 2010), ix-xii.
20. Gibler, *From the Beginning*, xi.
21. Gibler, *From the Beginning*.
22. Gibler, *From the Beginning*, x - xi.
23. See http://www.abc.net.au/news/science/2017-07-20/aboriginal-shelter-pushes-human-history-back-to-65,000-years/8719314, accessed 26/7/2017
24. See Bill Gammage, *The Biggest Estate on Earth, How Aborigines made Australia* (Crows Nest, NSW: Allen & Unwin, 2012).
25. See Bruce Pascoe, *Dark Emu: Black Seeds: Agriculture or Accident?* (Broome, WA: Magabala Books Aboriginal Corporation, 2018).
26. From the story that accompanies the painting. We are also told that Mark Nodea paints his mother, artist Nancy Nodea's Ngarrgooroon country which extends around Texas Station and down South to Purnululu.
27. The story is narrated by John of God Sister Alice Dempsey. Wirrimanu Adult Education and Training Centre, *A People's Learning Place, First*

Twenty Years at Balgo Hills, 1981-2001. (Halls Creek, WA: Wirrimanu Adult Education and Training Centre, 2002) 11
28 Denis Edwards, *Breath of Life, A Theology of the Creator Spirit* (Maryknoll, NY: Orbis Books, 2004), 64.
29 Patrick Dodson, 'The Land our Mother, the Church our Mother', Peter Malone, ed., *Discovering an Australian Theology* (Homebush, NSW: St Pauls, 1988), 83.
30 Patrick Dodson, 'The Land our Mother, the Church our Mother', 83.
31 Graham Paulson 'Towards an Aboriginal Theology', *Pacifica* 19, (2006), 310-321.
32 Paulson, 'Towards an Aboriginal Theology', 313.
33 Miriam-Rose Ungunmerr-Baumann is an artist, former school principal, and Catholic elder from Daly River.
34 Miriam-Rose Ungunmerr, '...Towards an Australian Spirituality', 12.
35 In remote communities, several months can pass between the death and a person and his/her funeral. Over that period many ceremonies take place, and the immediate relatives go into 'sorry camp' where their mourning includes fasting and isolation until the funeral is over.
36 Rainbow Spirit Elders, *Rainbow Spirit Theology: Towards an Australian Aboriginal Theology* (Blackburn, VIC: Harper Collins Religious, 1997), 38
37 V. Grieves, *Aboriginal Spirituality: Aboriginal Philosophy, The Basis of Aboriginal Social and Emotional Wellbeing,* Discussion Paper No. 9, (Darwin: Cooperative Research Centre for Aboriginal Health, 2009), 11.
38 Patrick Dodson, 'The Land our Mother, the Church our Mother', 84.
39 Stories told by women from the Balgo community, 18 June 2012.
40 The birth and funeral rituals were also told the writer by the same Balgo women.
41 Miriam-Rose Ungunmerr, '...Towards an Australian Spirituality', from an edited unpublished text. Address given at the International Liturgy Assembly in Hobart, 1988, 13.
42 John D. Zizioulas, *The Eucharistic Communion and the World* (London: T & T Clark International, 2011), 123. See also Teilhard de Chardin, *Hymn of the Universe* (London: Harper and Row, 1965).
43 Zizioulas, *Eucharistic Communion*, 125.
44 Pope Francis, *Laudato Si'*, 235.
45 General Instruction of the Roman Missal 2002, No. 281.
46 Thomas Berry, 'The Meadow across the Creek' in 'The Great work', 17. www. thomas+berry+quotes&oq=Thomas+Berry+q&gs_l=psy-ab.1.0.0j0i22i30k1l3.1711.84. Accessed 6.8.2018.
47 The same could be said of ritual objects in other indigenous nations, for example the eagle feather of the Native American and Canadian Aboriginal peoples, or the tambua (whale's tooth) for Fijians.

10

Ritual Apologies and Reconciliation in Australian Society

John Francis Fitz-Herbert

This essay considers a diverse yet select range of ritual acts between the 1990s and the first decade of the twenty-first century as examples of an emerging public response to Australia's past treatment of the First Peoples of this country. For many First Australians, contemporary words, actions, gestures and symbols at public events and ceremonies, and on occasions in Christian liturgy, are a response to their personal experience of being separated from their family. These rituals can speak to their experience and the consequences of the separation from family, kin and land throughout their life. For other First Australians, who may not have been personally separated from their families, they may carry stories within themselves from family members, past and present, who suffered similarly.

The ritual acts that I will consider, in and of themselves, publicly acknowledge the reality of the systematic dispossession of Australia's indigenous peoples since the arrival of the first European settlers in 1788 and the many effects for Aboriginal and Torres Strait Islander people personally, communally and nationally. They also recognise the effect of the dispossession throughout generations of indigenous Australians and, at times, make a commitment to stand in solidarity with them and to do better into the future.

a. Prime Minister Paul Keating and the Redfern Speech of 1992

The Australian Prime Minister Paul Keating, launching the Year of the World's Indigenous People in Redfern Park, Sydney, 10 December 1992, delivered what is now known as 'The Redfern Speech'. It is an early example in contemporary Australian public discourse by the elected leader of the Federal Parliament of Australia who acknowledged the truth of what non-indigenous Australians did to the First Australians following the arrival of the Europeans in 1788, and much more since colonial settlement began. Telling the truth about the past, no matter how painful the truth may be, is an essential part of the process of reconciliation.

In his introductory remarks, Paul Keating appeals to Australia's social goals and national will, our ability to say to ourselves and the rest of the world that Australia is a first rate social democracy, that we are what we should be – truly the land of the fair go and the better chance.

Here, Paul Keating draws on the self-understanding of many Australians who believe that in this nation, each person is to be accorded respect and dignity, given *a fair go* in the local Australian vernacular.

Similarly, he draws on another self-understanding in naming the social reality that many people who came to Australia did so for *a better chance*. To have *a better chance* may mean different things for different people such as escaping difficult circumstances which threaten human freedoms; ethnic, cultural, religious or political persecution; threats to life in one's country of origin; different opportunities for work and/or education. This is part of the success of this speech in terms of ritual words, that Paul Keating identifies part of the grand narrative which resonates historically with many people's experiences in the past and their hopes for the future.

Keating goes further in proposing that the fundamental test the nation faces is one of self-knowledge, of...

> How well we know the land we live in.
> How well we know our history.
> How well we recognise the fact that, complex as our contemporary identity is, it cannot be separated from Aboriginal Australia.
> How well we know what Aboriginal Australians know about Australia.[1]

He muses that the point of the Year of World's Indigenous People is

> to bring the dispossessed out of the shadows,
> to recognise that they are part of us, and

that we cannot give indigenous Australians up without giving up many of our own most deeply held values, much of our own identity – and our own humanity.

Paul Keating then suggests that the nation must be prepared to resolve these issues. He appeals to the national memory and to a sense of reasonableness in each citizen:

> We non-Aboriginal Australians should perhaps remind ourselves that Australia once reached out for us.
>
> Didn't Australia provide opportunity and care for the dispossessed Irish? The poor of Britain? The refugees from war and famine and persecution in the countries of Europe and Asia?
>
> Isn't it reasonable to say that if we can build a prosperous and remarkably harmonious multicultural society in Australia, surely we can find just solutions to the problems which beset the first Australians – the people to whom the most injustice has been done.

For the purposes of my enquiry into ritual acts of reconciliation, a final selection shows Paul Keating suggesting an initial starting point to address the problem as he sees it:

> And, as I say, the starting point might be to recognise that the problem starts with us non-Aboriginal Australians.
> It begins, I think, with that act of recognition.
> Recognition that it was we who did the dispossessing.
> We took the traditional lands and smashed the traditional way of life.
> We brought the diseases. The alcohol.
> We committed the murders.
> We took the children from their mothers.
> We practised discrimination and exclusion.
> It was our ignorance and our prejudice.
> And our failure to imagine these things being done to us.
> With some noble exceptions, we failed to make the most basic human response and enter into their hearts and minds.
> We failed to ask – how would I feel if this were done to me?
> As a consequence, we failed to see that what we were doing degraded all of us.
> If we needed a reminder of this, we received it this year.
> The Report of the Royal Commission into Aboriginal Deaths in Custody[2] showed with devastating clarity that the past lives on in

> inequality, racism and injustice.
> In the prejudice and ignorance of non-Aboriginal Australians, and in the
> demoralisation and desperation, the fractured identity, of so many Aborigines and Torres Strait Islanders.
> For all this, I do not believe that the Report should fill us with guilt.
> Down the years, there has been no shortage of guilt, but it has not produced the responses we need.
> Guilt is not a very constructive emotion.
> I think what we need to do is open our hearts a bit.
> All of us.
> Perhaps when we recognise what we have in common we will see the things
> which must be done – the practical things.[3]

To conclude, this part of the Redfern Speech is a powerful public confession of wrong-doing before all Australians, especially to the First Peoples of Australia. It is a truthful telling of what has happened between indigenous and non-indigenous Australians. I also suggest that Paul Keating's confession in this speech became an important stage in the process of national reconciliation. We can see reconciliation being advanced in Keating's recognition of past actions and in his acknowledging the contemporary consequences of such actions as is detailed in the extensive National Report of the Royal Commission into

Aboriginal Deaths in Custody of 15 April 1991.[4] His twinfold proposal that (a) everyone – *all of* us – open our hearts to one another and (b) recognise *what we have in common* so as to see the necessity of practical action, sets before the nation an ongoing 'act of penance', that is, making satisfaction for the sins of the nation and amending our national life.[5]

b. *Bringing Them Home: Reparation, Acknowledgment, Apology and Commemoration*

On 5 April 1997, the Human Rights and Equal Opportunity Commission presented 'Bringing Them Home' the Report of the National Inquiry into the Separation of Aboriginal and Torres Strait Islander Children from their Families to the Federal Government. The 'Terms of Reference' dated 2 August 1995, by the Attorney-General of Australia, Michael Lavarch, requested the Commission

> to trace the reality of past laws, practices and policies which resulted in the separation of Aboriginal and Torres Strait Islander children from their families by compulsion, duress or undue influence, and the effects of those laws, practices and policies.[6]

The Report first attends to the scope and process of the Inquiry (Part One), then traces the history of separation of indigenous children from their families in all States and Territories of Australia (Part Two) which is followed by evidence given to the Inquiry of the experiences of the children and the effects on their well-being, both as children and as they developed into adulthood (Part Three). Much of the evidence is first-hand testimony given at Commission hearings conducted throughout the nation and gives a public voice to those who were separated from their families.

It is in Part Four of *Bringing Them Home,* entitled 'Reparation' that the Commission addresses 'Grounds for Reparation' in chapter thirteen and next 'Making Reparation' in chapter fourteen. Broadly speaking, within 'Grounds for Reparation', a wide range of grounds are identified as reasons for reparation and this is done in two parts. In the first part, government actions are evaluated according to the legal values prevailing at the time of British colonisation of Australia and subsequent law developed by Australian parliaments and courts.[7] These include: deprivation of liberty of children by detaining them and confining them to institutions; depriving parents of their parental rights; abuse of power in legislation and in court hearings; breaches of duties by guardians (whether the guardian be a Protector, Protection Board, the State, foster families, or an institution); failure to care for people according to standards of the day; failure to prevent harm; failure to involve parents; and finally, the act of forcible removal as a breach of the duty to care for children.

In the second part, the Commission identifies the charters, declarations and conventions Australia pledged to uphold following the conclusion of the Second World War.[8] The official government actions of indigenous child removal, especially the assimilation policy, continued until the early 1970s, and the Commission, out of an awareness of international human rights agreements to which Australia voluntarily subscribed, identifies the following grounds for reparation: systematic racial discrimination and genocide which includes the forcible transfer of children, planning and attempting destruction of a group.

It is in Chapter Fourteen 'Making Reparation' that the Commission makes various Recommendations. After defining 'reparation' in a wide sense of the term, which includes 'compensation', it identifies components of reparation, and Recommendation 3 says:

> That, for the purposes of responding to the effects of forcible removals . . .; that reparation be made in recognition of the history of gross violations of human rights; and that the van Boven principles guide the reparation measures. Reparation should consist of,
> 1. acknowledgment and apology,
> 2. guarantees against repetition,
> 3. measures of restitution,
> 4. measures of rehabilitation, and
> 5. monetary compensation.

It is clear from this Recommendation that the commission believes that acknowledgment and apology is a primary response to all who are affected by forcible removals. Claimants are all who suffered because of these policies: individuals, family members, communities, and descendants of those removed.[9] As will be seen below, these two actions of acknowledgment and apology may occur with a ritual setting, whether that be in federal or state parliaments, territorial places of assembly, courts of law, churches or other institutional settings.

The Commission reported that throughout the process of the hearings, whilst there was 'no uniform view on reparations'[10] they heard a consistent view from Indigenous Australians regarding the necessity for apologies from government and non-government agencies, including the churches and the missions. This was heard in individual submissions, such as that given by a woman from Victoria who was removed as a young child in 1967:

> The Government has to explain why it happened. What was the intention? I have to know why I was taken? I have to know why I was given the life I was given and why I'm scarred today. Why was my Mum meant to suffer? Why was I made to suffer with no Aboriginality and no identity, no culture? Why did they think that the life they gave me was better than the one my Mum would give me?
>
> And an apology is important because I've never been apologised to. My mother's never

been apologised to, not once, and I would like to be apologised to.[11]

The Aboriginal and Torres Strait Islander Commission (hereafter ATSIC) submitted that

> reconciliation must surely begin with this one elementary condition: an apology. Indigenous people may then feel that the issue of separation, and the injustices it caused, have been acknowledged by those present-day government and non-government organisations . . . [12]

We can see it even more clearly certain ritual components of reconciliation in the recommendation of the Western Australian Aboriginal Legal Service:

> That the State government [and the Commonwealth government] **make a public statement** in Parliament **acknowledging** the devastating impact of the policies and practices... and **express regret**, and **apologise** on behalf of the people of Western Australia [and Australia].[13]

In further Recommendations within *Bringing Them Home,* the Commission asserts that acknowledgment and apology be offered by all Australian Parliaments (Recommendation 5a) and by State and Territory police forces (Recommendation 5b). Of note here is that contemporary Australian parliaments acknowledge that their predecessors enacted laws, policies and practices of forcible removal. Similarly for police forces in State and Territory jurisdictions who implemented these laws, policies and practices, that they also acknowledge their role and formally apologise to the claimants. The Commission recommends that these bodies are to negotiate with ATSIC in the formulation of the words for official apologies and the Commission also specifies the publicity which is to be given to those apologies.[14]

The Commission next recommends that churches and other non-government agencies which played a role in the administration of the laws and policies [of forcible removal of indigenous children] acknowledge that role and in consultation with [ATSIC] make such formal apologies and participate in such commemorations as may be determined. It is significant that during the process of the Inquiry itself, many of the churches who played a role in removing children from their families and who also ran missions for the removed children, such as agencies within the Roman Catholic Church, the Anglican Church of Australia, and the Uniting Church of Australia, as well as other non-government agencies, such as the Australian Association of Social Workers, acknowledged their role and apologised to claimants.[15] Once again, we see that it is those who were involved and who kept the systems of the removal of children in place being encouraged to tell the truth about their role, to apologise to those affected, and to ensure that this doesn't happen again in the future.

The final part of chapter fourteen concludes with Recommendation 7, which addresses the issue of commemoration. This addresses a number of suggestions made during the Inquiry which were concerned with what may occur following a single action of apology. One of the submissions made by Link-Up (NSW) suggested a national 'Sorry Day' *commemorating Aboriginal survival of the Holocaust which is accorded the same recognition as ANZAC Day. On a local level, communities may wish to establish commemorative places.*[16]

So we see in Recommendation 7a: That the Aboriginal and Torres Strait Islander Commission, in consultation with the Council for Aboriginal Reconciliation, arrange for a National 'Sorry Day' to be celebrated each year to commemorate the history of forcible removals and its effects. Recommendation 7b calls for the same two bodies to seek proposals for further commemorating the individuals, families and communities affected by forcible removal at the local and regional levels. The final part of this recommendation urges widespread consensus within the indigenous community when implementing proposals.

In recommending commemoration nationally, regionally and locally, the Commission places importance on these ritual actions for victims themselves and for society as a whole. They speak of the healing of a rupture internally for victims and a rupture between the survivors and society. The emphasis here is very much on everyone sharing: *a shared context, shared mourning, shared memory. The memory is preserved; that nation has transformed it into part of its consciousness. The nation shares the horrible pain.*[17]

c. The question of Parliamentary apologies following the submission of *Bringing Them Home*

The Report that I have been considering in the previous section was tabled in the Federal Parliament on 26 May 1997. Despite the Recommendation of a national apology, the new Prime Minister of Australia , John Howard, did not act upon the recommendation of the Commission to acknowledge and apologise for the role of the Federal Government in the forcible removal of children. Instead, on 26 August 1999, John Howard offered a 'Motion of Reconciliation' in the Federal Parliament, more than two years after the tabling of *Bringing Them Home*. The First Peoples of Australia and the nation were to wait until 13 February 2008 for the Federal Parliament to offer the national apology, by the Prime Minister of Australia, Kevin Rudd.

Despite the decision of the Prime Minister in this instance, the opportunity to acknowledge and apologise for their role in the forcible removal of children from their families was taken up by leaders in State and Territory legislatures around the nation. I note that these apologies were intentional speech-acts in response to Recommendation 5a of the *Bringing Them Home* report. Below, I will consider seven texts of apologies given to indigenous Australians by then-elected representatives of

New South Wales, South Australia, Queensland, Western Australia, Victoria, Tasmania and the Australian Capital Territory. My aim in now reviewing these apologies is to intentionally attend to what was included in each apology – the content – while at the same time recognising what was not included and, therefore, omitted. At this stage, I recognise each 'apology' is different in tone, language and content. The reader will also see that two apologies are detailed whilst the other five are less detailed.

In the State of New South Wales on 18 June 1997, Premier Bob Carr, offered the following apology:

> I move that this House, on behalf of the people of New South Wales:
> 1. apologises unreservedly to the Aboriginal people of Australia for the systematic separation of generations of Aboriginal children from their parents, families and communities.
> 2. acknowledges and regrets Parliament's role in enacting laws and endorsing policies of successive governments whereby profound grief and loss have been inflicted upon Aboriginal Australians
> 3. calls upon all Australian governments to respond with compassion, understanding and justice to the report of the Human Rights and Equal Opportunity Commission entitled 'Bringing Them Home',

4. reaffirms its commitment to the goals and process of reconciliation in New South Wales and throughout Australia.[18]

Premier Carr's apology is a fine example of an apology because it names clearly what has been done by previous New South Wales governments in the past. It then speaks the language of both regret and acknowledgment of laws and policies while aiming to situate its future responses within the context of implementing the Recommendations of *Bringing Them Home* and the ongoing work of reconciliation locally and nationally. I also note that it doesn't use the word 'sorry' nor ask forgiveness of indigenous Australians.

In the State of South Australia, two days after the tabling of *Bringing Them Home* in the Federal Parliament, on 28 May 1997, Dean Brown, Minister for Aboriginal Affairs apologised in these words:

> I move that the South Australian Parliament expresses its deep and sincere regret at the forced separation of some Aboriginal children from their families and homes which occurred prior to 1964, apologises to these Aboriginal people for these past actions and reaffirms its support for reconciliation between all Australians.

This apology is unique amongst these seven apologies now being considered because it was not given by the

Premier of South Australia – John Olsen – but by the Minister of Aboriginal Affairs. The other six were offered by the Premiers and the Chief Minister. Whilst Minister Brown spoke of 'deep and sincere regret' there are various conditional elements in this apology such as 'some Aboriginal children . . .' and his reference to 'prior to 1964'. It may be possible that we see in this apology the diminishment of apology which I understand to be an important stage in the process of reconciliation.

In the State of Queensland on 26 May 1999, Premier Peter Beattie, offered the following apology:

> This house recognises the critical importance to Indigenous Australians and the wider community of a continuing reconciliation process, based on an understanding of, and frank apologies for, what has gone wrong in the past and total commitment to equal respect in the future.

We see Premier Beattie situating his apology within the broader reconciliation process underway between indigenous Australians and the broader community. It is significant that his apology is given on 26 May 1999 which is the second anniversary of *Bringing Them Home* being delivered in the Federal Parliament. I wish to underscore that two years passed between the Recommendation for an apology and the Queensland parliament delivering one. It is also significant that the following is omitted in his apology: reference to the 1997 report; expressions of regret; and the very mention of the forced separation of children from their families in the State of Queensland. This last omission is galling given the evidence within *Bringing Them Home* regarding the laws, policies and practices within Queensland.[19]

In the State of Western Australia on 27 May 1997, Premier Richard Court acknowledged the forced removal of indigenous Australians in these words and with a gesture:

> It is appropriate that this House show respect for Aboriginal families that have been forcibly separated as a consequence of government policy in the past, by observing a period of silence.

Premier Court's motion in the State Parliament is not an apology. It is, however, a call to those present to 'show respect' for indigenous Australians by 'observing a period of silence'. Alongside the other examples of apology being considered while at the same time remembering Recommendation 5a within *Bringing Them Home,* it is striking that this is not an 'apology'. It is also noticeable that there is no expression of regret nor any mention of engaging in present or future acts of reconciliation, healing, or seeking forgiveness for actions, laws and policies of former Western Australian parliaments.

In the legislature of the Australian Capital Territory, on 17 June 1997, Chief Minister Kate Carnell, offered the following apology:

I move that this Assembly:

1. apologises to the Ngunawal people and other Aboriginal and Torres Strait Islander people in the ACT for the hurt and distress inflicted upon any people as a result of the separation of Aboriginal and Torres Strait Islander children from their families

2. assures the Aboriginal peoples and Torres Strait Islanders of this Territory that the Assembly regards the past practices of forced separation as abhorrent and expresses our sincere determination that they will not happen in the ACT

3. affirms its commitment to a just and proper outcome for both the grievances of Aboriginal and Torres Strait Islander people adversely affected by those policies and to the recommendations of the Bringing Them Home Report,

4. acknowledges that the Government is negotiating a Regional Agreement with the Ngunawal people in relation to the Ngunawal Native Title claim in the ACT, and

5. by this resolution seeks to take an important step in the healing process which is fundamental to reconciliation between Aboriginal and Torres Strait Islander peoples and the non-indigenous members of the ACT community.

Chief Minister Carnell's apology is the second of the seven apologies being considered here that demonstrated an understanding of the importance of apologising to indigenous Australians and to set it within the context of *Bringing Them Home*. It is noteworthy that in this apology, she names the local people, the Ngunawal people. This is unique amongst the seven apologies under consideration and that she situates her apology within a number of other important negotiations already under way with the same people, specifically a Regional Agreement and their Native Title Claim. I note here strong language which acknowledges the 'hurt and distress' caused by government policies to persons and families, her 'commitment to a just and proper outcome' for those adversely affected, and that this apology 'seeks to take an important step in the healing process fundamental to reconciliation . . .'. This apology is unique amongst the seven considered here in that in the name of the present Assembly the past practices are named as 'abhorrent' along with a determination they will not be repeated in the future in the Australian Capital Territory.

In the State of Victoria, on 17 September 1997, Premier Jeffrey Kennett, apologised in this way:

> By leave, I move: That this House apologises to the Aboriginal people on behalf of all Victorians for the past policies under which Aboriginal children were removed from their families and expresses deep regret at the hurt and distress this has caused and reaffirms

its support for reconciliation between all Australians.

In the State of Tasmania, on 13 August 1997, Premier Anthony Rundle, moved in the House, the following apology:

> That this Parliament, on behalf of all Tasmanians, expresses its deep and sincere regrets at the hurt and distress caused by past policies under which Aboriginal children were removed from their families and homes, apologises to the Aboriginal people for those past actions and reaffirms its support for reconciliation between all Australians.

In these final two apologies, I note there is specific reference within both to 'past policies' enacted by the respective States of Victoria and Tasmania which resulted in the removal of indigenous children from their homes. It is noteworthy that both do not describe the removals as 'forcible' as defined in *Bringing Them Home*. It is more striking, however, that both are strikingly similar in wording and content. Let us recall that Recommendation 5a of *Bringing Them Home* asked all Australian parliaments *to negotiate with the Aboriginal and Torres Strait Islander Commission a form of words for official apologies to Indigenous individuals, families and communities . . .*[20] I wonder if this recommendation was taken up by these two States as the history of forced removal of indigenous children from their families was particular to Tasmania and Victoria. As such, both of these parliamentary acknowledgments would have had the potential to address the particular histories of each State. This may be considered a lost opportunity and a diminishment of an important stage in the process of reconciliation.

I have shown in both the texts of the seven apologies and my brief analysis following each that the content as well as the sentiments within these Australian States and Territory acknowledgments and apologies are varied. Those offered by the leaders of New South Wales and the Australian Capital Territory are fuller apologies than the other five States. In light of my brief analysis of the apologies by the States of Tasmania and Victoria, I am left wondering what process was entered into by each government and whether or not they acted upon Recommendation 5a.2: *[That all Australian Parliaments] negotiate with the Aboriginal and Torres Strait Islander Commission a form of words for official apologies to Indigenous individuals, families and communities and extend those apologies with wide and culturally appropriate publicity.*[21]

d. Sorry Day celebrations

Across the nation, in work-places, schools, cities and suburbs, Sorry Day commemorations are held every year on 26 May. The date was chosen for this national day of commemoration because it was the anniversary of the Federal Parliament's acceptance of the Report *Bringing Them Home* in 1997. This is the national commemoration referred to in Recommendation 7a of *Bringing Them Home*.

In Brisbane, for example, local community groups, schools and workplaces are encouraged by the National Sorry Day Committee[22] to plan celebrations of Sorry Day. There are also specific Sorry Day celebrations held at different times of the day at the sites of former church and state run homes for indigenous children. All have now been demolished but there are stone markers erected by the Brisbane City Council to mark their former locations. This is known as the Stolen Generations Commemorative Plaques Project which commenced in 1998.[23]

In the past few years, I have attended Sorry Day celebrations in various communities and at some primary and secondary schools. I have found them to be quite moving commemorations for all present. One of the commemorations was held near the shoreline of Moreton Bay on the east-side of Brisbane, at Cleveland, close to the site of a former home for children. I will provide a short description of my experience.

A small group of about thirty people gathered early in the morning at 7.00am so that those working could attend and continue on to work. After the 'welcome to country' was given to those assembled by an Indigenous elder, a few words were then spoken by the leader about the significance of the day. We were next invited to listen to an audio recording of a song by Australian Indigenous singer, Archie Roach, titled *Took the Children Away* and which was written in 1990. Part of the song lyrics are:

> One dark day on Framlingham
> Came and didn't give a damn
> My mother cried 'go get their dad'
> He came running, fighting mad
> Mother's tears were falling down
> Dad shaped up and stood his ground.
> He said 'You touch my kids and you fight me'
> And they took us from our family.
> Took us away
> They took us away
> Snatched from our mother's breast
> Said this was for the best
> Took us away.
>
> Told us what to do and say
> Told us all the white man's ways
> Then they split us up again
> And gave us gifts to ease the pain
> Sent us off to foster homes
> As we grew up we felt alone
> 'Cause we were acting white
> Yet feeling black. [24]

Many people were visibly moved during the song. Many were quietly crying. After the song finished, someone said a few words about the meaning of Sorry Day for themselves, their family and the community. The ritual finished with the leader inviting all present to take a flower and to place it on the edge of the shoreline in memory of someone they knew. Once this had happened, breakfast was shared. The commemoration lasted for close to forty minutes.

The annual commemoration of Sorry Day is part of the broader ongoing work of reconciliation and healing and is not only for Indigenous Australians but for all Australians. It is public ritual that differs for every group and every gathering. It can be complex as the one I have described above. It can also be very simple.

One example of a simple Sorry Day ritual was related to me recently. I spoke to a male Indigenous worker who told me how his work-place commemorated this annual day. At morning tea on 26 May, the staff gathered together. His boss then invited him to share something of being an Indigenous Australian as well as saying a few words for the non-Indigenous work colleagues about the Sorry Day commemoration and its significance. After ten minutes of personal sharing, they then cut a cake and shared it amongst the workers.

It is important to recognise that in the two settings described, a group of people gathered together to commemorate Sorry Day. They remember what happened in the past. They think about the effects on Indigenous Australians. They support each other by being present to one another on this day and being in solidarity with each other.

Conclusion

Might it be possible the Church in Australia – in all its glorious diversity and with its long revered and emerging customs and liturgical traditions – undertakes a new or a renewed Spirit-led journey into these contemporary Australian 'rites of becoming reconciled' with our First Nation peoples? We in the Church may indeed have to admit we still have much to learn about actual 'practices of reconciliation' from society: words, language, actions, songs, witness, story and silence. As disciples of the crucified and risen One, we can learn what to avoid from other local 'practices of apology' that never really 'got there', especially for future liturgical celebrations. It may be prophetic yet all the more Christian as well as all the more human to seek honest, creative and open dialogue with First Peoples about our gathering on land and water courses that have never been 'vacant' nor 'available' for the outsiders who first came in ships.

What might we actually discover about our Christian practices of confession and liturgical reconciliation (as they are currently enacted or celebrated and also set out in ritual books) if we entered into listen to, enquire appreciatively and learn from those who feel dispossessed and unreconciled, as much as we can learn from these ritual apologies in our nation?

Endnotes

1 I have retained the layout of the text as it appears in the transcript. This highlights for me the spoken reality of the speech. In the following select quotes, I will retain the layout from my source document.

2 The National Report of the Royal Commission into Aboriginal Deaths in Custody was delivered to the Governor-General of Australia on 15 April 1991.
3 https://antar.org.au/sites/default/files/paul_keating_speech_transcript.pdf
4 *National Report of the Royal Commission into Aboriginal Deaths in Custody* (1991), http://www.austlii.edu.au/au/other/IndigLRes/rciadic/
5 *Rite of Penance* (1973) #44.
6 *Bringing Them Home* (1997) unnumbered page between Contents and page one.
7 *Bringing Them Home*, 249.
8 These include: The United Nations Charter of 1945, the Universal Declaration of Human Rights of 1948, the Convention on the Punishment and Prevention of the Crime of Genocide of 1948 and the International Convention on the Elimination of All Forms of Racial Discrimination of 1965.
9 *Bringing Them Home*, Recommendation 4, p. 283.
10 *Bringing Them Home*, p. 285.
11 *Bringing Them Home*, p. 277.
12 *Bringing Them Home*, p. 285.
13 *Bringing Them Home*, p. 285, additional emphases added.
14 *Bringing Them Home*, p. 287.
15 *Bringing Them Home*, p. 288-292.
16 *Bringing Them Home*, p. 292.
17 *Bringing Them Home*, p. 293.
18 The statements made in the various State and territory legislatures share a common source: http://web.archive.org/web/20061013043929/http://home.alphalink.com.au/~rez/Journey/parliam.htm
19 See further in *Bringing Them Home*, chapter 5 'Queensland' p. 71-90 and 'Appendix 3 Queensland' p.617-624.
20 *Bringing Them Home*, p. 287.
21 *Bringing Them Home*, p. 287.
22 See their website: http://www.nsdc.org.au
23 The park sites are at West End, Wynnum Foreshore, Everton Park, Nundah, Sherwood and the Brisbane CBD. See further information on: http://www.brisbane.qld.gov.au/community/community-support/aboriginal-torres-strait-islander-programs/stolen-generations-commemorative-plaques-project
24 http://songmeanings.com/songs/view/3530822107858710354/

11

Looking for the Body's Language

Bryan Cones

'In the restoration and promotion of the sacred liturgy the full and active participation by all the people is the aim to be considered *before all else*'.[1]

Since the authorisation of the Episcopal Church's *Book of Common Prayer 1979* (hereafter BCP-79),[2] there has been wide reflection on its ground-breaking 'baptismal ecclesiology', described by Ruth Meyers as 'an understanding of the Church as a community formed by baptism and empowered by baptism and the eucharist to carry out the reconciling ministry of Christ in the world'.[3] This focus on baptism as 'full initiation by water and the Holy Spirit into Christ's Body the Church',[4] as it is described in the liturgy for Holy Baptism, finds liturgical expression in the expansion of the BCP-79's 'Baptismal Covenant' beyond the Apostles' Creed to a number of promises related to the common life of the church and the ethical demands of gospel living.[5]

This approach to ecclesiology also appears in the BCP-79's Catechism, with its elaboration of the 'ministers of the church' as 'lay people, bishops, priests, and deacons'. This identification of 'ministers' achieves further contour in the articles dealing with each ministry. Thus, '[t]he ministry of lay persons is to represent Christ and his Church; to bear witness to him wherever they may be; and, according to the gifts given them, to carry on Christ's work of reconciliation in the world; and to take their place in the life, worship, and governance of the Church'.[6] 'Their place' in the worship of the church is among the primary issues this essay seeks to explore.

Given that the foundation of a *baptismal* ecclesiology must be liturgical – since almost all baptisms and every ordination takes place within a liturgical assembly – liturgies drawn from a resource grounded in a baptismal ecclesiology should, with some consistency, pray in ways that shape and propose such believing about the church. Episcopal liturgical theologian Leonel Mitchell asserts this fundamentally liturgical foundation of ecclesiology in his influential *Praying Shapes Believing: A Theological Commentary on the Book of Common Prayer*: 'The church is first and foremost a worshiping community'.[7] He goes on to note the role of the rubrics of the BCP-79 to guide the liturgical embodiment of this ecclesiology: '[T]he individual services provide the specific directions for participation, but the principle of common participation by the entire assembly, a principle which stands at the very centre of the grassroots liturgical movement of the twentieth century, is there established'.[8] Indeed, the baptismal ecclesiology of the BCP-79 is a particular contextual expression of the recovery of the assembly as a whole as the primary agent of the liturgy. Louis Weil, among the elders of the Episcopal Church's liturgical renewal, for example, often insists, 'limiting the term "celebrant" and "concelebrant" to bishops and priests sends the message that only the priests are celebrating the eucharist, and it fails to recognise that *all* the people gathered are celebrants'.[9]

Yet, long experience across many Episcopal assemblies suggests that is not often the case. Many liturgies drawn from the BCP-79 and enacting its rubrics continue as a matter of performance[10] to be focused on the functions of what Robert Hovda refers to as 'specialised ministers'[11] – presider, readers, choir, acolytes and other assistants – as distinguished from the primary ministry of the assembly as a whole. Thus William Seth Adams has characterised the ecclesiology of the BCP-79 as 'entangled', caught between the Baptismal Covenant and the 'clericalising rubrics' found elsewhere in the book.[12] While the BCP-79 is rich in *spoken* language that proposes a renewed liturgical baptismal ecclesiology, it has yet to find a parallel liturgical *body* language animated by the contention that baptism is the foundation of Christian ministry, liturgical and otherwise.

Agreeing with the introductory materials to the Episcopal Church's 1998 expansive language liturgical resource, *Enriching Our Worship*,[13] that '[n]on-verbal language—the language of gesture, movement, sign—will always override the text of the prayer',[14] it is reasonable to guess that the instructions guiding liturgical performance might be thwarting a fuller liturgical expression of the

BCP-79's baptismal ecclesiology. Given that liturgical performance is likely the primary experience of the church for most Episcopalians, reimagining and rewriting these instructions offers pastoral liturgical theologians and assemblies opportunities to seek that fuller expression. The BCP-79 itself supports this instinct when, in its introductory 'Concerning the Service of the Church', it notes that '[i]n all services, the entire Christian assembly participates in such a way that the members of each order within the Church, lay persons, bishops, priests, and deacons, fulfil the functions proper to their respective orders, *as set forth in the rubrical directions* for each service'.[15]

Follow the directions...

Among the first noticeable qualities of the BCP-79's rubrics and directions is their relentless attention to 'orders', particularly who may do or say what, and who may not. As 'Concerning the Service of the Church' notes, 'The leader of worship in a Christian assembly is normally a bishop or priest'.[16] Thus almost every note 'concerning the service' begins with the presumed ordained minister, often a bishop, then a priest, with their liturgical ministry usually named by some form of 'celebrant' or 'officiant', titles absent from the 1928 BCP and introduced in 1979.[17] If based on orders and titles alone, such an overly critical reading would perhaps appear under-supported and overstated. Yet given that the rubrics and directions assign almost all words and actions to the celebrant or officiant of whatever order of ministry, the claim deserves further exploration. A close reading reveals well-defined ritual actions according to order, regarding not only who can preside at a particular liturgy, but what ritual gestures may be taken and postures assumed, and which words may be used. The BCP-79 is clear, for example, that only a bishop may preside at a confirmation or ordination,[18] is the normative presider at liturgies of baptism[19] and eucharist[20] – where the bishop is the 'principal celebrant' – and is the only minister authorised to 'consecrate' chrism.[21] In the absence of the bishop, a priest presides at baptism and eucharist, and along with the bishop, may use particular forms of absolution[22] and blessing.[23] These two orders of ministry are also the only ones directed by the BCP-79 to engage in 'manual acts' related to prayer, for example, laying on hands during baptism[24] or confirmation,[25] blessing water or consecrating chrism,[26] holding or touching bread and wine during part of the eucharistic prayer,[27] and setting aside an object for use in the liturgy, for example, during the dedication of a font or an altar.[28]

The rare exceptions to these directions are found in the *Book of Occasional Services* (herein BOS), such as in 'A Public Service of Healing', in which 'lay persons with the gift of healing' may also lay hands upon those being anointed,[29] and in the materials concerning the catechumenate, which have several occasions for sponsors to lay hands on catechumens and candidates for baptism as the 'celebrant' voices a prayer, such as the admission of persons to the catechumenate, when a sponsor 'place[s] a hand upon the shoulder of the one they are sponsoring, while the Celebrant extends a hand toward them'.[30] Given that these rubrics appear in a resource that has been continually updated, the inclusion of more fulsome opportunities for the baptised who are not also ordained to take a 'full, conscious, and active' part in newer liturgies indicates the beginning of ritual gestures that point away from a clerical focus.

While noting such exceptions, the weight of rubrics tend to reinforce an 'active' role for the leader of prayer – whether officiant or celebrant – and a passive one for everyone else. This instinct is reinforced by a regular and repeated use of an active-voice rubric common in many liturgies, such as: 'The Officiant begins the service . . .'[31] or 'The Celebrant begins the liturgy . . .'.[32] Even in the spare outline provided by 'An Order for Celebrating the Holy Eucharist', which includes the possibility of an extemporaneous eucharistic prayer, the rubrics for that prayer indicate that *the 'Celebrant* gives thanks to God the Father for his work in creation and his revelation of himself to his people. . . . *The Celebrant* now praises God for the salvation of the world'.[33] These active-voice rubrics almost always render the subject of the liturgical action the celebrant, often 'saying' something to the people.[34] In effect, these instructions undermine any strong claim that the liturgy is the collective work of an assembly, served in its work when necessary by members appointed to certain roles. This tendency is magnified when an abundance of clergy is expected to participate, as in the instructions for the Easter Vigil, which go so far as to specify 'active' parts in the liturgy, with the insinuation of passive ones.[35]

The work of 'the people'

When a user of the BCP-79 finally arrives at any instruction given to 'the people' or, more rarely, 'the congregation' or simply 'all', the rubrics and directions are minimal, as if presuming that the people are present and active to a degree, but not necessarily terribly busy. In general their 'full, conscious, and active' part is restricted to posture, whether obligatory – 'all stand',[36] 'the people standing'[37] – or optional, 'may stand or kneel', as in the case of the eucharistic prayer.[38] Often, however, these rubrics differentiate the posture of the people from that of the celebrant, such as at the absolution after the confession, when 'the Priest alone stands and says',[39] thus also indicating a difference of posture according to order.

Beyond posture, some texts are provided with the presumption that they will be 'said' together, often marked 'Celebrant and People', including various dialogues and 'Amen', as well as some longer texts, such as the confession and the creed, portions of the eucharistic prayer, the prayer that Jesus taught, and, in Rite Two, the prayer after communion.[40] Model forms of the prayers of the people are unique in that they are perhaps the only time the BCP-79 imagines members of the assembly praying in their own extemporaneous voices, with rubrics indicating, 'The People may add their own petitions' or 'The People may add their own thanksgivings'.[41]

That is not to say that the people would be limited only to those texts directly indicated as voiced by the whole assembly. Other texts and prayers – forms of the Kyrie and Trisagion, psalms and canticles in the daily offices, and the Fraction Anthem before communion – might well be voiced by all the people. The rubrics regarding these texts, however, and unlike those for the officiant or celebrant, are curiously styled in the passive voice: '. . . is sung or said', '. . . the following is used . . .', and the like.[42] Such rubrics raise the question, 'By whom?' and at most celebrations of evensong and sometimes eucharist, the answer will likely be, 'by the choir, of course'—again reducing the people to the passive (if appreciative) role of observing someone else's liturgical work. Read narrowly, there is little in these passive-voice rubrics that would prevent a near-complete takeover of all the 'active parts' of the liturgy by specialists, whether ordained ministers or trained musicians, which hardly suggests a church enlivened by and embodying an ecclesiology rooted in a common baptism.

Indeed, further descriptive rubrics may in effect reinforce the opposite, suggesting as they do a certain 'ritual architecture' and likely reflecting and reinforcing the actual architecture of the church building. Numerous rubrics imagine some 'at the front' with others elsewhere: These include directions to the celebrant to 'face the people' for the preface dialogue of the eucharistic prayer and then 'face the Table' for the prayer itself, implying a table pushed up against a wall at some distance from the people,[43] along with a marked difference in degree of participation in the eucharistic prayer itself. Other rubrics indicating that the celebrant should 'face' the people, such as at absolution, or that 'representatives of the people' 'present' a candidate for baptism 'to the Celebrant',[44] all signal a presumption of different liturgical 'locations' for celebrant and people.

Some of these lend themselves easily to rendering the people into a watching audience. This is most obvious in the 'Additional Directions' for baptism: 'At the Thanksgiving over the Water, and at the administration of Baptism, the celebrant, whenever possible, should face the people across the font, and the sponsors should be so grouped that the people may have a clear view of the action'[45] – of which they are clearly not directly a part. It would be hard to argue in this case that the people are the active common subject initiating a new member.

The cumulative effect of these rubrics, repeated virtually without change regardless of the mode of language used (Rite I or Rite II) or the liturgy in question, is to inscribe a heavily 'ordered' liturgical ecclesiology, marked both by the dominance of the ordained offices (especially bishop and priest) and the liturgical roles (celebrant and officiant) they would most often undertake. While many roles may be granted to others – and most instructions indicate that 'other persons' should read readings and lead prayers, and these 'should normally be' lay persons 'appointed by the Celebrant'[46] – there is a general presumption that a 'minister' in the liturgy would not reflect the definition found in the catechism (which, after all, begins with 'lay persons') but that provided by the ordinal.

This tendency is so common that, in the absence of a bishop or priest, the alternative officiant is routinely styled '*a deacon* or a lay person', even though 'Concerning the Service of the Church' explicitly states that deacons do not officiate by virtue of their order. So why keep repeating 'a deacon or . . .'? The emphasis on the roles of the ordained can make it hard to find 'the assembly' at all. It further suggests the danger of what Gordon Lathrop refers to as a hierarchical *antiliturgica,* assembly practices that undermine liturgy's reconciling and liberating power: 'Every one of us – bishop and priest included – do not first of all participate in the liturgy "according to our order". We first of all participate, hands out as beggars, for the sake of once again encountering mercy, once again coming to faith'.[47] Such an *antiliturgica* is particularly disturbing, given that most of the directions regarding the roles of different orders found in 'concerning the service' and 'additional directions' were *added* to the BCP-79; such texts were mostly absent from the 1928 book.

All together now

Many would rightly insist that it is unjust to ask a resource of liturgical spoken language compiled at the midpoint of the ecumenical liturgical reform to propose a liturgical body language then only barely imagined.

Given that, as William Seth Adams and Louis Weil have noted, the compilation of the BCP-79 was driven primarily by clergy, the significance of gestures toward a baptismal ecclesiology ought not be understated.[48] Yet given the further work and reflection that has been done since the BCP-79 was authorised in 1979, not least the widespread reflection on the Baptismal Covenant that is the liturgical foundation of the BCP-79's ecclesiology, now seems an acceptable time to seek a new whole-body language shaped by the praying proposed in the spoken language of the Baptismal Covenant. In this the Episcopal Church would be wise to heed the warning of Leonel Mitchell: 'If the church's theology of ministry is not manifested in the liturgical actions of the ministers . . . the theology of ministry which is expressed in the liturgy will eventually supplant the official theology in the minds of worshipers'.[49]

One obstacle may be that the BCP-79, given its spare rubrics, is only marginally a 'ritual book' and might better be described as an 'Anthology of Common Prayer'.[50] While it contains plenty of texts for use in liturgy and their order in relation to each other, it contains comparably fewer directions for the liturgical action through which these texts become embodied prayer. What is there generally directs the actions of the clergy, often limited to 'laying a hand' on this or that object or person. In this, the BCP may signal an underlying Anglican approach to liturgy that sees it finally as, in the words of Pierre Whalon, 'oral recitation of a text', and a prayer book as 'above all a collection of authoritative texts, mostly texts to be recited aloud'.[51] This stands in contrast to a strong emphasis in contemporary liturgical theology and practice on liturgy as embodied ritual event, as articulated by Aidan Kavanagh in relation to the BCP: '[L]iturgy is not a text, much less a book. It is an act of worship in faith done repeatedly by countless thousands of people from Sunday to Sunday, year in and year out'.[52] Granting the strength and beauty of much of the liturgical spoken language of the BCP and successive resources, and the pioneering baptismal ecclesiology they inscribe, the relative lack of a parallel body language suggests that a further revision is now due.

Proposals toward such a liturgical whole-body language might begin with the presumption of the assembly as its common active subject, with every liturgy simply beginning with, 'The assembly gathers . . .' From there, all ritual directions might well presume that the assembly is its active agent, collectively processing, praying, proclaiming, singing, blessing, preparing gifts, and so on: 'The assembly enters the church singing a song of praise'; 'The assembly sits to hear God's word'; 'The assembly reflects in silence'; 'The assembly acclaims the presence of Christ in the gospel'; 'The assembly rises to offer prayers for the church, the world, and those in need'. Where the current rubrics suggest a 'representative of the people present' the eucharistic gifts to the deacon (or an assisting priest), who in turn 'prepar[es] and plac[es] . . . the offerings of bread and wine',[53] assembly-driven rubrics could imagine the whole assembly doing so, led by the deacon if necessary: 'The assembly processes with gifts of bread and wine and other offerings, and prepares the table for the Great Thanksgiving'.

When the assembly requires one of its members to act on its behalf, for example, to proclaim a reading or lead prayers, no distinction beyond 'a member of the assembly' would be required: 'A member of the assembly leads the preaching or other response to the readings'. Even in these cases, there is ample opportunity for communalised leadership that might better suggest the whole church doing its liturgical work. If the worship aid includes the texts of the prayers of the people, for example, each petition might be preceded by 'one so moved', indicating that different members of the assembly might lead different petitions, with ample opportunity for members to voice particular needs or thanksgivings, as is already imagined in the current rubrics. This echoes what Charles Price proposed in 1976 when the BCP-79 was still in draft form: 'Leadership in the liturgy should be widely shared'.[54]

By and large, this shift would mean the elimination of directions that distinguish between presider and the rest of the assembly except when absolutely necessary – and these would likely be rare and limited only to those roles that require particular orders in addition to that conferred in baptism. Even then, such rubrics would emphasise the relation of the ordained person to the whole: 'Gathered at the table, the assembly prays the Great Thanksgiving, *led by its presider.*' Further, as much as possible, a whole-body liturgical language would presume that actions which can be communalised, for example the *orant* posture for prayer, are made available to all so moved. There would little need to note that 'a lay person *may* . . .' if the default position is that any baptised person so moved *can:* lay hands, process, voice prayer, bow, lie prostrate, proclaim a reading, dance, light and bear a candle, and announce a word of blessing, lament, or forgiveness.

Each of these gestures may well need rubrics that communalise or extend their embodiment beyond the presider, if only to overcome the presumption that they are restricted to the ordained: 'The assembly lays or extends hands upon the person to be blessed'. Further, rubrics and directions concerning the service must emphasise that access to every 'location' in the place for liturgy, especially the font and table, is presumed to be open to all members of the assembly, never restricted by order or function: 'The assembly gathers around the font with the candidates for baptism, their sponsors, and its presider'. Above all, rubrics would unfailingly reinforce the 'aim before all else' – the 'full, conscious, and active participation' in the liturgy of the entire assembly through its diversity of gifts.

Such a reorientation would likely require a profound review of the ordinal ecclesiology that is arguably present in the current BCP-79, as well as serious reflection on the relationship between the fundamental order of Christian ministry entered through baptism and the ordained manifestations of that baptismal ministry in the offices of deacon, presbyter, and bishop. As Charles Miller argues, this will require a more robust and primary liturgical theology of 'the laity', or, better, of the liturgical ministry of the baptised.[55] Superficially, this reorientation would require the elimination of distinctions between presider and assembly that suggest the former is not first and always part of the latter, as well as the unfortunate title 'celebrant' or 'principal celebrant' in relation to the presider. It will also demand reflection on the limits of the ministry of presider (of whatever order) and the primary function of that 'specialised ministry' among others, and always in relation to the common ministry of the whole.

This should call into question ways in which that presidential and other liturgical ministries gets parcelled out among bishops and presbyters in ways that suggest clerical concelebration rather than the common celebration of the assembly.[56] Beyond these, however, current expressions about normativity in relation to leadership require further examination. For example, what does it mean to say, 'The leader of worship in a Christian assembly is normally a bishop or priest'? All 'worship'? Which parts? And how does that reflect a 'baptismal ecclesiology', much less that the assembly itself is the collective subject and symbol of the liturgy? It is likely that there is much unfinished business of renewal in relation to the orders of deacon, presbyter and bishop, and how those offices appear and function in the assembly.[57]

These are likely only the first of many questions that will require attention if the hierarchically ordered church imagined by many of the rubrics of the current BCP is to take further steps toward the baptismally ordered church prophetically proposed in some of it. Yet the Episcopal Church will have to engage these issues and likely many others if it wishes to disentangle the rival ecclesiologies found in its liturgical resources – or simply unravel a hierarchical one. Such effort would allow praying the spoken language of a baptismal ecclesiology to be animated by an equally poetic and prophetic whole-body liturgical language that further forms the baptised in their believing.

Endnotes

1. Constitution on the Sacred Liturgy *Sacrosanctum concilium*, para. 14, in *Vatican Council II: The Conciliar and Post-conciliar Documents*, Austin Flannery, gen. ed. (New York, NY: Costello Publishing, 1975), 8.
2. New York, NY: Church Publishing, 1979.
3. Ruth A. Meyers, Continuing the Reformation: *Re-visioning Baptism in the Episcopal Church* (New York, NY: Church Publishing, 1997), 225.
4. BCP-79, 'Holy Baptism: Concerning the Service', 298.
5. BCP-79, 304-5. Eugene R. Schlesinger has explored the baptismal liturgy for both its new ecclesiological and missiological dimensions, arguing that it 'represents . . . a recovery of the laity as fully Christian members of the Church with a positive ministerial contribution, rather than merely passive recipients of the clergy's ministrations'. See his 'Baptismal and Missional Ecclesiology in the American Book of Common Prayer', *Ecclesiology* 11 (2015): 177-198.
6. BCP-79, 855.
7. Leonel L. Mitchell, *Praying Shapes Believing: A Theological Commentary on the Book of Common Prayer*, Revised Anniversary Edition, Ruth Meyers, ed. (New York, NY: Church Publishing, 2016), Mitchell, Kindle location 165.
8. Mitchell, *Praying Shapes*, Kindle Locations 214-16.
9. Louis Weil, *A Theology of Worship* (Cambridge, MA: Cowley, 2002), 30-31.
10. I take for granted the widely held position that, while often rooted in resources such as the BCP-79, liturgy is an action best described as a common 'performance', with that term's many meanings. See, for example, Richard McCall's *Do This: Liturgy as Performance* (Notre Dame, IN: University of Notre Dame Press, 2007).
11. See his 'Liturgy's Many Roles: Ministers? . . . Or Intruders?', John Baldovin, ed., *Robert Hovda: The Amen Corner* (Collegeville, MN: Liturgical Press, 1994), 152-57.
12. William Seth Adams, *Moving the Furniture: Liturgical Theory, Practice, and Environment* (New York, NY: Church Publishing, 1999), 35.
13. New York, NY: Church Publishing, 1998.

14 EOW, 16.
15 BCP-79, 13, emphasis added.
16 Ibid.
17 The 1928 BCP generally uses 'minister' to denote the liturgical leader; the rubrics and 'Additional Directions' of 1979 broadly expand both references to three orders of ordained ministry and to the liturgical roles of 'officiant' and 'celebrant'. See, for example, the comparison of rubrics and additional directions for the celebration of eucharist in Paul V. Marshall, *Prayer Book Parallels: The Public Services of the Church Arranged for Comparative Study* (New York, NY: The Church Hymnal Corporation, 1989), especially 311-15 and 381-85.
18 BCP-79, 'Confirmation', 412-19; and, for example, 'The Ordination of a Priest', 524-35. References to BCP-79 liturgies throughout reference their "Rite Two" manifestations, as its contemporary language is the most widely used, and, when possible, to liturgies of baptism and eucharist. With rare exception, almost all these rubrics are generally and consistently repeated verbatim across liturgies, at times adapted for the particular rite.
19 Ibid., 'Holy Baptism: Concerning the Service', 298.
20 Ibid., 'Holy Eucharist: Rite Two: Concerning the Celebration', 354.
21 Ibid.
22 Ibid., 'A Penitential Order: Rite Two', 353. Other forms are provided for leaders who are deacons or lay persons outside the celebration of eucharist.
23 While the order for eucharist indicates that 'The Bishop when present, or the Priest, may bless the people', it does not give a specific formula (BCP-79, 366). "The Holy Eucharist: Rite One" (339) provides two options indicating, 'The Bishop, when present, or the Priest, gives the blessing'.
24 Ibid., 'Holy Baptism', 308, where the 'Bishop or Priest places a hand on the person's head, marking on the forehead the sign of the cross' after the baptism.
25 Ibid., 'Confirmation', 418.
26 Ibid., 'Holy Baptism', 307, where 'the Celebrant touches the water' during the Thanksgiving over the Water, and the bishop 'consecrate[s] the oil of Chrism, lacing on hand on the vessel of oil'.
27 Ibid., 'Holy Eucharist: Rite Two', 362.
28 Ibid., 'The Dedication and Consecration of a Church', 569 and 573, respectively. In both instances, the bishop 'lays a hand' upon the object set aside.
29 BOS, 170.
30 BOS, 118.
31 Ibid., 'Daily Morning Prayer: Rite Two', 75.
32 Ibid., 'Ash Wednesday', 264.
33 Ibid., 402-3.
34 Ibid., 'Holy Eucharist: Rite Two', 357 (the dialogue introducing the collect), 360 (invitation to the Peace).
35 Ibid., 'The Great Vigil of Easter: Concerning the Vigil', 284. Similar specifications of liturgical role by order occur elsewhere, especially in liturgies of ordination.
36 Ibid., 'Morning Prayer: Rite Two', 80.
37 Ibid., 'Holy Baptism', 299.
38 Ibid., 'Holy Eucharist: Rite Two', 362.
39 Ibid., 'Morning Prayer: Rite Two', 80.

40 Ibid., 'Holy Eucharist: Rite Two', 361-65. Regarding the prayer after communion, the Rite One Eucharist indicates the 'People may join in saying this prayer' (339).
41 Ibid., 'The Prayers of the People: Form VI', 393. All the model forms suggest a response by the people and generally include pauses for free intercession or thanksgiving.
42 Ibid., 'Holy Eucharist: Rite Two', 356; these are but two of many examples.
43 Ibid., 'Holy Eucharist: Rite Two', 333.
44 Ibid., 'Holy Baptism', 307.
45 Ibid., 313.
46 Ibid., 'Holy Eucharist: Rite Two: Concerning the Celebration', 354.
47 See his *Holy Ground: A Liturgical Cosmology* (Minneapolis, MN: Fortress Press, 2003), 187. 'Beggars' refers to a phrase written on a piece of paper found in Martin Luther's pocket after his death: 'We are beggars, this is true'. http://www.iclnet.org/pub/resources/text/wittenberg/luther/beggars.txt [accessed 26 April 2018].
48 See, for example, Louis Weil's 'Scope and Focus in Eucharistic Celebration', in Ruth A. Meyers, ed., *A Prayer Book for the Twenty-first Century* (New York, NY: Church Publishing, 1996), 35 and 43.
49 Mitchell, *Praying Shapes*, Kindle Locations 237-241.
50 Benedictine Aidan Kavanagh, in his 'appreciation' of the BCP after its release in draft, notes that the BCP 'begins to verge on becoming a library of liturgical books—a missal of 227 pages, a pontifical of 77 pages, a ritual of 82 pages, and a breviary of 344 pages, all of which accounts for three-quarters of the Book'. See his '"The Draft Proposed Book of Common Prayer": A Roman Catholic's Appreciation' *Anglican Theological Review* 58:3 (1976): 360-368.
51 See his 'The Future of Common Prayer' in *The Oxford Guide to The Book of Common Prayer*, 551-57. A review of the changes in rubrics from 1928 (not including the 'Additional Directions' added in the BCP-79), suggests only minimal editing and updating of those directions.
52 Kavanagh, 'Roman Catholic's Appreciation', 368.
53 BCP, "Holy Eucharist: Rite Two: Concerning the Celebration," 354, 361.
54 Quoted in Mitchell, Kindle location 228.
55 Miller notes that Anglicanism has, for a variety of reasons, struggled to articulate a 'theology of the laity'. He argues, following John Zizoulas, that baptism constitutes an 'ordination': '[B]aptism establishes the lay status of a believer by ordaining that person into the lay order. It is, moreover, an order which is not simply foundational to the church as the People of God, but distinct from, though complementary to, other orders'. See his 'The Theology of the Laity', 223-24.
56 See, for example, BCP-79, 'Holy Eucharist: Rite Two: Concerning the Service', 354, which directs, 'At all celebrations of the liturgy it is fitting that the principal celebrant, whether bishop or priest, be assisted by other priests, and by deacons and lay persons. It is appropriate that the other priests present stand with the celebrant at the Altar, and join in the consecration of the gifts, in the breaking of the bread, and in distributing communion'.
57 Eugene Schlesinger, for example, while arguing in favor of the BCP-79's baptismal ecclesiology, also robustly argues for maintaining robust theological distinctions between the grace conferred in baptism and that

received in ordination, echoing (in a footnote) Roman Catholic teaching asserting that 'the common and ministerial priesthoods differ "in essence and not only in degree" (*Lumen Gentium*, para.10)." See Schlesinger, 'Baptismal and Missional', 185-89.

12

Confessing More than Sin

Stephen Burns

My reflections are evoked by Gail Ramshaw's recent *Pray, Praise, and Give Thanks*,[1] in which she provides six brief liturgical texts of lament: about disease and infirmity, injustice in society, damage to the earth, the grip of melancholy, dread of mortality, and weight of guilt.

These recent offerings can be read alongside Ramshaw's 1989 article, 'Sin: One Image of Human Limitation,'[2] in which she sets sin – 'in the West the dominant image for our creatureliness', but nevertheless just one image – next to mortality, injustice, disease, and meaninglessness as experiences by which human limits may be acknowledged. I am intrigued by her work and her ideas over time about what she has called in other contexts 'confessing more than sin',[3] and I have my own questions to place in conversation with Ramshaw's work about how confession of sin in liturgy is 'heard' and how it functions in contemporary cultures of which I am a part. So in what follows I (i) introduce the work of Gail Ramshaw; (ii) consider Ramshaw's suggestion that Christian liturgy may 'confess more than sin' and her own development of that suggestion; and (iii) survey and reflect on the invitation to repentance as it presents in prayer books and liturgical settings in both old-line and new settings, asking how sin, and maybe more than sin, are indeed and might yet be confessed. While the latter section is less directly related to Ramshaw, I doubt that I would questioned any of it if it were not for her.

Gail Ramshaw, liturgical theologian

Gail Ramshaw is a contemporary ecumenical liturgical scholar whose writing features in prayer books across a variety of traditions, and whose writing about Christian assembly has significantly shaped what happens in Christian assemblies.

She is now retired from her role as professor of religion at La Salle University, a Roman Catholic institution in Philadelphia, Pennsylvania, USA. She is herself a member of the Evangelical Lutheran Church in America, in which she had an influential hand in shaping *Evangelical Lutheran Worship* (ELW),[4] contributing to its texts for prayer and the resources around it to suggest its best practice: *A Three Day Feast*,[5] *A Three Year Banquet*,[6] *Keeping Time*,[7] for example. More widely, she made major contributions to Protestant appropriation of the Roman Catholic Lectionary for Mass in the Revised Common Lectionary (RCL), with extensive work on using the lectionary: *Readings for the Assembly*[8] are 'emendments'[9] to the RCL, while *Treasures Old and New*[10] is a magisterial exploration of it. So her books have shaped how other books – of scripture – are read in the liturgy.

Beyond her work on the lectionary and specific contributions to Lutheran liturgical resources, however, Ramshaw has contributed to the genre of liturgical spirituality[11] through her early – and latest – work, often for Roman Catholic presses: notably the trio of book *Words Around the Font*, *Words Around the Table* and *Words Around the Fire*,[12] and latterly *Saints on Sunday*.[13] And she has been determined in publishing her concern that liturgical language be metaphoric, as well as inclusive. So *Liturgical Language*[14] complements *God in Sacred Speech* and *Reviving Sacred Speech*[15]—and this mirrors her attention to *who* constitutes Christian assembly: she writes very consciously as a layperson, a woman, and a feminist,[16] with the latter perspective at the fore of *God Beyond Gender*,[17] amongst other examples.

Just as Ramshaw's writing embraces different concerns, so it develops further genres. On the one hand, she has produced textbooks specifically geared at audiences among university students, 'the 3900 students who wanted, or did not want, to take my courses.'[18] These involved not only texts for prayer and texts about prayer and scripture, but also things sometimes approaching 'objective', at least carefully non-partisan, writing about Christian doctrine, in which she sets views from 'a scholar' alongside (notably always plural) views from 'the churches'.[19] On the other hand, she has also covered doctrinal ground in highly personal ways, such as in her account of 'the religion of a feminist Christian', *Under the Tree of Life*, organised as much of it is around liturgical tropes. Beyond her own writing in books and articles,[20]

Ramshaw's texts for prayer feature in at least official Anglican,[21] Presbyterian,[22] United Church,[23] and World Council of Churches sources.[24]

I appreciate Gail Ramshaw's work for many reasons, and especially because (a) as a layperson who neither preaches nor presides in eucharistic celebration, she has had very considerable influence on Christian worship – perhaps in some ways a kind of Egeria for our own times?[25] (b) While she writes prayer, she brings to that work an evident depth and breadth of learning as her bibliography bears witness – and this can be a caution to students straight out of college – and the rest of us – not to rush in as if wording public prayer requires little discipline.[26] (c) Her work's appearance in prayer books from across traditions raises good questions about the complexities involved in identifying a prayer as belonging to a particular tradition: Is a prayer Lutheran because its author is Lutheran? Anglican because it appears in an Anglican book? And what if it came to an Anglican book via a United Church one, without the Anglican compilers necessarily knowing it was written by a Lutheran? Ramshaw well represents something of the ecumenical treasure[27] the churches share.

Confessing more than sin

Each of Ramshaw's lament texts are shaped in the same way: an opening stanza begins with a strong scriptural allusion, a three line long petitionary litany, silence and then trinitarian ending. So the lament for 'the grip of melancholy' begins:

> With Job of old we cry out:
> Everywhere the innocent suffer.
> Our desires and efforts achieve us little.
> O God, are you good, yet do nothing to help us?
> Our answers have holes, and we fall though.

After *Kyrie, Trisagion*, brief petition and quiet, it then ends:

> Hear these words, and receive their power:
> The majesty of God the Father undergirds all that is.
> The mercy of God the Son accepts our despair.
> The comfort of God the Spirit embraces us in communities of care.
> **Thanks be to God.**[28]

Ramshaw suggests that her texts might be used either in a gathering rite, intercessions, or devotional setting.[29] Her brief excurses on these laments notes that Christian communities accustomed to praying for forgiveness can find many appropriate texts to hand, though in another place she praises (as 'stunning') a confession with which many Christians may not be familiar: the abecedary of the *Ashamnu* prayed by Jews at Yom Kippur. In translation, it begins: 'We abuse, we betray, we are cruel.

We destroy, we embitter, we falsify', then speaking of gossip, hate, insult, jeering, killing, lies, mocking, neglect, oppression, perversion, quarrelling, rebellion, stealing, transgression, unkindness, violence, wickedness, xenophobia, yielding to evil and zeal for bad causes.[30] Whatever the scope of their own prayers for forgiveness, however, Ramshaw suggests that more recent demand for provision of texts 'for other matters of communal lament' are less readily found.[31] And she uses a biblical allusion to frame her hope for her laments in *Pray, Praise and Give Thanks*: 'Mark 2:4 tells of those who opened up a hole in the roof of a house so as to lower a paralysed man to Jesus. The hope is that these texts will assist your assembly as it presents the needs of the world to God.'[32]

Paying attention to the invitation to repentance

Ramshaw's work invites a fresh look at the invitation to repentance, including the question of what may need if not to replace it, then to enrich it – that more than sin may be confessed. But we might also consider questions like where it best fits (if at all) and how it might best be worded. Though what follows in the rest of these reflections wanders around wide ranges of liturgical practice, and though space given to different practices is uneven, as I follow one lead or turn in a particular direction that interests me, I keep what I have to say in dialogue with Ramshaw's insights.

The limits of 'sin'

A first cluster of considerations unfold from recognition of the loss of language of sin from wider cultural parlance – at least in the west.[33] Not least for this reason, Ramshaw's search for language to express human limits while putting sin among a skein of other images is highly valuable.

Insight into some of the trouble of communicating albeit biblical and traditional ideas about both sin (broadly conceived as distance from divine holiness) and sins (specific immoral acts) can be tracked through the way that the Church of England's baptismal rites, in which while as yet the language of sin has survived, now allow for omission of reference to 'the devil.'[34] This suggests that the language-cluster that stories or makes some sense of sin has been recognised as not communicating in a wider milieu less biblically-literate than when earlier liturgies of baptism were commonly sought by the general population. Moreover, in such a context, regular expression of repentance of 'all our sins' (as the default general confession in both *A Prayer Book for Australia* (APBA) and *Uniting in Worship 2* (UiW2), with one subtle difference between them)[35] may seem especially over-reached. In part in response to this may be that the various volumes of the *Common Worship* range of the Church of England now provide many alternative confessions,[36] perhaps in an attempt to allow fresh wording to pique what a flat default confession may not now do so well.

Gail Ramshaw notes that "'confession of sin" is not the same thing as "confession of sins",' and that she 'hesitates when confessions particularise sin into sins.'[37] If the accent of regular, general confession falls on acknowledgment of specific sins, worshippers – not least 'believers and doubters alike'[38] which, notably, liturgies of the Sydney diocese of the Australian Anglican tradition at least admit may both be present[39] – may, believers and doubters alike, need help to identify what their specific sins may be, which 'general' confession may do less to facilitate than it once might have. And while writing local prayers may allow greater specificity and so address possible or felt-need for such help, closely attending to local writing of specific confessions is the risk that prayer may become 'clunky'[40] – long, losing care for sense lines, and so on – while another is a more serious danger of perceived accusation by the pastor/presider/prayer-writer. Ron Anderson's suggestion that good use of silence may be the best way to enable pray-ers make connections between specific personal experience and what can be said in more generic forms of words seems to me to remain the best kind of wisdom.[41] Gail Ramshaw would seem to agree.[42]

If the point of regular general confession is perceived more as highlighting human distance from divine holiness, more generic forms of words may be more appropriate in any case. But different ways of wording what may be understood as the larger narrative or nodal points of Christian theology about God can be seen in contrasting antipodean Anglican attempts to provide prayer of confession that includes children. *A New Zealand Prayer Book* (NZPB) opts in its 'family prayer' to echo the great commandments:

> Loving God, we are sorry that we have not always done what you wanted us to do. We have not loved you with our whole heart, and we have not cared enough about other people. Forgive us, for Jesus' sake.[43]

By contrast, the Anglican Church of Australia pursues a 'shepherd theme' which draws in disturbing images:

> God our Shepherd,
> we are lost in the darkness and danger of sin.
> We are hungry and afraid,
> and we cannot find our own way home.
> We are sorry for our sins.
> Search for us,
> save us,
> forgive us,
> and bring us back to life, we pray,
> through Jesus Christ our Lord.[44]

The question of including children – perhaps now even less familiar than their elders in the general population with how 'sin' was once more widely understood – in prayer might bring to the fore issues with the general confession within a wider culture largely out of touch with Christian doctrine. Ramshaw has herself been more engaged than most in crafting liturgical resources for children, and it would be interesting to hear her address directly the cultural gulf across which children may have increasing trouble making sense of sin.

Placing confession

A second cluster of considerations circle around the placement of confession in varied Christian liturgies.[45] Some traditions, the Roman Catholic for example, tend to place the confession in the gathering rite. Here placed, it may be that 'the penitential act at the beginning of the liturgy insists on an initial purification as the condition of being in the presence of God",[46] but doing so as part of a larger sequence through the gathering rite drawing worshippers into sense of presence (greeting), mercy (invitatory, silence, confession and absolution) and glory (*gloria*), as Goffredo Boselli suggests. The gathering rite's collect for purity, asking God to 'cleanse the thoughts of our hearts / by the inspiration on your Holy Spirit', drawn into Anglican, and from it, to other, liturgies after the greeting keeps echoing in some prayer books, with *A New Zealand Prayer Book* deftly using the unison line 'Spirit of God, search our hearts' as a response to the great and/or new[47] commandments.[48] While in the Roman tradition, as others, the gathering rite concludes with a collect prayer, variants within the Reformed tradition conclude the gathering with the sign of peace, conceived as seal on the prayers that preceded it.[49]

In some traditions, likely also influenced by theological priorities of the Protestant Reformation, an invitation to repentance follows reading and exposition of scripture, so that it functions as part of response to the gospel announced earlier in the ministry of the word.[50] Some commentators relate the confession of faith in the creed and the confession of sin in the invitation to repentance,[51] juxtaposed in this 'Reformed' ordering. Some traditions might then imagine confession of faith as related to offering of selves, gifts, money and prayer for others, all conceived as part of ministry of the word and response to the gospel story.[52] And when Boselli speaks of the collection as a 'manifestation of the mystery of the church',[53] ways to imagine the offertory as a form of confession, alongside creed and invitation to repentance, may follow. Such possibilities notwithstanding, whereas Boselli begins his 'mystagogy of the penitential act' with reference to the *Didache* and its call to 'confess offences' before breaking bread,[54] perhaps of greater influence on much contemporary thinking about eucharistic celebration has been Justin's *First Apology*, in which its well-known account of Sunday worship in mid-second century Rome omits reference to confession in its account which has been so influential on constructs of the *ordo*.[55] Hence, corresponding to Justin's witness, the World Council of Churches' 'Fundamental Pattern of Eucharistic Celebration'[56] minimises confession, placing it in parenthesis among the elements of the *ordo*. The coterminous International Anglican Liturgical Consultation ranked elements of the eucharist on a scale of 1-4, placing confession only at 3, that is, neither 'indispensable' nor 'integral', but something that 'would not be omitted in principle, [but] may be limited or varied.'[57] Ramshaw suggests options for any such variation.

Replacing confession?

On any Sunday, the suppressed, perhaps about to be rehabilitated[58] 1998 Roman sacramentary allows for *asperges* as remembrance of baptism. Gail Ramshaw's own Evangelical Lutheran Church in America follows its lead. These cast 'sin' in a different tone from general confession, with a stronger, certainly tactile, dimension of baptismal grace in play: 'shower us with your Spirit' is one of its evocative lines.[59] Experimental texts towards *Evangelical Lutheran Worship* also allowed for an extended form of lament in some services. Although they did not appear in the final publication of *Evangelical Lutheran Worship*, the example they set may have migrated as it were to other traditions, with the Uniting Church in Australia's *Uniting in Worship 2's* laments now providing one of few examples of official provision of what Ramshaw calls for. The UiW2 form is one of two default rites of gathering placed side by side as pathways into 'A Service of the Lord's Day.' While not an adoption of the ELW materials, UiW2 has some striking parallels, notably the repeated use of the refrain 'How long?': the Lutheran form associates this question with Psalm 13, which shapes its whole provision of lament-related texts (including the repeated transliteration of the Hebrew, '"Ad 'anah 'Adonai"). UiW2 associates the same question with Zechariah 1.12. While the Lutheran form suggests that prayers of both lamentation and intercession are spoken on behalf of the world, society and local community, UiW2 has very creative rubrics that draw in both 'newspaper headlines' and visual art ('slide shows') of contemporary events alongside its use of scriptural texts, silence and song. And whereas the Lutheran form pairs lament with 'petition', UiW2 wends from lament to (albeit at this point optional) 'affirmation of hope in Christ' alluding to 1 Corinthians 1:22-4's talk of stumbling blocks and folly and Matthew 11:19's affirmation of wisdom being vindicated by deeds before an arresting presidential text:

> In faith, we appeal to God.
> In hope, we will not let God go.
> In love, we claim God's attention.
> Let us honour the God who receives our cries,
> and gathers us to herself even as we continue
> to call.[60]

The default text which then concludes the gathering rite in UiW2 is based on Mechtild of Magdeburg's 'The Nine Choirs: How They Sing', with its line 'in your wisdom, you place us', before concluding 'in your love, you lift us up.'

The UiW2 forms are more integrated into its wider resources than, for example, the Church of England's lament rite, 'Facing Pain',[61] which remains highly ancillary, tucked away among the many more visible aspects of the *Common Worship* range. By contrast, UiW2 allows for lament to be a major aspect of the gathering rite, regularly if need be, significantly shaping the liturgy as a whole. Interestingly, a rubric in UiW2's provisions suggests that where lament is used, a prayer of confession remains part of the Service of the Lord's Day following proclamation of the word, but no form for it (nor reminding rubric) is included after the preaching. Gail Ramshaw may well not agree with the need for this.

Enacting confession

While UiW2 suggests use of imagery from various media, rites of lament in other traditions sometimes involve bringing biblical images and local concerns into collision. An interesting example can be seen in laments from the Anglican Church of Kenya's *Our Modern Services*, which make strong allusion to Habakkuk 3:17-18's woe at wizened olive trees, but switches the reference to mangoes and lack of abundance in the local crops and context.[62] And in other contexts again, local 'pagan' ceremonies may be adopted into the liturgy. Malaysian Tamils, for example, have incorporated a wider cultural practice of smashing coconuts during confession, and then picking up the pieces after absolution. The thrown-down coconut symbolises the heart, broken by sin, and picking up pieces represents a resolution never to commit the same sin again, and purity of heart retrieved.

Pacific Islanders at worship have sometimes appropriated a wider cultural tradition of sitting under a large straw mat as a sign of sorrow, awaiting forgiveness. The mat is removed with absolution, representing the movement to new reconciliation.[63] While the whole assembly may not sit under the mat, nor each person smash coconuts, these representative actions may vivify and deepen experience of confession in communities whose cultures mediate reconciliation through such ritual modes. And these ritual practices raise questions to ask of Western rites of confession, in which beating of the breast may be directed in the rubrics of the Roman rite, but most are devoid of ceremonial dimensions. Moreover, they suggest that while the question 'whatever happened to sin?' resounds in some – western – cultures, in others the question is strange. Reception of Gail Ramshaw's work has perhaps largely been in the west – the context in which she identified sin as just one way of naming human limitation. Yet she states: 'I do not confess my sin alone, but with centuries of the penitents around the world: does that help the ritual to find meaning?'[64]

Engulfing confession

It is worth observing that some Christian traditions in the west – and notably ones often growing more quickly than old-line ones – have some distinctive ways of dealing with an invitation to repentance. These may be as 'inculturated' as the examples from the Asia-Pasifika, just cited. In neo-Pentecostal communities, perhaps the only use of scripted, written-down, prayer may be a 'prayer of commitment' as part of an 'altar call', as in the Australian Hillsong church. In practice, such prayer may display more 'traditional' elements than other aspects of their liturgies: for example, naming towards God with the metaphor of fatherhood, whereas other prayer may be addressed more directly simply to 'God'; carefully reflecting very particular understanding of atonement, whereas other prayer may be more loosely expressive of worshippers' feeling, and so on.[65] In these respects, such prayer may conform to a wider liturgical dynamic: of parts deemed to be most important being most conservative. At the same time, a regularly used 'penitential act' inviting repentance of those deemed to have committed themselves may be missing from regular worship in neo-Pentecostal settings, which can hardly be an oversight when their liturgical events and environments are so highly sensitive to the mores of popular culture with respect to music (rock music, often with a 'wall of sound aesthetic'[66]), space (meeting in cinemas), dress (not vestments, but current fashions), leisure (with prominent imagery of surfing and skateboarding in the promotion of Hillsong, for example), registers of language,[67] and so on. However, the opening section of worship may – though unlikely to be called a gathering rite – involve a sequence akin to that identified in the Roman mass by Boselli: greeting, mercy, glory, with song focusing on divine mercy and divine glory and skateboarders and surfers et al's response to it. Arguably, this song-driven arc may effectively convey human limits, acknowledging human creatureliness, wording dependence upon God, and taking joy in divine gifts.

Swee Hong Lim and Lester Ruth point out how Hillsong's theological themes can also be mapped onto musical tempo and mood in the music sets in which they are sequenced.[68] For example, down tempo Hillsong 'The Stand' begins with praise of God acknowledged as being before creation, holding eternity, bringing forth the earth, before becoming personal: 'I'll stand, with arms high and heart surrendered.'[69] 'With all I am' praises God who holds the singers' 'world in the palm of [God's] hand.' Commitment to a 'way', a newness of life, not so much ethical as intimate, is commonly scripted into the songs: 'I'll walk upon salvation, your Spirit alive in me', 'I'll walk with you wherever you go, through joy and pain, I'll trust in you', 'I will live in all of your ways, your promises, for ever.'[70] These songs, by no means confined to Hillsong given that the church's music has now become a global brand, convey a sense of divine grandeur, of gifts that come from divine care, and reception of and correspondence to such benevolence – albeit whilst inviting an experience worded by participants in terms like being 'unexpectedly lost' in the song.[71]

The point seems to be that the experience of worship, not least being 'lost' in a 'wall of sound', opens an amplified sense of divine encounter, as it were 'in stereo', with Jesus and the Spirit presumed to be moving worshippers beyond the realm of 'conscious human behaviour' into some deeper feeling of salvation. Language like 'conversion' – and perhaps by extension, 'confession' – may be considered by advocates of Pentecostalism as too tied in with conscious behaviours, while their style of worship frees them up for something more.[72]

Such worship is likely to include some kind of 'altar call', with the altar understood in Pentecostal theology not as liturgical furniture but 'a soteriological metaphor'[73] and one which has had shifting manifestations in the history of Pentecostal worship: 'a walking of the aisle or jumping on pews' among the possibilities, but most typically perhaps associated with space between front pew and stage. As Wolfgang Vondey has suggested, in neo-Pentecostalism it is possible to discern a relocation of the altar 'from clear architectural identifiers at the back end of a church building to the more symbolically and experientially identified centre of worship of the congregation.'[74] But whatever its spatial identifiers within Pentecostal assembly rooms, the notion of the altar as divine encounter remains firm, and as Daniel Tomberlin speaks from within this tradition:

> each time we approach the altar to meet with God we are faced with an opportunity to carefully examine ourselves. We must sincerely seek to maintain *shalom* in our family, our church, and in the greater human community. As we bow before God at the altar, we express humility. But we must remember that before we bow before God at the altar, we may need to seek out an enemy, or someone we have injured, and bow in humility before

them. The altar becomes a witness to the ministry of reconciliation.[75]

To my mind, Pentecostal worship beckons curiosity about participation in communal penitential acts (whether or not particular songs are regarded as such) in a wider culture that does not speak or perhaps not know how to talk theologically about sin. And in Hillsong and other neo-Pentecostal contexts, while formal confession, less again word of absolution, may be absent, presumably for some if not many of the worshippers in such communities, it is the music which the words of these songs accompany that begins to invite affective involvement in the words' sentiments. Of course, coming to an understanding of the altar may seem no less obvious than coming to appreciate any other theological approach to sin – distance from divine holiness, or whatever – though the merit of the former may be that it may sometimes, by some, be felt to more immediately yield the experience it purports to pry open.[76]

When other traditions allow for song to replace spoken words of confession in a liturgy, as in UiW2 for example,[77] this should not be correlated with all that is going on for Pentecostals with a complex notion of the altar, and whose understanding may well include both confessing sin and confessing more than sin, as well as unmediated encounter to propel the change for which their songs and prayers say they yearn. Gail Ramshaw notes that neither she 'nor any Christian whom she knows well' has experienced the 'second baptism' of the Spirit characteristic of contemporary Pentecostal experience, yet she echoes Symeon the New Theologian's insight that the Spirit is the key to the door which is Christ and urges in her own voice, 'let's use it more than was our wont.'[78] Further, she asks a pertinent question about experience from which she says she is distant, which might well include contemporary Pentecostalism: 'what is the process, and how many centuries does it take, for an extraordinary personal experience to become grafted into and thus influence future growth in church tradition?'[79]

Official deficiencies

Finally, and I think most significantly, is the stark challenge which churches – in so much of the west – face with regard to their own moral authority and hence their capacity to speak meaningfully or guide trustworthily about sin/s.[80] Here, more – and painful – reflection is needed on children. The churches have at least three-fold deficiencies in relation to abuse of the vulnerable young, and the deficit is so stark it can be stated bluntly: first with their representatives inflicting abuse, second with their overseers failing to confront it or covering it up, and third now frustrating legislation in the so-called secular realm to mandate the reporting of its incidence – in which confession to a priest is the principal disputed context. In such circumstances, one might not be surprised that the confessional box is disappearing.[81] Monika Hellwig's encouragement of 'lay and mutual confession that takes place over the kitchen table between neighbours and friends'[82] is part of the picture that has emerged since the Second Vatican Council, and may go some way to addressing at least some of the mistrust – at least among some persons sufficiently churched to take up such responsibility for one another.

Whether it gives voice to a wider sense of human limits than is possible through the image of sin is of course another question. And the more recent wider public impact of the churches' deficiencies in care of children – allied as it often is in public space with what are widely perceived as churches' intolerant views of diverse adult consensual sexual expression[83] – is, because now such a grave cause of public mistrust, an overwhelming reason why the invitation to repentance needs new care. Nothing less is at stake than whether the churches can be trusted to know what wrongdoing is, let alone offer anything to address the depth of harm it may cause. Whether this complex of problems can be addressed in ways that suggest to the wider public a credible dimension of repentance on the part of the church, in which language of sin persists where it does not elsewhere – should be expected to impact how confession of sin in liturgy is received. Albeit with feminist clues as to both what is wrong and what needs to be put right in human relationships, Gail Ramshaw has not yet written on the scandal of abuse. I hope she will. My own sense is that the new care that is needed in the churches' wording of sin goes beyond all liturgical possibilities – either tinkering or more wholesale – that I have mentioned hitherto.

Grateful thanks

Gail Ramshaw claims that it may be her questions that are most helpful,[84] and she invites our attention to things that matter: to matters of communal lament, to knowing and wording human limits, to enabling sense of sin, to inviting confession of sin and more than sin. I thank her for evoking my own questions shaped by my reading and thinking about her writings.[85]

Endnotes

1 Gail Ramshaw, *Pray, Praise and Give Thanks: A Collection of Litanies, Laments, and Thanksgivings at Font and Table* (Minneapolis, MN: Augsburg Fortress Press, 2017).

2 Gail Ramshaw-Schmidt, 'Sin: One Image of Human Limitation', Mary Collins and David Power, eds, *The Fate of Confession / Concilium* 190 (Edinburgh: T & T Clark, 1987), 3-10. Reprinted in Gail Ramshaw, *Worship: Searching for Language* (Washington DC: Pastoral Press, 1988), 139-150.

3 http://www.naal-liturgy.org/meetings/seminars/85-meetings/seminars/108-liturgical-language

4 Minneapolis, MN: Augsburg Fortress Press, 2006. Ramshaw's own contributions to *Evangelical Lutheran Worship* (ELW) are anonymous, though as Frank Senn notes in *Eucharistic Body* (Minneapolis, MN: Fortress Press, 2017), 120, certain parts of ELW suggest Ramshaw's influence.

5 Gail Ramshaw, *A Three-Day Feast: Maundy Thursday, Good Friday, Easter* (Minneapolis, MN: Augsburg Press, 2004).

6 Gail Ramshaw, *A Three-Year Banquet: The Lectionary for the Assembly* (Minneapolis, MN: Augsburg Press, 2004).

7 Gail Ramshaw and Mons Teig, *Keeping Time: The Church's Years* (Minneapolis, MN: Augsburg Press, 2007).

8 Edited with Gordon W. Lathrop, *Readings for the Assembly: A, B & C* (Minneapolis, MN: Augsburg Fortress Press, 1995, 1996, 1997, respectively).

9 Lathrop and Ramshaw, eds, *Readings... A*, vii-viii.

10 Gail Ramshaw, *Treasures Old and New: Images in the Lectionary* (Minneapolis, MN: Fortress Press, 2002).

11 She defines this as one in which 'life in the spirit of Christ is sought through the rhythm, forms, words and melodies of the liturgy' (*Words Around the Font* [Chicago, IL: LTP, 1994], vii), and employs an image to depict its construction: 'a quilt – one swatch from an old linen tablecloth, one from grandma's flowered housedress, one from grandpa's plaid shirt. Liturgical

spirituality is such a quilt. Wrap yourself up in it. It is wondrously warm in a shivering world' (*Font*, x).

12 Gail Ramshaw, *Words Around the Fire* (Chicago, IL: LTP, 1990; Gail Ramshaw, *Words Around the Table* (Chicago, IL: LTP, 1991); Ramshaw, *Font*. Also, Gail Ramshaw, *Words That Sing* (Chicago, IL: LTP, 1992).
13 Gail Ramshaw, *Saints on Sunday: Voices from the Past Enlivening Our Worship* (Collegeville, MN: Liturgical Press, 2018).
14 Gail Ramshaw, *Liturgical Language: Keeping it Metaphoric, Making it Inclusive* (Collegeville, MN: Liturgical Press, 1996).
15 Akron, OH: OSL, [2] 2000. This is a revision of *Christ in Sacred Speech*, with interesting "second thoughts."
16 Albeit what she calls a 'minimizer' one: Gail Ramshaw, *Under the Tree of Life: The Religion of a Feminist Christian* (New York, NY: Continuum, 1998), 17.
17 Gail Ramshaw, *God Beyond Gender: Feminist Christian God-language* (Minneapolis, MN: Fortress Press, 1995)
18 Gail Ramshaw, *What is Christianity?* (Minneapolis, MN: Fortress Press, 2014),vii. For another of her textbooks, *Christian Worship: 100,000 Sundays of Rituals and Symbols* (Minneapolis, MN: Fortress Press, 2009)
19 Her method in *What is Christianity?*
20 Footnotes to this essay mention most – but not all – of Ramshaw's books, but there is also a wealth of articles, only few of which are mentioned here.
21 As she notes in her valuable review of Buchanan, *Anglican Eucharistic Liturgies*: Gail Ramshaw, 'A Look at New Anglican Eucharistic Prayers', *Worship* 86 (2012): 161-7.
22 Several of Ramshaw's prayer, including the laments are included in *The Book of Common Worship* (Louisville, KY.: WJKP, 2018).
23 'Triple Praise' is found in *Pray, Praise…*, 54-6, and also *Celebrate God's Presence: A Book of Services for The United Church of Canada* (Etobicoke, Ont.: United Church of Canada Press, 2000), 256-258, as well as my *Liturgy (SCM Study Guide)* (London: SCM Press, 2006, rev. 2018): I agree with Kimberly Bracken Long's assessment of Triple Praise as 'exquisite': Kimberly Bracken Long, 'Beyond Merely Adequate: Poetic Sensibility in Liturgical Language',*Liturgy* 25 (2010): 3-10, 3. Compare Ramshaw's prayer in Thomas F. Best and Dagmar Heller, eds, *Eucharistic Worship in Ecumenical Contexts: The Lima Liturgy – And Beyond* (Geneva: WCC, 1994), 155-157 and that of the Anglican Church of Southern Africa in Colin Buchanan, ed., *Anglican Eucharistic Liturgies, 1985-2010: The Authorized Rites of the Anglican Communion* (Norwich: Canterbury Press, 2012), 168.
24 Thomas Best and Dagmar Heller, eds, *Eucharistic Worship in Ecumenical Contexts: The Lima Liturgy—And Beyond* (Geneva: WCC, 1994).
25 See Ramshaw, *Saints on Sunday*, 157-64.
26 I note Robert Gribben, *Uniting in Thanksgiving: The Great Prayers of Thanksgiving of the Uniting Church in Australia* (Melbourne: Uniting Academic Press, 2008), 177: 'the Uniting Church permits a presider to offer their own "Great Prayer", but the result is too frequently much poorer than the church's authorised provision… it is a permission that should be taken extremely rarely, and on the basis of being told by the church that you *have* the relevant gift,' as well as his most marvellous story about celebrating the eucharist with Jesuit priest Henri Nouwen, who used a Lutheran book of worship, as related on pages 34-5 of *Uniting in Thanksgiving*.

27 Gordon Lathrop's term in his 'Strong Center, Open Door: A Continuing Vision of Liturgical Renewal', *Worship* 75 (2001): 35-45, 36.
28 Ramshaw, *Pray, Praise...*, 25.
29 Ramshaw, *Pray, Praise...*, 11. They were originally written and published in the Presbyterian Church (USA)'s worship journal. More detail here: https://easternsynod.org/ministries/worship/files/2012/06/Ramshaw_Laments.pdf
30 Ramshaw, *Saints on Sunday*, 38
31 Ramshaw, *Pray, Praise...*, 10.
32 Ramshaw, *Pray, Praise...*, 11.
33 Karl Menninger, *Whatever Became of Sin?* (New York, NY: Hawthorn Books, 1978) is a classic in this mode. I note in Ramshaw's own work, *100,000 Sundays*, 211; *What is Christianity?* 56-9, *Saints on Sunday*, 34-40, while much of her work does not much employ the term 'sin' – no doubt enacting her conviction that human limits can be conveyed in other images.
34 https://www.theguardian.com/world/2014/jun/20/church-of-england-baptism-service-no-devil
35 APBA, 120 / UiW2, 154: While APBA follows mention of sin 'in thought and word and deed', with 'what we have failed to do', UiW2 does not include the expanded failure of omission.
36 Among various possible examples, *Common Worship: Services and Prayers for the Church of England* (London: CHP, 2000), 122-37 and 275-278, though 'authorisation' remains tighter around confession than most other aspects of the services, as 26 and 331.
37 Ramshaw, *Saints on Sunday*, 37.
38 Archbishop of Sydney's Liturgical Panel, *Sunday Services: A Contemporary Liturgical Resource* (Sydney: Anglican Press, 2001), 28.
39 *Common Prayer: Resources for Gospel-shaped Gatherings* (Sydney: Anglican Media, 2012),
40 Brian Wren, 'Clunky Prayers and Christian Living: Reflections on Writing, Prayer, and Practice', in E. Byron Anderson and Bruce T. Morrill, eds, *Liturgy and the Moral Self: Humanity at Full Stretch Before God: Essays in Honor of Don E. Saliers* (Collegeville, MN: Liturgical Press, 1998), 181-192.
41 E. Byron Anderson, 'Linking Liturgy and Life', in E. Byron Anderson, ed., *Worship Matters*, Volume I (Nashville, TN: Discipleship Resources, 2000) 63-69, 67.
42 Ramshaw, *Saints on Sunday*, 38.
43 *He Karakia Mihinare o Aotearoa / A New Zealand Prayer Book* (Auckland: Collins, 1989), 189.
44 https://www.anglican.org.au/data/An_Order_for_Holy_Communion_where_Children_are_present_-_Shepherd_theme.pdf
45 Interestingly Ramshaw discusses sin in her reflection on the communion rite, in *100,000 Sundays*, 212.
46 Goffredo Boselli, *The Spiritual Meaning of the Liturgy: School of Prayer, Source of Life* (Collegeville, MN: Liturgical Press, 2014).
47 Harriet Harris, "Confession," in Stephen Burns, ed., *Liturgical Spirituality: Anglican Reflections on the Church's Prayer* (New York, NY: Seabury, 2015), 35-55.
48 NZPB, 406. The default placing of the Gloria is, however, between collect for purity and recitations of the great and/or new commandments, though a rubric on 405 allows for the Gloria to be moved until after absolution.

49 See the Presbyterian Church (USA)'s *Book of Common Order* (Louisville, KY: WJKP, 2003) for examples of this: 36 and 57. Oddly, given the Church of England's resources' suggestion of variant placing of the peace (e.g. *Common Worship: Services and Prayers...*, 333), this position is not included (alongside opening, close, beginning of the liturgy of the sacrament, and following immediately on from eucharistic prayer).
50 A number of traditions present the two positions – that is, in the gathering rite, and following reading and preaching in the liturgy of the word – as alternatives.
51 Boselli, *Spiritual Meaning*, 23-46.
52 See *Uniting in Worship 2*, 134 (and 133 on placing of confession in the order).
53 Boselli, *Spiritual Meaning*, 192-3.
54 Lawrence J. Johnson, ed., *Worship in the Early Church; An Anthology of Historical Sources* (Adelaide: ATF Press, 2009), Volume 1, 39.
55 Johnson, ed., *Early Church*, 68.
56 Best and Heller, eds, *Ecumenical Contexts*, 34.
57 See David Holeton, ed., *Our Thanks and Praise: The Eucharist in Anglicanism Today* (Toronto: ABC, 1998), 292-3.
58 See Gerald O'Collins with John Watkins, *Lost in Translation? The English Language and the Catholic Mass* (Collegeville, MN: Liturgical Press, 2017). On the last (never authorised) missal see Mark R. Francis and Keith Pecklars, eds, *Liturgy for the New Millennium: A Commentary on the Revised Sacramentary* (Collegeville, MN: Liturgical Press, 2000) and especially Mark Francis' own chapter 'Well Begun is Half Done: The New Introductory Rites in the Revised Sacramentary', 65-76. On the current Roman provisions, in which *asperges* is found only in an appendix for use 'from time to time': see Ed Foley, et al, eds, *A Commentary on the Order of Mass in the Roman Mass: A New English Translation* (Collegeville, MN: Liturgical Press, 2011), 107, 120.
59 *Evangelical Lutheran Worship*, 97. See also Lorraine Brugh and Gordon Lathrop, *The Sunday Assembly* (Minneapolis, MN: Augsburg Fortress, 2008), 121-3. The prayers included in the trial-use *Holy Baptism and Related Rites* (Minneapolis, MN: Fortress Press, 2004) were more notable for their playful tone, and their theological constructs suggest some influence of Ramshaw. Sadly, this resource is out of print. On other kinds of recasting of confession, note also the Church of England's configuring of reconciliation of a penitent within initiation services, as 'recovering baptism' (see *Common Worship: Initiation Services* [London: CHP, 2007]), and these including thanksgiving for baptism.
60 UiW2, 202.
61 *New Patterns for Worship* (London: CHP, 2002), 442-8.
62 *Our Modern Services* (Nairobi: Uzuma Press, 2002), 5.
63 Both examples as found in I-to Loh, *Hymnal Companion to Sound the Bamboo: Asian Hymns in their Cultural and Liturgical Contexts* (Chicago, IL: GIA, 2011), 35-6.
64 Ramshaw, *Saints on Sunday*, 40.
65 See my account at https://www.exploringliturgy.org/hillsong-melbourne/
66 Mark Evans, 'Hillsong Abroad: Tracing the Songlines of Contemporary Pentecostal Music', in Monique M. Ingalls and Amos Yong, eds, *The Spirit of Praise: Music and Worship in Global Pentecostal-Charismatic*

Christianity (University Park, PA: U. Penn. Press, 2015), 179-198, 183.
67 For a good discussion of registers of language, see UiW2, 9-10.
68 Swee Hong Lim and Lester Ruth, *Lovin' on Jesus: A Concise History of Contemporary Worship* (Nashville, TN: Abingdon Press, 2017), 76-78 summarising aspects of research by Tanya Riches.
69 http://www.worshiptogether.com/songs/the-stand/
70 http://www.worshiptogether.com/songs/with-all-i-am/
71 Tanya Riches, 'Liturgical Inculturation in Urban Aboriginal Pentecostalism', *Liturgy* 33 (2018): 54-62, 58.
72 See Wolfgang Vondey, *Pentecostal Theology: Living the Full Gospel* (London: T & T Clark, 2017), 48, with the 'stereo image' there attributed to MykHabets. Vondey discusses notions of conversion in relation to conscious behaviour, I extend his reference to confession.
73 Vondey, *Full Gospel*, 41.
74 Vondey, *Full Gospel*, 41.
75 David Tomberlin, *Pentecostal Sacraments: Encountering God at the Altar* (Cleveland, OH: CPLC, 2010), 23.
76 This is not the prying open Gail Ramshaw discusses in her 'Pried Open by Prayer', in E. Byron Anderson and Bruce T. Morrill, eds, *Liturgy and the Moral Self*, 169-178, though see *Saints on Sundays*, 20-26.
77 UiW2, 347.
78 Ramshaw, *Saints on Sunday*, 26.
79 Ramshaw, *Saints on Sunday*, 23.
80 Two recent engagements of my own with these issues are: 'Liturgy After the Abuse', Jione Havea, ed., *Resistance and Vulnerability: Body and Liberating Theologies* (Lanham, MD: Lexington, 2019) and 'Ordination Services, After the Abuse', *Liturgy* 34 (2019), 41-50.
81 The decline of participation in the sacrament of penance/reconciliation has a longer recent history, not least with respect to evident widespread disagreement among Roman Catholics with the papal encyclical *Humanae Vitae* of 1967, on which Jack Maloney, *The Making of Moral Theology: A Study of the Roman Catholic Tradition* (Oxford: Clarendon, 1987) remains an important treatment, suggesting as it does the grounds for popular operation of, and acting upon, conscience at odds with official church teaching.
82 Monika Hellwig, *Sign of Reconciliation and Conversion: The Sacrament of Penance for Our Times* (Wilmington, MD: Michael Glazier, Inc., 1982), 112.
83 Note, for instance: 'the majority of young people [in Australia] look at the churches with some suspicion and even disdain. Many see them as irrelevant and out of date. They see them as exclusive and intolerant, even repressive, particularly in relation to different expressions of sexuality' (Philip Hughes, Stephen Reid and Margaret Fraser, *A Vision for Effective Youth Ministry: Insights from Australian Research* [Nunawading, Vic.: Christian Research Association, 2015], v).
84 Ramshaw, *Saints on Sunday*, viii.
85 Cf. Ramshaw, *Saints on Sunday*, viii.

13

'Thou Shall Not Chant': Prayer Book, Musical Authority and Parish Practice

Peter Campbell

Liturgy and ritual have been matters of constant debate within the Anglican Church since the English Reformation. Arguments became particularly heated during the nineteenth century as those associated with what became known as the Oxford Movement sought to refocus worship on the sacraments, including restoration of the Eucharist as a central and frequent form of worship.[1] What caused particular offence was the reintroduction of ritual elements such as candles, crosses, copes and chants, vestiges of pre-English Reformation Roman Catholic practice. These objects were designed to heighten the drama of and add depth to worship, but in the eyes of many merely widened the divide between the clergy and the congregation. 'Popish' rituals got between the people and their God, serving only to make services – and priests – fancy and mysterious, and further removing most worshippers from active participation in the liturgy, precisely the sort of thing that the Reformation had sought to eliminate.

Investigating practices at several of Melbourne's Anglican parish churches during the 1860s allows these tensions to be examined from a colonial perspective. The actions of the people, the clergy and the bishop are presented in order to show the attitudes toward the Prayer Book at the time, and to highlight issues that still cause discomfort today, more than 150 years later. The legal framework for liturgical approval is provided to enable debate on liturgical practice and the shape of the Prayer Book tradition in the future.

The settlement at Port Phillip was founded in 1835, and Melbourne became a city in 1847 with the appointment of Charles Perry as the first Bishop. As was the usual for members of his class, Perry grew up attending church and described his mother as a 'religious woman'. She had not, he said, 'herself enjoyed the privilege of an evangelical ministry', but had a 'strong prejudice against the Methodism, as she called it, which had invaded the Church'.[2] Perry's personal study of the Bible led him to beliefs that aligned directly with 'the so-called evangelical school', and he agreed entirely with their commitment to both the 'advancement of true religion and piety in our Church at home and for the promulgation of the Gospel in foreign lands'.[3] It is against this background that Perry, after some ten years in Melbourne, found it necessary to issue a stern injunction to his clergy regarding the conduct of services within his diocese.

An early biographer described Perry as 'always anxious to preserve simplicity of worship'.[4] Perry's circular to the clergy, issued in June 1857, noted that his attention had been drawn to 'some practices ... in the mode of conducting divine service' in a few churches that fell outside what was sanctioned by the Book of Common Prayer. He identified two matters in particular: 'the intoning of the service, or parts of the service, such as the responses and particularly the *Amen* at the close of every prayer; and the chanting of the responses after the Commandments'. Perry's made his views clear:

> The use of these practices at cathedrals and collegiate chapels in England has naturally led some of the clergy, either in compliance with the wish of their choirs, or from their own taste, to adopt them: but they are altogether unauthorised by the Rubric; they give offence to many of our people, and cause them to absent themselves from our services; and they are, in my opinion, wholly unsuitable for ordinary congregational worship. I would therefore request you ... immediately to discontinue them and to require the choir (for whom, as being under his control, a minister is responsible) to discontinue them also.[5]

With the authority given to bishops in the Preface to the Book of Common Prayer, Perry thus 'took order' over his flock. Despite the directness of his order, Perry was at pains to show reasonable tolerance for some variation in worship:

> First ... I do not regard an absolute uniformity in all particulars as essential to the wellbeing of the Church, and some variety (provided the spiritual character of the service is not affected by it) may be considered as justified by custom; and secondly, because I am very unwilling to recognise, and thus perhaps promote among the members of the Church, both clerical and lay, a division of opinion and feeling upon matters of ritual.[6]

There was evidently some wriggle room, but not much, and Perry at first expressed his reluctance to act at all. But others certainly demanded action, telling the Bishop of the goings on in his diocese while he had been away in England. Perry does not specify which parish was in his sights, but then, as now, the leading high church parishes were known by all: All Saints', Prahran (now East St Kilda); St Peter's, Eastern Hill; St Andrew's, Brighton; and Christ Church, South Yarra. Of these, All Saints' was considered the 'highest of the high' in the 1860s.[7]

Sir George Stephen, an All Saints' parish representative in the Church Assembly, wrote immediately to the vicar, the Revd John Gregory, objecting to the Bishop's remarks, prefacing his own letter with the information that he had 'been brought up from infancy in those principles which are usually described as belonging to the Low Church, ... full freedom of conscience, unfettered by rubrical dicta or priestly authority, except so far as I am convinced that they are founded on the basis of the Scriptures'. Stephen then presented his chief discomfort:

> I object firstly to this restriction because it is an innovation on the practice of our congregation, and, as I believe, on the general usage of the English Church. It is true that at Prahran we have not been in the habit of intoning, not even in the Amen, nor have we chanted the entire service, as in strict conformity with cathedral usage we ought to do, but we have certainly gone beyond the limits of the prohibitory circular, and therefore the restriction it enjoins is an innovation; yet, under the system we have pursued, your congregation has visibly increased ... Why, then, is the performance of the services to be varied in its character? I also conceive that it is an innovation on the general usage of the English Church, and even of the Low Church section of it.[8]

Stephen goes on to suggest that the bishop's 'alterations' would, rather than improve worship, actually make it poorer, offering the examples of Rowland Hill (who, 'though the very impersonation of Low Church principle, exulted in having the best choir and the finest music in the metropolis') and the Wesleyans as models of great musical worship.[9] Are we, asked Stephen, to:

stand alone in our opinion, and to render our services stern, cold, and gloomy, that we may give due honor to our Saviour and our God? It appears to me that this is degrading to our ritual, and needlessly divesting it of a dignity and a charm for which it is peculiarly adapted.

While Perry did not wish to incite division, that is precisely what Stephen foresaw as the result. He told Perry that: 'We are a very different people here from our countrymen at home. We are more independent – more impatient of restraint – more republican in feeling – and especially more averse to everything in the nature of ecclesiastical control'. Perry had already caused concern when he had requested changes to the music heard in the Cathedral services ('the suspension of the anthem in the Cathedral Church in Melbourne was most unpopular, and for a time alienated many'). If such episcopal interference in 'matters so unimportant' was maintained, Stephen felt that it would not be long before a 'Free Church of England' was established in Melbourne, as it had recently been in Geelong.[10]

But to what, exactly, was Perry objecting? The protestant desire for all members of the congregation to participate fully in the service – being supported by a choir, rather than being replaced by one – had already been expressed strongly in the Australian colonies by this time. The *Church of England Messenger* had reported in 1854 that at St Paul's in Melbourne (not yet designated the site for the Cathedral), the Revd Septimus Chase had preached several sermons on congregational music:

> We feel much pleasure in noticing an effort ... to improve Congregational Psalmody. Heretofore, that portion of the service was left almost entirely to the choir. With a view to remedy[ing] this ... two sermons ... were immediately followed by the establishment of a weekly meeting in the Church, for instruction and practice ... Of the capacity of the system to effect the object aimed at, not a doubt can be felt, as on the second evening, the persons present sang a psalm in full harmony and with fine effect, accompanied by the harmonium.[11]

Hymns were also gradually being introduced, with local hymnbooks such as *Psalms and Hymns Selected for Public Worship, in the Diocese of Melbourne* (London: J.J. Guillaume) appearing in 1855, dedicated to Bishop Perry. Gregory at All Saints' published his own hymnbook in 1858 to bring a more 'catholic' flavour to the selection, pre-empting the printing of *Hymns Ancient & Modern*, which appeared in 1861 and was first used in Melbourne at All Saints' in August 1863.[12] Perry had little problem with these innovations, but after visiting St Stephen's, Richmond, in November 1858, he again complained of intoning, as well as expressing his view that had 'no love for an anthem sung by a few – frequently hired – performers in the presence of the congregation'.[13]

In June 1859, a correspondent to the *Argus*, identifying himself only as 'X', attempted to inject a positive note to the debate that had seen 'numberless complaints ... raised condemnatory of the utter neglect of the choral part of the service'. He commended the clergy at St Peter's, Eastern Hill, who had 'sought to render to their congregations in as complete and agreeable a manner as possible the glorious service of the Anglican Church', and where now 'the service in that church is sung in a manner that is most acceptable, and is nearly all that can be desired'. 'Praiseworthy efforts' were being made also at St James', at All Saints' and at Brighton, while the Choir of Christ Church, South Yarra, had 'lately been, perhaps, the most efficient of any, and it is to be hoped in a few Sundays, when the new building is completed, the choral service of our Church will swell through its aisles in all its integrity'.[14] Yet even this drew the criticism that 'it is to be wished that more anxiety were displayed to enable the congregation to join with the choir in all the choral parts of the music'.[15] Another complained that at South Yarra the choral service was a 'spectacle' with the 'praises of Almighty God to be sung by a handful of the congregation, and the rest to stand as mute as if they had no interest in the matter'. When last visited, 'there was scarcely a voice raised by the congregation, and little wonder, for the tunes were so new and difficult that only practiced singers could take part in the service'. This was 'not the singing that is wanted' at all, he said; rather, 'let us have simple music, such as our people are already accustomed to, and which they can join in'.[16]

Both the organist, Charles Compton, and a parishioner named 'S.B.V' responded to these accusations, defending the service with detailed commentaries explaining how standard and approachable the music at Christ Church had been on that day, despite it being a Feast Day commemorating Trinity Sunday: all was done 'with the sanction of its respected minister', and there was 'no intoning or attempt to intone'. The writer noted that the object of the choir was to 'make our choral service really congregational, but at the same time effective and expressive', and he could 'assure the public generally that no spectacle is presented in Christ Church, South Yarra, but that the service is conducted in that church in strict conformity to the Church of England, as usually and ordinarily conducted in parish churches in England'.[17] A correspondent called 'J.' then wrote on 4 July 1859 that:

> The true ground of complaint is that much of the music now attempted to be introduced by many choirs is of a character totally unfitted for congregational worship, and choirs are fast becoming a nuisance, as, instead of being content with the good work of leading the people in giving praise to God, they seem anxious to convert themselves into orchestras for the public performance of music.[18]

All this was, however, a mild-mannered and friendly exchange compared with what was to come in 1861 at St Andrew's, Brighton. In September that year, Bishop

Perry appointed the Revd Lorenzo Moore as 'officiating minister' while the Incumbent was on leave. On 7 October 1861, soon after his arrival, Moore wrote to the 'ladies and gentlemen comprising the choir' asking them to make changes to the practices he had observed the previous Sunday:

> 1. No parts of the service or of the responses, including the 'Amen', to be sung or intoned as at present, but said in the natural voice. 2. The anthem and the music, as the minister goes from the reading-desk to the communion rails, to be discontinued; a hymn for the congregation to be substituted. It is desirable to have the singing in our churches as congregational as possible, and everything done in so simple and natural a manner that the most humble worshipper may be able to join with ease in our beautiful and devotional services.[19]

The likelihood that Perry has sent Moore to Brighton precisely to bring the parish into line with the liturgical boundaries set out in his *ad clerum* is supported by Moore's plea that the choir 'continue kindly to assist in leading the psalmody, and aiding in the responses in the service in the simpler form which I wish to be adopted, and which is the usual way in our parish churches'.

On the same day, Moore wrote to the organist, Mr T.G. Goold, seeking his support in making the changes. He appended a sheet setting out 'the way in which I think it desirable the services at St Andrew's shall be conducted for the future', and that he 'shall feel much obliged by your kindly adhering to the plan'. At morning service, the 'Venite', 'Te Deum' and 'Jubilate' were to be chanted, while the 'Gloria Patri' in the Psalms and the 'Glory be to Thee' before the Gospel were to be sung. Not to be intoned were the Creed, Lord's Prayer, alternate verses of the psalms, the prayer after each Commandment in the Communion Service or the 'Amen', instead these always being 'repeated along with, or after, the minister, in the natural voice'. A hymn was to be sung after the prayers, to be 'given out by the minister before he leaves the reading-desk'. In the evenings, the 'Magnificat', 'Cantate', 'Nunc dimittis' and 'Deus misereatur' (whichever were used) were to be chanted, along with the 'Gloria' in the Psalms. As in the morning, no other part of the service was to be intoned. A hymn would follow the third collect, and the Evening Hymn would be sung after the sermon.[20]

Responses to his letters were received a few days later. Frederick G. Moule wrote on 11 October that he had been deputed by members of the choir to inform him that 'they cannot comply with your request, feeling that by so doing they would be acting inconsistently with the principles which have been successfully maintained by them during the last six years'.[21] Neither was Goold as organist happy about the 'musical portion of the services ... being confined to singing chants and hymns' nor that the 'anthem, sanctus, and responses hitherto intoned, shall henceforward be discontinued'. He knew of no other case where a temporary minister had 'exercised any power suddenly to alter the mode of conducting Divine service'.²² Moore naturally pointed out that in the absence of the Incumbent, 'I am responsible for the way in which Divine worship is conducted; and the power of regulating the services is invested in me'.²³ Moore reminded Goold that it was his 'duty to carry out the minister's wishes, and is responsible to him alone'.²⁴Moule thought Moore's actions arbitrary and detrimental to good order, considering that he had not accused them of having 'done anything contrary to the rubrics or the usage of the church'. Moore had also acted 'without consulting the wishes of anyone but the bishop, whose conduct in the matter I believe to have been unbecoming his high office'.²⁵

George Walstab, a member of the choir, also wrote to Moore, seeking to set out more clearly the view from the pews:

> The choir never desired to monopolise the responses, they desired merely to lead the congregation; and it has been a source of gratification to them to observe how much more and more regular the responses became. The choir do not intone the responses, they monotone them, intoning the 'Amen' only; and I submit that it would be an impossibility to keep the congregation together except upon some such principle.²⁶

Walstab noted that Bishop Perry had 'upon more than one occasion, sought to interfere, unsuccessfully, with our mode of conducing Divine service', but that he had never gone so far as proposing 'such sweeping alterations as you seek to enforce'. He continued: 'I am aware that there is a feeling on the part of a few to bring down our "Anglican Church" to the rank of the lowest dissenting bodies. I trust I shall not live to see the attempt succeed'. He and Moule dug in against the reforms, intoning parts of the service from the congregation. Moule wrote on 1 November to tell Moore that he would 'reserve to myself the right to say the responses and all the parts of the service appointed to be said by the people, in any tone of voice convenient to me'.[27] Walstab stated that he was 'prepared to resist to the upmost any attempt to interfere with my mode of worship'.[28] Needless to say, the whole saga descended into farce.

Having received a memorial from 39 seat-holders (representing 135 parishioners), calling on him to remove Moore from the Parish, Bishop Perry went to Brighton, but could only respond to the request by stating that 'the changes which had been carried out he himself should have effected had he been in Mr. Moore's place'.[29] Perry explained his position in detail:

> It was not a question of right or taste, but he deliberately expressed his conviction that, for a large portion of the congregation, the intoning of the responses was destructive of all devotion. He did not say that no persons could intone the responses in a devotional manner. He knew there were spiritually-

minded persons who delighted in the cathedral service, but he unhesitatingly affirmed that, in every parochial congregation, there would be found a large number – he believed the larger number – of the congregation having a strong distaste for that mode of response, and also feeling that their devotions were absolutely impaired and destroyed by it ... He did not ask the clergy to make any change, or discontinue any practice, where the church allowed an alternative. He did not ask the clergy to discontinue the anthems, or the chanting of the service, he simply asked them, by the authority which the church vested in him, to put an end to a practice which was not sanctioned by the rubric in any way.[30]

The *Argus* editorial the next day tried to score political points, tying the 'very anomalous despotism under which the church labours in Victoria' to its campaign against state aid for religion. The normally Conservative paper then took up a decidedly anti-establishment tone:

There is no heresy in an anthem, and nothing against any article of faith in intoning ... They are things purely congregational, on which the congregation alone has a right to be consulted. But the Bishop of Melbourne, by his dictum, has ... deliberately used his arbitrary and irresponsible power to over-ride the free will of his people. What is this but a part of that policy which is rapidly separating the people of the Church of England from their ministers and hierarchy? What man of honour and self-respect, in this free country, will submit to such a petty and wretched despotism as this – a despotism which prescribes in what way we shall sing in our churches, and in what form we may make our responses?[31]

Needless to say, the papers continued to be filled with letters on both sides of the argument. A satirical poem appeared in the Melbourne *Punch*,[32] reports were written for the Church Assembly (the precursor to the current Synod), and Perry himself wrote to the papers:

I am painfully sensible of my incapacity, from the want of a musical ear, to treat it scientifically. But I believe ... that good music speaks with power to the hearts even of those who cannot appreciate its artistic excellency; and I know, from my own experience, that the music which I have ventured to condemn grates upon the feelings of one who desires to sympathise with and give utterance to the devotional sentiments which the beautiful words, with which it is so incongruously united, so eloquently express.[33]

Despite Perry's support, Moore finally left the parish, fleeing to New Zealand, after which, according to *Punch*, the choir was able to 'revel in any choral luxuries they think fit'.[34] This did not, however, come in time to stop a proportion of disaffected parishioners from seceding from Brighton and attempting to establish a new parish, having been 'forcibly prevented from entering the choir gallery'. The matter of the extent of a bishop's reach in such liturgical matters was again debated in the Church Assembly in January 1863, leading to the appointment of a Committee of Enquiry, during which Perry admitted that while Moore had 'committed faults' in his handling of the issue, he still deserved the thanks of the diocese for 'liberating St Andrew's Church, Brighton, from the tyranny of the choir'.[35]

Notwithstanding the endless inquiry, the leading high-church parishes across the city continued to press the boundaries of allowable liturgical practice. On 27 July 1865 the reopening of the organ at St Peter's, Eastern Hill, was celebrated with the choir wearing surplices for the first time in Victoria. Women singers were also 'dispensed with' in order to form a choir only of men and boys. The music was of the 'full cathedral service' style, leading one correspondent to advise that:

> in the selection of 'services' and anthems, care should be taken to avoid those which are very elaborate and scientific in their construction, at all events until the congregation get more accustomed to join in the singing; for we

hold it to be of very great importance that the congregation should join in the church service.[36]

It is perhaps this particular service that forced Perry in August 1865 was once again to issue an injunction against unauthorised practices during parish services:

> Whereas it hath been represented to me that certain diversities in the mode of conducting the services of the Church other than are authorised by the Rubric of the Book of Common Prayer have arisen in this diocese; know ye therefore that for the *appeasing of all such diversities*, I have by my discretion taken order as follows:—No portion of the service of the Church shall be sung or intoned, except such as is expressly authorised by the Rubric; and there shall not be introduced into the service, either on the ground of ancient usage, or because it has been adopted in some churches in England, or on any pretext whatever, any ceremonial which is not directed or sanctioned by the Book of Common Prayer.[37]

So exactly what does the Prayer Book say about music during services? Very little, it turns out. The earliest versions, prepared by Cranmer under Edward VI, removed almost all reference to music, liturgical vestments and non-biblical texts, leaving only the surplice and the 'Te

Deum'. No particular music or chant was ever prescribed in the Prayer Book, and therein lay the problem of it being open to a variety of methods of implementation. Protestant reformers in England had already grappled with variety, giving approval to certain anthems, as long as they were simple, sober and intelligible. A royal commission into music at Lincoln Cathedral in 1548, for example, issued an injunction requiring that:

> they shall from henceforth sing or say no anthems of our lady or other saints, but only of our Lord. And then not in Latin but choosing only the best and most sounding to Christian religion they shall turn the same into English, setting thereunto a plain and distinct note, for every syllable one.[38]

Ten years later, following the passing of the Act of Uniformity, Queen Elizabeth ordered a visitation to ensure that her new Prayer Book was being followed. The subsequent report noted that:

> [F]or the comforting of such that delight in music, it may be permitted that in the beginning, or in the end of common prayers ... there may be sung an Hymn or such like song, to the praise of Almighty God, in the best sort of melody and music that may be conveniently devised, having respect that the sentence of the Hymn may be understood and perceived.[39]

Elizabeth is clearly encouraging of appropriate music being heard in church, particularly those that had exiting choral foundations. Reformers were not trying to throw everything out, merely getting rid of the unnecessary trappings.[40] Let us concentrate, however, on the 1662 version of the Prayer Book, produced after the Restoration, that was still the authority in Melbourne in the 1860s. The introductory matter – keeping the words of the 1559 Prayer Book – makes clear the purpose of the new book: 'And whereas heretofore there hath been great diversity in saying and singing in Churches within this Realm ... now from henceforth all the whole Realm shall have but one Use'. Use here refers to the specific words and the types, forms and frequency of services, the 'rites', rather than necessarily to any mode of their delivery. Then follows the statement relied on by Perry:

> And forasmuch as nothing can be so plainly set forth, but doubts may arise in the use and practice of the same; to appease all such diversity (if any arise) and for the resolution of all doubts, concerning the manner how to understand, do, and execute, the things contained in this Book; the parties that so doubt, or diversely take any thing, shall always resort to the Bishop of the Diocese, who by his discretion shall take order for the quieting and appeasing of the same; so that the same order be not contrary to any thing contained in this Book.

The instructions for the Order of Morning and Evening Prayer clearly allow for the singing of these services, even by a lay person when a minister is unavailable. The sections of Morning and Evening Prayer appointed to be 'said or sung' included the Psalm(s), Apostles' Creed and canticles. After the Third Collect, come those famous words 'In Quires and Places where they sing here followeth the Anthem', which had not in fact appeared in any editions of the Prayer Book before 1662 (an indication that there was already diversity requiring approval). In the Order for the Administration of the Lord's Supper, the sections mentioned specifically as being sung are the Creed, the Sanctus (including its introductory clauses, beginning 'Therefore with Angels and Archangels ...') and the Gloria.[41] There appear to be no other instructions given as to the manner in which the congregation should make their 'Answer', as they are indicated to do at many points. The modern Prayer Book Society in England offers a series of videos designed to assist people 'seeking guidance on how to conduct services' according to BCP, but even they note: 'While it is customary for music to be used to enhance worship, the style and format of this varies considerably: for the sake of simplicity, therefore, all the services are presented here without any music or singing'.[42]

It is interesting to note that even the Roman Catholic Church was grappling with issues of music in the liturgy throughout these years, the rise of the 'Cecilian movement' and a restoration of Gregorian chant being the greatest innovations. This culminated in the 1903 *motu proprio* by

Pope Pius X containing a formal 'Instruction on Sacred Music'. Every local church was expected to maintain the 'decorum and sanctity of the sacred functions' where the public came to 'unite in the common prayer of the Church'. Yet, the Pope observed that there had been 'a general tendency to deviate from the right rule, prescribed by the end for which art is admitted to the service of public worship' and an 'abuse affecting sacred chant and music' though the 'fatal influence exercised on sacred art by profane and theatrical art', by which was meant, in general terms, opera. (Complaints of 'theatrical performances' in church, presumably reference to the many operatic soloists engaged to sing during the service or to provide professional support to the choir, had been made by Perry in Melbourne in 1857, and appeared in the newspapers regularly in ensuing years.)[43] Pius stated that music was a 'complementary part of the solemn liturgy'. Its chief object was to 'add greater efficacy to the text, in order that through it the faithful may be the more easily moved to devotion' and thus be allowed an 'active participation in the most holy mysteries and in the public and solemn prayer of the Church'.[44]

For Anglicans, no revisions to the 1662 Prayer Book reached publication until 1928, but even that, after some 20 years of work, fell at the last hurdle – the House of Commons—and was not adopted. At precisely the same time as the Pope was issuing his *moto proprio*, a Royal Commission had been established in England to examine discipline within the church. The finding that 'Prayer Book rubrics were being ignored in almost countless ways, most of them completely devoid of doctrinal significance, by clergymen of all shades', led to the eventually fruitless decision to revise the Prayer Book.[45] Finally, in 1978, the Standing Committee of the General Synod of what was then known as the Church of England in Australia released *An Australian Prayer Book*.[46] Its subtitle provides further information on its purpose: 'for use together with the Book of Common Prayer, 1662'. The Australian publication was not to supersede the 'traditional' text, but merely supplement it. AAPB provided revised forms using modernised language as well as a communion service that would 'restore the balance of worship envisaged in the Prayer Book within a time span that would be realistic for contemporary Australian Church life'.[47] In essence, though, the editors did not alter any of the rubrics regarding the singing of parts of the service, nor offer any advice on the manner of the congregation's answer. At Evening Prayer, for example, the 'First Form' indicated that the Psalm(s), Canticles, Creed and Litany 'may be said or sung'.

This form of words had been in use back not just to 1662, but to 1549, where at Matins Psalm 95 is introduced with the words: 'Then shal be saied or song without any Invitatori [a refrain] this Psalm ... in Englishe'. But this instruction is curiously absent in any edition when introducing the Preces or Responses, texts early on having musical settings attached to them during the Reformation period, including those by Merbecke in 1550.[48] Proctor and Frere's detailed description of the development of the Book of Common Prayer, observes that there is sometimes a confusion involving the terms reading, saying and singing in the revision of the rubrics from one edition to the next:

> To *say*, however, does not necessarily mean to *intone* ... The distinction intended by the rubrics is that which has been recognised since 1549, between 'choirs and places where they sing' – churches where there are choral establishments, and where the service is chanted – and ordinary churches, 'where there be no clerks', and where the service is read. But in each case the XIVth Canon (1603) directs that the Common Prayer be 'said *or* sung distinctly and reverently.'[49]

This distinction between places with and without choral foundations accords directly with the remarks of Perry in attempting to ensure uniformity across his parish churches. The fact that some parishes were eager to introduce skilled choirs and to contribute more complex music to services might be applauded rather than derided, and, while Perry's position is defensible, his arguments regarding the prohibition of such practices by the Prayer Book cannot be wholly supported. Two streams of interpretation are possible. On the one hand, Perry is arguing that anything not specified in the rubrics should be eliminated; those of the other view would hold that a practice not specifically prohibited in the Prayer Book might be acceptable.

What does this all mean for today's church, of any denomination that holds to an authorised prayer book? We now hear a wide divergence of liturgical practice, despite services following similar approved forms. The Prayer Book is now not the only source of information regarding the conduct of services within the Australian Anglican Church. In Melbourne, the *Parish Governance Act 2013* sets out clearly certain matters under the heading 'Public Worship'. Section 2 allows for worship to be conducted according to a 'a form of service' contained in BCP, APB or APBA, but also enables the Archbishop to allow 'deviations from any of those forms', as authorised under Section 4 of the Constitution of the Anglican Church of Australia,[50] or other variations that are 'not of substantial importance' authorised under a Canon adopted by the Diocese.

But there is also a final paragraph that allows two matters to be determined between the vicar and the parish council: the time or 'mode' of conducting the principal service. That term goes undefined in the legislation, and it seems unlikely to correspond to its use in nineteenth-century reports (see above); it could here refer to the choice between a service of Matins or Eucharist, rather than to the 'way' in which the particular service was to be conducted. This is clearer in the earlier *Parishes Act* of 1987, where S.44 (2) stated: 'The mode of conducting the service shall not be contrary to the rules of the Book of Common Prayer' or another authorised form.

Other Australian dioceses have similar provisions. In Brisbane, a *Diocesan Handbook* has enforceable status.

Its Section B.1 deals with Prayer Books, with essentially the same authorisations as for Melbourne, but there are additional paragraphs of interest here:

> B.1.9. The Archbishop has set up a Liturgical Advisory Committee, which is available for guidance on liturgical matters and may be consulted at any time. Creative liturgy is always encouraged. These are to be used within the framework of authorised liturgies.
> B.1.10. From time to time the Archbishop may give general authorisation within the Diocese for particular liturgical experimentation recommended by the Liturgical Commission or by his Liturgical Advisory Committee.[51]

Note that experimentation is at all times to be done within the limits of the authorised forms. Brisbane is allowing a variety of expression, as long as the theological framework is maintained. Further, in the section on Parish Committees, the suggestion of a parish having a Worship Committee is made, to assist in the 'ordering of worship' and to 'explore other forms of worship' such as healing services or family services, all the while acknowledging that the parish priest should be the chair 'as he is directly responsible to the Archbishop for the conduct of public worship in the parish'.[52]

Three hundred years after the English Reformation, congregations came to physical blows over the conduct of their service. At St George's-in-the-East in London in 1859, an angry mob threatened to tear down the choir stalls. They objected to a liturgy that reintroduced elements of ritual they had thought stamped out by the Reformation. One anonymous threat read: 'We will never, never rest until St George's ... is stripped of all drapery, crosses, candles, choristers, intoning, preaching in the surplice, or any one thing tending to Popery'.[53] The situation at St Andrew's, Brighton, just a year later, was similar in terms of its emotional fervour and its disruptive effect. In most cases today, however, battle lines are drawn on matters of theological belief rather than liturgical practice, although those lines of dispute are still as contested as ever, and outward symbols, such as vestments or incense or singing in Latin, can still cause discomfort and distress to some, as does the lack of them to others.

Yet these are matters that fall almost entirely outside of the scope of the Prayer Book; they are matters of practice, not belief; of how, not what. In the 1990s, the Diocese of Sydney was right to question on theological grounds some of the most novel aspects of *A Prayer Book for Australia*, the next attempt at providing modern service forms.[54] What is perhaps less clear – as indeed was the case with Bishop Perry in the 1860s – is raising objections to differing modes of practice relating to the acting out of these agreed orders of common prayer. Adopting a policy of unity of faith while allowing diversity of practice would certainly have avoided much turmoil over the long history of the Church of England. As the original prayer book noted, where there has been great diversity, the whole realm would now have but one use, as long as there was room given for different modes of expressing that tradition of common prayer.

Endnotes

1 See, for example, Geoffrey Rowell, *The Vision Glorious: Themes and Personalities of the Catholic Revival in Anglicanism* (Oxford: OUP, 1983); Peter Benedict Nockles, *The Oxford Movement in Context: Anglican High Churchmanship 1760-1857* (Cambridge: CUP, 1994); John Reed, *Glorious Battle: The Cultural Politics of Victorian Anglo-Catholicism* (Nashville, TN: Vanderbilt UP, 1996), W.N. Yates, *Anglican Ritualism in Victorian Britain 1830–1910* (Oxford: OUP, 1999); Dominic Janes, *Victorian Reformation: The Fight Over Idolatry in the Church of England, 1840–1860* (Oxford: OUP, 2009).

2 Charles Perry, 'Some Reminiscences of My Religious Experience, and of God's Spiritual Dealings with Me', May 1888, reproduced in George Goodman, *The Church in Victoria during the Episcopate of the Right Reverend Charles Perry* (Melbourne: Melville, Mullen & Slade, 1892), 53; A. de Q. Robin, *Charles Perry, Bishop of Melbourne: The Challenges of a Colonial Episcopate, 1847–76* (Nedlands, WA: University of Western Australia Press, 1967), 7.

3 Perry, 'Some Reminiscences', in Goodman, *Church in Victoria*, 58. See also F.W.B. Bullock, *History of Ridley Hall, Cambridge* (Cambridge: Ridley Hall, 1941), vol. 1, 96.

4 Goodman, *Church in Victoria*, 369–70.

5 Charles Perry, *Ad Clerum*, 23 June 1857, reproduced in Robin, *Charles Perry, Bishop of Melbourne*, 136.

6 Note the comments by Charles Sherlock elsewhere in this volume as to the 'oppressive uniformity' that the Prayer Book was designed to instil across the English church.

7 Stuart Soley, '"The Highest of the High": All Saints, St Kilda as Melbourne's Original High Church', Colin Holden, ed., *Anglo-Catholicism in Melbourne* (Parkville, VIC: University of Melbourne, 1997), 21–31.

8 Letter, George Stephen to J.H. Gregory, 29 June 1857, 'Church Music', *The Age*, 27 July 1857, 5.

9 Rowland Hill (1744–1833) was a leading non-conformist preacher in London, drawing vast crowds to his Surrey Chapel.

10 A congregation worshipping under the designation 'Free Church of England' and thus not under the control of the Bishop had been founded at Chilwell near Geelong the previous month. See, *The Argus*, 24 June 1857, p. 5. The Free Church had been created in England in 1844 by conservative Low Church clergy. Having at one stage more than 90 congregations, there are currently about twenty in England and five elsewhere in the world. In January 2016, a congregation was licenced in Brisbane, and a new jurisdiction called the Reformed Episcopal Church in Australia was formed within the Free Church of England.

11 *Melbourne Church of England Messenger*, 1 Feb. 1854, 64. The rehearsals were conducted by local retailer George Allan, later to found Melbourne's Allan's music empire.

12 Soley, 'The Highest of the High', 22-23; Geoffrey Cox, 'Church Music in the Anglican Diocese of Melbourne, 1847–1997', Colin Holden, ed., *People of the Past? The Culture of Melbourne Anglicanism and Anglicanism in Melbourne's Culture*, (Parkville, VIC: University of Melbourne, 2000), 68–69.
13 Letter, Charles Perry to J.C. Holm, Secretary, Anglican Parish of St Stephen, 13 Nov. 1857, cited in Robin, *Charles Perry, Bishop of Melbourne*, 137; Cox, 'Church Music'.
14 'X.', 'Church Music', letter to the Editor, *The Argus*, 30 June 1859, 7.
15 'A.Z.', 'Church Music', letter to the Editor, *The Argus*, 1 July 1859, 7.
16 'M.', 'Church Music', letter to the Editor, *The Argus*, 4 July 1859, p. 6. See also 'Church Music', *The Argus*, 13 July 1859, 1
17 'S.B.V.', 'Christ Church, South Yarra', letter to the Editor, *The Argus*, 5 July 1859, p. 6.
18 'J.', 'Church Music', letter to the Editor, *The Argus*, 4 July 1859, p. 6.
19 'The Brighton Church and its Minister', *The Argus*, 18 Mar. 1862, 7. The entire correspondence between Moore, the choristers and the congregation of St Andrew's during October and November 1861 was published here.
20 Letter, Lorenzo Moore to T.G. Goold, 7 Oct. 1861, *The Argus*, 18 Mar. 1862, 7.
21 Letter, Frederick Moule to Lorenzo Moore, 11 Oct. 1861, *The Argus*, 18 Mar. 1862, 7.
22 Letter, T.G. Goold to Lorenzo Moore, 11 Oct. 1861, *The Argus*, 18 Mar. 1862, 7.
23 Letter, Lorenzo Moore to F.G. Moule, 15 Oct. 1861, *The Argus*, 18 Mar. 1862, 7.
24 Letter, Lorenzo Moore to T.G. Goold, 15 Oct. 1861, *The Argus*, 18 Mar. 1862, 7.
25 Letter, Frederick Moule to Lorenzo Moore, 17 Oct. 1861, *The Argus*, 18 Mar. 1862, 7.
26 Letter, George Walstab to Lorenzo Moore, 18 Oct. 1861, *The Argus*, 18 Mar. 1862, 7.
27 Letter, Frederick G. Moule to Lorenzo Moore, 1 Nov. 1861, *The Argus*, 18 Mar. 1862, 7.
28 Letter, George Walstab to Lorenzo Moore, 2 Nov. 1861, *The Argus*, 18 Mar. 1862, 7.
29 *The Argus*, 18 Mar. 1862, 4.
30 'St Andrew's Church, Brighton – The Bishop, the Officiating Minister, and the Parishioners', *The Argus*, 18 Mar. 1862, 6.
31 *The Argus*, 19 Mar. 1862, 4.
32 'The Choir of Saint Andrew's', *Punch*, 20 Mar. 1862, 59. A typical verse read: 'The singers were desired to cease / Unsanctified intoning, / And join the inharmonious Moore / In inharmonious groaning.'
33 Charles Perry, letter to the editor, 13 Oct. 1862, *Church Gazette*; reprinted as 'Bishop Perry on Church Music', *The Argus*, 18 Oct. 1862, 6.
34 *Punch* [Melbourne], 9 Oct. 1862, 84.
35 'Church of England Assembly', *The Argus*, 15 Jan. 1863, 6. See also the editorial, *The Argus*, 16 Jan. 1863, 4.
36 *Church Gazette*, Diocese of Melbourne, no. 84, 1 Aug. 1865, 141. A shorter report had appeared in the *Argus*, 28 July 1856, 5. Surpliced choirs would be introduced at All Saints' in 1869 (also soon to move to a male-only choir),

and at St Paul's in 1886, where the women processed alongside the men, a practice perhaps even more shocking. See discussion in Cox, 'Church Music in the Anglican Diocese of Melbourne', 71–73.

37 See, for example, *The Age*, 5 Sep. 1865, 5 [emphasis added]. See also letters to the editor, 'Protestans' and 'A Churchman', 'Choir Singing in Churches', *The Herald*, 9 Sep. 1865, 4.

38 Injunction 25, *Lincoln Cathedral Statutes*, ed. H. Bradshaw and C. Wordsworth, vol. 2, 592–93.

39 W.H. Frere and W.M. Kennedy, eds, *Visitation Articles and Injunctions of the Period of the Reformation* (London: Alcuin Club, 1910), vol. 3, 8; Nicholas Temperley, *The Music of the English Parish Church* (Cambridge: Cambridge University Press, 1979), 39.

40 For the historical background to the anthem specifically, see Jason Smart, 'In Quires and Places where they Sing ... Here Followeth the Anthem', *News and Notes* (Sep. 2003). See also, Jonathan Willis, *Church Music and Protestantism in Post-Reformation England: Discourses, Sites and Identities* (Abingdon: Routledge, 2016).

41 The rubrics note that Communion should be taken 'at least three times in the year, of which Easter to be one'.

42 https://www.pbs.org.uk/resources/videos

43 See, for example, 'W.P.A.', 'Church Music', letter to the Editor, *The Argus*, 4 July 1859, p. 6. He also complained of the 'utter disregard to the Psalter, and the substitution of a few miserable hymns, the majority of which are entirely devoid of anything like devotion and utterly incomprehensible to the poor and unlearned'.

44 Pope Pius X, 'Tra Le Sollecitudini', 22 November 1903. The various kinds of acceptable sacred music were explained, singing in the vernacular (or by women) forbidden, and any 'musical compositions of modern style which are admitted in the Church' would have to be 'free from reminiscences of motifs adopted in the theaters'. See also, Paul Collins, ed., *Renewal and Resistance: Catholic Church Music from the 1850s to Vatican II* (Bern: Peter Lang, 2010).

45 Paul Nicholls, '"Supporting the Book without Reservation": Melbourne, Mother and the 1927–8 Revision of the B.C.P.', *Anglo-Catholicism in Melbourne,* ed. Colin Holden (Parkville: University of Melbourne, 1997), 49–68.

46 See also the comments by Elizabeth Smith elsewhere in this volume.

47 Preface, *An Australian Prayer Book* (Sydney: Church of England in Australia, 1978), 10.

48 John Merbecke, *The Booke of Common Praier Noted*, 1550.

49 Francis Proctor and Walter Frere, *A New History of the Book of Common Prayer* (London: Macmillan, 1910), ch. 10, 'The Order for Daily Morning and Evening Prayer', fn 65. The first edition, by Procter alone, dates from 1966.

50 Ch. 2 'Ruling Principles', s. 4: 'a bishop of a diocese may, at his discretion, permit such deviations from the existing order of service, not contravening any principle of doctrine or worship as aforesaid, as shall be submitted to him by the incumbent and churchwardens of a parish'.

51 Diocese of Brisbane, *Diocesan Handbook* (Brisbane, 1987 with rev.), s. B.1, 2.

52 Brisbane, *Diocesan Handbook*, s. C.4, 1.

53 William Crouch, *Bryan King and the Riots at St George's-in-the-East* (London: Methuen, 1904), 54.
54 See *Report from the Diocesan Doctrine Commission on A Prayer Book for Australia*, Synod of the Diocese of Sydney, Synod Summary, 1996.

14

'Becoming We': Exploring Liminality

Amelia Koh-Butler

Leader   Talatala (*tr.* Minister)… when are we going to start?
Me   Whenever you are ready to sing.
Leader   [*pause…*] oh
      [*the congregations starts singing*]
Woman   What happened? What's she doing?
Leader   *We* are doing it Fijian-style.

The first time I led worship with the Parramatta Fijians was after several months of sitting in the pew, learning how to *be in the* community. I was surprised when I was welcomed every week, but came to learn it is part of being a *Talatala*. I will always be welcomed. I wonder if it is because for so long Talatalas were foreigners, not part of the community? The congregation were surprised I did not default to starting worship with words, as most English-speakers did. After they sang, I herded a young boy to the front to help light the candle, sent him back and signalled for everyone to bow their heads in prayer… *Bula! Let's pray.*

Waiting for the community, the sung call, the visual action, the greeting in 'mother' language... were all part of worship that acknowledged *who we were* before God. My congregation were initially concerned about what I might be doing. (I don't look Fijian.) The moment of waiting and not knowing had transformed them and me into *us*. Once they realised I knew who *we* were, *we* were able to worship together.

In July 2018, I reported on behalf of the Worship and Liturgy Committee of the World Methodist Council (WMC),

> ...Many of our churches offer a great gift in their preservation of historical forms and some translate those into vibrant expressions that engage people in contemporary life and service.
>
> What is noticeable is that those Churches who have the longest-established Books of Order/ Books of Discipline often have liturgies with deeply historical roots, whereas the more recently-established Churches often have more flexibility and more options for liturgical components.[1]

Coordinating WMC Worship in Seoul, I described the scope of our difference. Some have set texts and narrow expectations, emphasising piety from the Wesleyan heritage.[2] Others have flexibility, prioritising community relationships. The Committee's task was curating worship[3] for our global context. Turning to established performative patterns (shaped by the rubrics of a prayer-book) and familiar words (exemplar texts), we also used more than twenty languages and symbols from six continents.

I write conscious of my Uniting Church heritage and formative years in an Anglican school using *An Australian Prayer Book*[4] which has automatic responses to trigger phrases. I write as worshipper, practitioner and missiologist. I am a Multifaith Tertiary Chaplain, worshipping in a Fijian-Australian UCA Congregation, as a Buddhist convert of Chinese-Scottish heritage with my Aussie-Spanish-Irish husband. My congregation has set a goal to decolonise worship.[5] This essay is my response.

At inauguration (1977), the Uniting Church in Australia had myriad resources.[6] Identity was summarised in *The Basis of Union*[7] and new logo, but negotiation and compromise left little energy for integrating offerings as subsequent communities entered union. In 1988, booklet-form services and the 'publication of a comprehensive collection of services and other resources' were released in *Uniting in Worship (UiW)*.[8] UiW tried to capture and embed the new 'Uniting' identity, using phrases from *The Basis of Union*. Adherence to set texts gave way to pockets of creativity as people used new language about themselves. The ecumenical DNA began to find expression, taking members beyond known catholic, reformed and evangelical traditions. Liturgists collaborated with partners in Aotearoa-New Zealand and Canada. Many embraced elements from the Pentecostal movement, with Hillsong events populated by Uniting Church worship leaders and musicians. Diversity was embraced with the declaration *'We are a Multicultural Church'* in 1985 (welcoming recent migrants and international partnerships). By 2005, the new edition, *Uniting in Worship 2 (UiW2)*[9] included core materials, with more comprehensive data-resources on CD.[10]

As Uniting Church members, we named *inclusion* as a core value.[11] Inclusion grew and tight boundaries around liturgical conformity (sticking to reading only English-language texts and performing habitual actions) were replaced with more hospitable ways of gathering diversity (including multilingual texts, negotiated verbal-visual language and contextualised movement). 'Ordered liberty'[12] marked the shift:

> *One of the highly significant aspects of these (reformed) traditions was their reassertion of that liberty to which we are all heirs through Jesus Christ (see, e.g. Gal.5:1 and 2 Cor.3:17.) Such liberty was and is valued, not only in belief and practice, but also in forms of worship so that dulling uniformity and 'vain repetitions' (Matt.6:7 KJV) are avoided.*

At the same time as it is the Holy Spirit's role to be 'the Lord and giver of life' we can be sure that the Spirit will enliven set orders and written prayers, including the words of the Lord's Prayer and of Scripture, and, just as readily, will inspire extempore forms.[13]

'Ordered Liberty' included following rubrics in the text advising whether something might or should happen. While liberty was implied in the rubrics in UiW, its first decade coincided with a period of identity-formation. Only ministers/presiders had copies of 'the UiW Red Leader's book', so creative input by worshippers, who had 'the UiW Blue People's book', was significantly restricted. Where UiW was less visible, a sense of pioneering saw freedom to draw upon international materials. The Canberra World Council of Churches gathering in 1991 inspired choreographers, actors, musicians and wordsmiths, resulting in pilgrimages to Taize, Glasgow, Singapore and Toronto. Affirming multicultural identity and covenantal relationships with First Peoples, new resources were created or sourced to suit emerging contexts.[14] Dorothy McRae-McMahon[15] exemplified creativity at Pitt Street Uniting Church in Sydney and in Worship Expos held at The ELM Centre[16] in the 1990s-2000s. Rich liturgies were trialed at Pitt Street and adapted, via the Expos, into other congregations. Once liturgical liberty was understood by local leaders, there was no going back. Dorothy used rocks, cloth, candles and other items, and she challenged us to experiment within our own environments. Members of Pitt Street shared how they had grown spiritually through such worship, developing new language to express their faith.

As a missiologist, I call locally-grounded worship 'liturgical contextualisation'. It involves making meaning, communicating and recognising who is making the 'sacrifice of praise'. It makes tangible our grappling with gospel and culture, carrying an expectation of God's inspiration everywhere. Contextualising liturgy becomes an act of faith, as we attend to God's revelation in situated time and place.

UiW2 gave permission to explore, to *liberate order*[17] from the perception that it was restrictive. We may recognise God's grace in different forms of physical greeting (a reverent bow or touching of forehead) or the way in which the seating and serving protocols of certain communities demonstrate relational respect. Despite expectation of cross-cultural integration with UiW2, the reality was more a sense of lost potential. Leaders sometimes stuck with published texts rather than treating them as examples. This lost opportunity was stark when UiW2 texts were translated into community languages, rather than using community cultural expressions and languages to realise the rubrics in UiW2.[18] Using English as the dominant language did not give us the tools to go beyond non-English-language concepts.

Words unite and divide:
'emerging', 'missional' and 'fresh'

With globalisation, English and American-English speakers were struggling with language too. The term, 'emerging mission' gained traction with The Gospel and our Culture Network (GOCN[19]) in the 1990s, as it focused on developing local missiologies.[20] Leaders in the Emerging Church movement worked with new forms of

Christian community, articulating faith anew in their contexts, with few assumptions about how Christianity was defined or the lens of Christendom applied.[21] 'Church-planting' and evangelistic initiatives referred to emerging models of faith communities, built on spiritual traditions but not bound by the constraints of inherited community expectations. While some church-planters had church-replication and site-inhabitation models in mind, others questioned what it meant to be church.

'Mission'-terminology appeared: 'missionary congregation',[22] 'missional church',[23] and 'missional leader'.[24] Both Warren and Roxburgh documented attitude shifts required for institutionally-enculturated leaders to be more missional. They made the case for transformation through experience.[25] Where I believe the movement lost momentum, was in emphasising leadership without sufficient attention to whole-community practices and liminal reformation.[26]

Archbishop of Canterbury Rowan Williams influenced the English church to consider being mission-shaped and mission-focused. Over a thousand fresh expressions of church developed since 1990. They were defined as:

> ... established primarily for the benefit of people who are not yet members of any church [which] will come into being through principles of listening, service, incarnational mission and making disciples [and] will have the potential to become a mature expression of church shaped by the gospel...[27]

In the Uniting Church, congregations are defined by *'worship, witness and service'*.[28] Despite a history of service-oriented Presbyterian and Methodist Deaconesses in pre-union community development work, church-planters post-union focused on starting worship services on new sites. During the 2000s people started talking about alternative faith communities.[29] However, it was 2009-2011 when service groups reported building new witnessing faith communities. In order to gain ecumenical support and blessing, Uniting, Lutheran and Anglican churches launched 'pioneer' mission-shaped-ministry training in Adelaide and Canberra.[30]

The Uniting Church's Mission and Evangelism Network looked at how *Fresh Expressions* (FX) connected with groups of different cultures, languages and philosophies. *FXs* often start as contextualised experiments outside churches. New initiatives were encouraged, but the blessing of sacraments was harder to come by.

Sitting at *the little table*

Growing up in Australia, I remember childhood Christmases where adults would sit at 'the big table' and children, not yet trusted with the crystal and silverware, would be seated at 'the little table.' There were advantages to being at the little table. Mess and noise were more acceptable, but the richer food and mysteries of the big table were lost. Likewise, some *FXs* failed due to lack of eucharistic access.[31] New believers might be baptised in small groups, but without communion in their own discipling groups, some felt starved or rejected. Few could imagine themselves as bearers of life for the world when the institutional church judged them too immature for the heavenly banquet.[32] Differing attitudes to church membership challenged ideas of how hospitality was respectfully given, received and shared. In the Uniting[33] Church, communion was understood to be nourishment for the baptised, but the practice sometimes was to welcome all to an open table whether they were able to confess faith or not.[34]

Sending via liminality - *Communitas*[35]

Ritual can invite participants into liminal space, offer a framework for liminal engagement, or provide response to liminal experience.[36] A characteristic of liminality is participant transformation. Victor Turner described the process as having a threefold pattern: (1) movement from structure into ambiguity and disorientation, (2) the experience of anti-structure, liminality or threshold space, and (3) reformation and renewal.[37] Experiencing eucharistic ritual can provide the opportunity to develop *communitas* (a transformed community with new internal relationships and identity).

In the work of salvation, liminality can provide room for conversion and repentance. Revisiting liminality is part of continuous re-formation in discipleship.[38]

Regularly and ritually breaking bread and sharing wine are necessary for the faithful to be God's transformed people. As disciples mature, they recognise their appetite for revisiting liminality in order to sustain *communitas*.

The *ordo* traces the movement from hospitality (invitation) to mission. The *communitas* transformation sees those who have participated as 'going into the world'. *Missio* (Latin: being sent) is linked to the intention of being brought together to partake of communion. We gather and receive and, in turn, are sent to share God's grace in the world. Example services in UiW include a missional 'Charge' or a 'Word of Mission' before the final blessing to highlight the sending of the people into the world.[39] Worship, whilst focusing on God, should also be evaluated for how it inspires communities to participate in God's mission. While drawing people to worship God is one of the core outcomes of mission, it is also part of a living cycle of 'worship, witness, and service' (UCA *Basis of Union*, Paragraph 1).

Mission's *big table*

How do we get a seat at *the big table*? The Uniting Church in Australia's *Basis of Union* states that baptism 'initiates people into Christ's life and mission in the world, so that they are united in one fellowship of love, service, suffering and joy, in one family of the Father of all in heaven and earth, and in the power of the one Spirit'

(*Basis of Union*, Paragraph 7). Through participation in Holy Communion, we claim that disciples are nourished to become missional nourishment, 'the people of God... are strengthened for their participation in the mission of Christ in the world' (*Basis of Union*, Paragraph 8).

Christ offers sustenance, so the people become the means of encountering Christ for others. Bosch argues the Church's essence is missionary. His work prompts the following questions in relation to such a missionary congregation's liturgical life:

- How do we address the tension between individualistic world-views and an emerging call to community-oriented mission?
- How important are liturgy and hospitality in shaping our missional identity?
- How important is our identification as 'local church'?[40]
- How are diverse groups being 'church' within our local experience of the world?
- How do we understand our location, cultural identity, life-stage, politics, demographic, as we bear light and life within a local community?

The movement towards ministry by the whole people of God[41] requires building connections between gatherings of individuals who then come to identify themselves as a people, bound in God's story. Hospitality and eucharistic experience provide opportunities to build connection, with liturgy articulating identity. These are also times when different world-views can lead to tensions and conflicts around language, culture, tradition and relationship. Addressing these differences are required for any ecumenical future.

In Rome 2017, the World Methodist Council Steering Committee celebrated fifty years of ecumenical dialogue between the Vatican and Methodism. Pope Francis issued us a challenge. He proposed nothing short of full communion should be the goal of our dialogue.[42] My thoughts went to the obstacles to be overcome. I imagined ecumenical worship teams moving beyond World Day of Prayer compromises (made possible by strong lay-women) to more courageous creativity. Bearing witness to Francis' prophetic words, I wonder why we cling to the security of past practice, when the vision of broader inclusion is before us? What do we fear? Do we think we will be corrupted by becoming too close to different cultures?

Bosch also offers a reminder to confront syncretism and broaden perspectives about diverse gifts and graces in our community. The way to avoid syncretism is to ensure the salvation is not narrowly defined for a chosen few. He advocates the re-articulation of salvation in each missional context: how gospel is mediated relates to fresh interpretations of justice, evangelism, context, liberation, and enculturation. Surely, these pleas apply, not just to theology-missiologist, but also to worship?

One year after the Rome meeting, the World Methodist Council gathered in Seoul. What did we hold 'in common'? Disappointingly, what was suggested as common was the singing of Wesleyan hymns. As much as I love a good sing, I longed for more than a hymnfest at the 'heavenly banquet'! I turned to our Nigerian members to share their abundant joy in a sung and danced Call to Worship, followed by a litany in eight languages. We heard the scriptures in the musics of different tongues and prayed a eucharistic prayer full of beautiful diverse imagery with different angles on the gospel story. The highlight, for me, however, was a prayer made meaningful through ritual action.

Contextual ritual reveals the *We*

Shared physical ritual can move community into *communitas*.[43] People can overcome difference by sharing a 'sympathetic' sensation of mutual 'fellow-feeling'.[44] They move beyond holding things 'in common' to experiencing community as sacred and blessed.[45] While Turner makes the distinction between phases of *communitas* as existential, normative and ideological, rituals are not always experienced in the same way, even within shared *communitas*.

In Newcastle, I worked with four distinct identity groups. Each participated in the same eucharistic worship services, but understood what was happening in different ways. Some emphasised being in God's presence, others saw the communal integration of their personal devotional lives, while others experienced a symbolic enactment of their life as God's community in the world. Their different experiences did not detract from the building of *communitas*, and neither did their understandings negate the understandings of the others. They held some things in common, but were not conformed to one another. People enter into *communitas* with different understandings and experiences of what is happening. *Communitas* can develop from competing discourses,[46] particularly as parties share journey or pilgrimage.[47]

Turner's work built on Arnold Van Gennep, who described three stages of movement from liminality to *communitas* in coming of age rituals: separation, liminal period, and reassimilation. He identified liminality as the space between stages or 'intermediate' place. It can also be thought of as the 'in-between' time.[48] *Communitas*, comes when those who have undergone liminality are reassimilated into a new expression of community.

Christian *Communitas* sees gathered people, moving from a community structure, through liminality, where they thank God for Jesus and receive gifted identity. In turn, they offer themselves to the society around them.[49] As people find themselves entering into and sharing God's story through art, wellness, cooking and musicking, they are sharing in new forms of communal prayer. In the eucharistic prayer, people find themselves invited to participate at the universal table. Here, people give thanks, not always through the presider's words, but certainly as they receive and experience grace.

Prior to leaving Australia for Korea, I had a moment of foolishness and inspiration. Knowing there would be Pacific Islanders at the gathering, I hijacked my suitcase to pack a Samoan fine-woven grass mat.[50] Such mats are used in ceremonies and gatherings. They carry histories of communities and memorialise sacred storying. When I packed, I did not know how the mat would be used, but I did know we wanted to include participants' diverse languages, musics, signs and symbols. While curating can produce badly fitting patchwork coverings rather than beautifully woven garments of praise, I went with the expectation wisdom would emerge from the gathering.

The first use of the mat was in the opening service. We read the story of lowering the paralytic through the roof and Jesus telling him to take up his mat and walk (Mark 2:1-12). In the magnificent Kwanglim Church in Seoul, we had covered the communion table with the mat, then covered the mat with stoles from around the world. The visual welcome was immediate. During the reading, the stoles were swept aside to reveal the mat. It became a sign of sweeping away our overlaid stories to allow other stories to be seen and told.[51]

The closing communion was when the impact of the mat became apparent. I approached a chiefly leader from Samoa to read the confessional prayer, developed by women from South Pacific fellowships, while the delegates from Oceania placed the mat over the leaders of our gathering, the President and General Secretary of the World Methodist Council. McPhearson describes the process as follows, 'in a form of exchange known in Samoa as the *ifoga*, one group submits to a ritual and public humiliation in return for the forgiveness by another offended one'.[52]

In Samoa, those confessing bring a mat and sit under it until the offended chooses to offer mercy. Under the mat, the supplicants do not eat or drink. They do not leave to relieve themselves or wash. There is a complete loss of dignity, a stripping of humanity, a sense of entering the tomb.

In *ifoga*, risk, faith and hope all come into play. Through ritual, forgiveness withheld and grace fulfilled are sharply contrasted. The whole community prayed as if under the mat, naming self-awareness and recognising brokenness. When God's forgiveness was proclaimed, the mat was removed. We were ritually given back the gift of our humanity, and able to be a whole community at the Lord's table.

The ritual came to be for all but came from part of the community. To create mat-language with integrity, we needed 'mat-Elders' to guide us, and the larger gathering respectfully and gently entered into wisdom held by a few, in that time and place. We layered meaning so the mat became part of our shared language.[53]

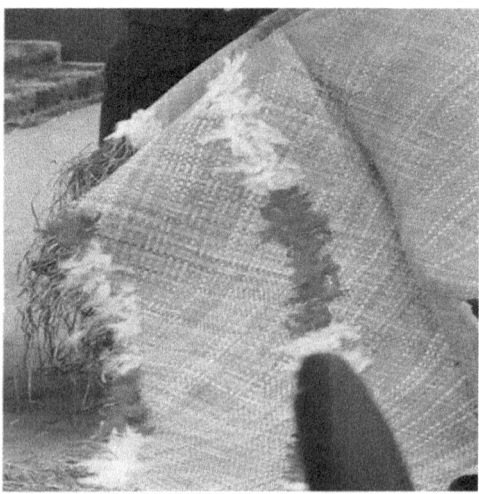

The 'fine mat' (with a President and General Secretary underneath) - July 14, 2018, Seoul, Korea

We go

Communitas sees people form community built through sharing together. The new *communitas* is declared as the restored spiritual people are named as those sent by God and with God's Spirit into the world. Turner referred to *communitas* where people articulate a sense of the 'essential We',[54] but *eucharistic communitas* is not simply a collection of people who have shared their liminal experience with one another. Rather, they become the Body of Christ, ready to engage in God's mission. I pray we may always be prepared to undertake this commission in fresh words and actions.

Endnotes

1   Amelia Koh-Butler, *Report of the Worship and Liturgy Committee to* the World Methodist Council, Seoul, 2018.
2   See https://www.oikoumene.org/en/folder/documents-pdf/fo_celebrationseucharist.pdf P.7
    The WCC "Fundamental Pattern of Eucharistic Celebration" (Ordo) was developed for a broad ecumenical family. In international conversations with Methodist/Wesleyan/Nazarene/United/Uniting colleagues, what and how to include worship elements had to be negotiated. e.g. particular themes of justice to be woven throughout, visibility of lay leadership, various spiritual disciplines (prayer, testimony, service and accountability practices from groups/class meetings).
3   Mark Pierson, *The Art of Curating Worship* (Minneapolis, Minn." Sparkhouse, 2010) and Jonny Baker, *Curating Worship* (London: SPCK, 2010) both use the term *'Curating Worship'*. Pierson was known as a Worship Curator at Cityside in Aotearoa-New Zealand, while Cheryl Lawrie was referred to as a Curator in Melbourne whilst working for the UCA Synod of Victoria-Tasmania (2006-2007). The term was also retrospectively used to describe the role liturgists played in developing Worship Stations in an interview Pierson gave on ABC radio in 2011,
    https://www.abc.net.au/radionational/programs/spiritofthings/stories-that-heal--worship-curators/2955854#transcript
4   Sydney: Church of England in Australia, 1978.
5   Migrant Fijians talk about having *'wet feet'*, an expression indicating the transformation that takes place when crossing the ocean.. Most migrating Fijians travel from their colonised birth-land to another colonised migration-

land. At the same time, Fijian colonial history is recent enough for many retain indigenous cultural knowledge. In relating to both birth-land and migration-land, they become adept at negotiating the requirements of colonial cultures while maintaining identity. The request of members of the congregation to *decolonise* is in keeping with their desire to acknowledge their own *wet feet* among the other wet feet of colonisers. Fijians mark indigeneity and seek permission to be on the sovereign country, negotiating welcome from indigenous Aboriginal and Torres Strait Islander Australians or Maori's in Aotearoa-New Zealand. In 'A New Zealand Prayer Book = He Karakia Mihinare o Aotearoa: A Study in Postcolonial Liturgy,' Claudio Carvalhaes, ed., *Liturgy in Postcolonial Perspectves: Only One is Holy* (New York, NY: Palgrave, 2015), 165-175, Storm Swain describes 'A New Zealand Prayer Book = He Karakia Mihinare o Aotearoa' as 'an expression of what it is to be a people of God in relationship within a complex space that both privileges the contextuality of the first peoples and socially marginalises them within the colonial legacy of the Anglo-centrism of that later settler peoples.' My Parramatta Fijian community seeks to cut through such spaces by attempting to decolonise multiple histories at the same time.

6   In 1977, Congregational, Methodist and Presbyterian Churches formed the new Uniting Church in Australia. They recognised 'the uniting Churches were members of the World Council of Churches and other ecumenical bodies, and will seek to maintain such membership. It remembers the special relationship which obtained between the several uniting Churches and other Churches of similar traditions, and will continue to learn from their witness and be strengthened by their fellowship.' (*Basis of Union*, Paragraph 2, 1977.)

The vision of Union involved seeing beyond the inheritance, *"We were Congregationalists, Methodists, Presbyterians, but that was not the most important thing about us. The most important thing was and is that we belong to the Church of God. What we did and do is 'in fellowship with the whole Church Catholic'."* (J. Davis McCaughey, Commentary on the Basis of Union, Melbourne: Uniting Church Press, 1980, p 7).

7   1971 edition: https://assembly.uca.org.au/images/stories/HistDocs/basisofunion1971.pdf

8   Melbourne: Uniting Church Press, 1988.

9   Sydney: Uniting Church Press, 2005.

10 The material is summarised in the Introduction to *Uniting in Worship 2*, with flexible options and examples for adaption.

11 Successive National Church Life Surveys report 'inclusion' as the prime self-identifier.

12 'Ordered Liberty' had been used in the UCA's sister Church, the United Church of Canada. See *Celebrate God's Presence* (Etioboke: United Church Press, 2000), 2, with the phrase *ordered liberty* ascribed to the 1932 *Book of Common Order*. The idea has many ecumenical parallels: British*Methodist Worship Book* (Peterborough: Methodist Publishing House, 1999) and Presbyterian Church USA *Book of Common Worship* (Louisville, Kenn.: WJKP, 2018), 'form and freedom'.

13 https://assembly.uca.org.au/images/stories/Theology_Discipleship/pdf/Ordered_Liberty_in_Worship.pdf

14 In *'Wide and Deep'* (Adelaide: MediaCom, 2017), a collection of liturgical resources, I sought guidance from several Elders' focus groups (indigenous

and migrant) about protocols around acknowledgements and welcomes in different situations. There was a desire for some to articulate adherence to a faith-informed Covenant (made by the Uniting Church in Australia and Uniting Aboriginal and Islander Christian Congress in 1994). Group participants made the distinction between the courtesy of secular acknowledgements in our wider society and the words and actions that might articulate a *'grounded'* spiritual relationship and commitment. I use the term *grounded* here intentionally, as aboriginal people reminded me of the importance of land links and naming relationships connected with land.

15 From 1993 to 2015, Dorothy McRae-McMahon published eleven books of liturgies or instructional volumes about developing worship, making her amongst the most prolific of UCA writers.

16 The ELM Centre (Education for Life and Ministry) was the Lay Ministry Education arm of the NSW-ACT Synod of the Uniting Church from 1977-2011. As a lay leader (1987-2002), the Associate-Director of ELM from 2003-2006 and Director from 2006-2011, I was heavily involved in the Worship Expos. The influence of participants shapes my thinking and practice.

17 The flipping of terminology, *liberated order* comes from conversations with UCA academic and worship curator, Craig Mitchell. He argues the concept of *ordered liberty* can have connotations about control of creativity, whereas *liberated order* respects the heritage while allowing the freedom of improvisation and innovation.

18 Examples of this tendency include standardisation of the Charge at Ordinations (2009) and the Declaration of Purpose of Marriage (2016). Rather than utilise the texts and nuanced actions from indigenous and migrant communities, English-language versions were translated, resulting in a narrowing of expressions. Emphasising English as normative was experienced as dominant-culture colonisation and a return to the 'white Australia policiy' of 1901-1973. There is an increasing awareness about colonisation in worship, with Carvalhaes, ed., *Liturgy in Postcolonial Perspectives*, Michael Jagessar and Stephen Burns, *Christian Worship: Postcolonial Perspectives* (Sheffield: Equinox, 2011), and Kristine Suna-Koro, *In Counterpoint* (Eugene, Ore.: Pickwick Press, 2017), suggesting we need to change the questions we ask and seek non-dominant perspectives.

19 Craig Ott, Stephen J. Strauss and Timothy Tennant note the development of the missional church movement, offering the following survey of available materials: "summaries of missional church concepts can be found in Roxburgh (2004) and Van Gelder (2004). Further material is available in Hunsberger and Van Gelder (1996), Guder (1998), Gibbs (2000), Frost and Hirsch (2003), Minatrea (2004) and a critique by Goheen (2002)" (Craig Ott, Stephen J. Strauss and Timothy Tennant, Encountering Theology of Mission: Biblical Foundations, Historical Developments, Contemporary Issues, Grand Rapids, MI: Baker Academic, 2010, pp. 197-201).

20 George R. Hunsberger and Craig van Guder, eds, *The Church Between Gospel and Culture: The Emerging Misison in North America* (Grand Rapids, Mich: Eerdmans, 1996).

21 Leonard I. Sweet, Andy Crouch and Brian Mclaren,*The Church in Emerging Culture: Five Perspectives* (Grand Rapids, MI: Zondervan, 2003).

22 Robert Warren in the UK in 1995 and Alan Roxburgh in the US in 1997.

23 Darrell L. Guder and Lois Barrett,. *Missional Church: A Vision for the*

Sending of the Church in North America (Grand Rapids, MI: Eerdmans, 2011).
24 Alan J. Roxburgh, Fred Romanuk, and Leadership Network, *The Missional Leader: Equipping Your Church to Reach a Changing World* (San Francisco, CA: Jossey-Bass, 2006).
25 See the similar thinking inRobert Warren, *Being Human, Being Church : Spirituality and Mission in the Local Church* (London: Marshall Pickering, 1995) and Alan Roxburgh, *The Missionary Congregation, Leadership and Liminality* (Harrisburg, PA: TPI, 1997). In Roxburgh's subsequent visit to the Uniting Church's School of Continuing Education in Sydney, he picked up on the idea of liminality, where people go through an 'in-between', transitional time/space, emerging changed. Roxburgh's description was similar to Victor Turner's concept of emerging from ritual experience as a community transformed = *communitas*. Communitas concept will be further explored later.
26 The rise of New Monasticism and a focus on Faith Practices represented by the like of Diana Butler-Bass, *Christianity After Religion: The End of Church and the Birth of a New Spiritual Awakening* (New York, NY: HarperCollins, 2012). may offer a corrective here.
27 Subsequently popularised in the literature: e.g. http://freshexpressions.org.uk/resources-3/quick-look-guides/quick-look-a02-mission-context/
28 Constitution of the Uniting Church in Australia, *Congregation* Definition, (2018 ed) p.43
29 Uniting Church Regulations changed to recognise non-congregational Faith Communities (2018 ed) 3.9.2
30 Mission-shaped-ministry education focuses on 'pioneers' establishing new forms of church for people previously unreached by the gospel. Cheryl Lawrie (from the Victoria-Tasmania Synod one Nicole Fleming (from the NSW-ACT Synod) led groups of potential experimenters to see what was going on in the UK. In 2011, David Male visited the South Australia Synod from the UK to talk about Fresh Expressions (FX). He returned on several occasions, building formal connections between Australian and UK networks.
31 See also Mark Earey's reflections in this volume.
32 Extending eucharistic hospitality beyond previous conventions is discussed by Barbara Glasson in *I am somewhere else* (2006) and *Mixed up Blessing* (2006) and Katherine Jefferts Schori in *Gathered at God's Table* (2012).
33 It is notable that the name is Unit-ing rather than Unit-ed. The hope for ongoing union implies ongoing welcome to those who are not yet identifying as members of the community. Whether we believe welcome invites outsiders in, or invites all into a renewing community, influences how the invitation is offered.
34 The Faith and Order Paper (No.111), *Baptism, Eucharist and Ministry* (Geneva: WCC, 1982), included a Confession of Faith/Creed as part of the eucharistic ordo. Yet, the dual influence of progressive theology and unchurched/de-churched people approaching the table presented a challenge.
35 *COMMUNITAS* refers to unstructured community who a liminal or *in-between* experience through ritual, emerging changed.
36 Ronald L. Grimes, *Ritual Criticism: Case Studies in Its Practice, Essays on Its Theory* (Columbia, SC: U. South Carolina Press, 1990)

'Becoming We': Exploring Liminality

37 Victor W. Turner, *The Ritual Process: Structure and Anti-Structure* (Chicago IL: Aldine Publishing Co., 1969), 94-95.
38 *Ecclesia Semper Reformanda* (Latin) – 'Reformed' traditions emphasise the need for disciples, individually and collectively, to be continually re-formed in Christ.
39 This moves beyond a release of the congregation and imbues the 'Dismissal' with missional imperative, focusing on their going into the world. It follows the World Council of Churches' 'Lima Text' (1982), found in *Baptism, Eucharist and Ministry*, Faith and Order Paper No. 111.
40 David Bosch,*Transforming Mission: Paradigm Shifts in Theology of Mission* (Maryknoll, NY: Orbis Books, 1991), 378.
41 Bosch, *Mission*, 467-474.
42 'We cannot speak of prayer and charity unless together we pray and work for reconciliation and full communion.' Pope Francis, 2017. For full text see http://worldmethodistcouncil.org/wp-content/uploads/2017/10/Papal_Address_To_Delegation_of_the_World_Methodist_Council-19-October-2017-_-Francis.pdf
43 Turner, *Process*, 96
44 Adam Smith, *The Theory of Moral Sentiments* (Amherst, NY: Prometheus Books, 2000)
45 Claudio Carvalhaes, "Communitas: Liturgy and Identity", *International Review of Mission* 100 (2011):37-47.
46 John Eade and Michael J. Sallnow, *Contesting the Sacred: The Anthropology of Pilgrimage* (Urbana, IL: U. Illinois Press, 2000), 5.
47 Michael A. Di Giovine, *Pilgrimage: Communitas and Contestation, Unity and Difference*. Tourism (Zagreb) Vol. 59 (2011): 247-386, 252-254.
48 Turner, *Process*, 196.
49 Turner, *Process*; also Guy Scott Shigemi Higashi, *Musical Communitas: Gathering Around the 'Ukulele in Hawaii and the Foursquare Church*. (Fuller Seminary, School of Intercultural Studies, 2011), 52-55.
50 The Samoan 'fine mat' is not a floor-covering, but a cultural symbol. See https://en.m.wikipedia.org/wiki/'ie_toga
51 I was told the placing of a mat on the Communion Table had probably caused some 'Divine shock... in a good way'.
52 http://www.jps.auckland.ac.nz/docs/Volume114/jps_v114_no2_2005/1%20The%20ifoga.pdf (Accessed July 2018)
53 In this setting we had Pacifica, African and Asian worshippers who all had 'mat-cultures'. Being led by a chiefly Samoan was key to holding in *ifoga* with integrity.
54 Turner, *Process*, 137.

Response

Processes of Liturgical Change:
A Roman Catholic Response

Jason J. McFarland

'When we pray', as Stephen Burns says in his introduction to this collection, 'we pray with others'. Nothing is more essential to the Christian tradition. It is our prayer in common that binds us. It constitutes the Church. Though expressed in a multiplicity of ways within a kaleidoscope of cultural forms informed by a fathomless collective tome of theological insight, being Christian means praying together.

As a Roman Catholic, in a certain sense, I pray most specifically with other Roman Catholics. Ritual forms and a particular understanding of revelation bind us together as a specific, if global, community of believers. More specifically, I pray within the Roman Rite (Ordinary Form). Even more specifically, I pray with other English-speaking Roman Catholics. This implies not only a linguistic but also a cultural connection. These connections unify, but also bring to the fore a complicated negotiation with the histories of colonialism and reformation that have led to the present-day reality of a community within a community of believers worshipping in one of the languages of a large island in the North Atlantic.

I also pray with all Christians. The ties that bind us together vary in terms of history, ritual, theology, ecclesiastical politics and the like, but bound we are in the person of Jesus Christ – indispensably and inescapably. Even further, I and we pray with all other human beings who pray: most closely with those who resonate with the idea of a God who is love, but indeed with all people who pray to assert a universe of meaning rather than of meaninglessness.

We pray both locally and universally, then. This collection of essays concerns quite specifically local (though local in a variety of senses) expressions of the global reality of Christian common prayer and the ongoing history of liturgical change. It is a truism that every context is local, as human beings can only ever express anything in their particular places with their particular bodies. But the local manifestation of liturgical practice is a topic that interests me greatly, and one that I am quite familiar with from an English-speaking Ordinary Form Roman Rite Roman Catholic perspective.

Of course, anyone who entered into Liturgical Studies around and after the time of the Second Vatican Council would be interested in and well-versed in such matters – why else this collection with this array of esteemed authors? As it happens, though, I was the full-time Assistant Editor at the International Commission on English in The Liturgy (ICEL) from 2005-2012. I say 'as it happens' because it was not an anticipated or sought after career move. But, as it happens, I ended up working there during the time of the preparation of the new translation of the *Missale Romanum* guided by the new liturgical translation principles of *Liturgiam authenticam*.[1] For these years, I was one of a very small team that facilitated the processes of liturgical translation, organising and providing resources and background research for translators and commentators, collating their work, planning meetings of various committees and of the bishops who led the organisation, keeping track of the results of various stages of the process. By no means do I want to overstate my influence or role at ICEL – but at the very least I was a witness to the process. I see the work of those years as serendipitous with a hint of dissonance, as I was and am a fan and proponent of *The Sacramentary* (1998), which has never seen the liturgical light of day, at least officially speaking. Depending on one's evaluation of the final result – *The Roman Missal* (2010) – my keen interest in the theology of the *Rite of Penance* might have relevance.

Whatever one's assessment of the final product, the procedural irregularities in its approval by the Holy See, and indeed the motivations behind the need for it in the first place, it is now the normative collection of texts and rites for the tens of millions of Roman Catholics who worship in English – not only for the celebration of the Eucharist, but also for many of the other rites of the Church because texts contained in the Missal pertain to many other rites. Its style and application of translation principles continue to be mirrored in ICEL's ongoing work. In one sense, *The Roman Missal* shows us how important it is to get it right (or as right as possible) the first time around. In another sense, it shows us how difficult getting it right actually is. Miscalculations of the politics of the process – and abuses of power – can mean decades of work end up sitting on the shelf unused, and even an inevitably inferior product (because of the inferiority of the translation principles undergirding it, not because of a lack of expertise or care on the part of ICEL and its collaborators) can itself be compromised at the very end.

The experience of translating the Missal also reveals how clericalism can derail liturgical reform and renewal. On one hand, the Congregation for Divine Worship and the Discipline of the Sacraments lacks the personnel and organisational structures to properly evaluate and revise the Church's rites translated into English by ICEL, let alone by ICEL's fellow organisations tasked with creating vernacular translations into the world's other major language groups.[2] On the other hand, there is an ever-present mistrust of ICEL – which has prominent roles in its processes for laypeople, religious, and ordained scholarly types who have little interest in hierarchy politics. Thus, the Congregation takes on the impossible task of review and revision anyway and the result is inevitably messy and flawed. There has been a serious failure in delegation and subsidiarity.

When We Pray's wide-ranging collection of essays touch on some of the issues I have raised so far, to be sure, and much broader issues as well. In what follows, it is this broad look at 'the future of common prayer' that has inspired my response, though of course whatever insights I have to offer are inevitably seen through the lens of the very specific process of creating vernacular-language liturgical books. It is clear that many of the same concerns pervade the variety of traditions represented in the book: Anglican, Episcopal, Uniting, Roman Catholic. This is to be expected, given our common liturgical roots. Nevertheless, it is worthwhile to be reminded of the commonalities – the same challenges permeate our experiences and thus (might) serve to unite us in collaboration for the good of the future of our common worship. In a more practical sense, noting common themes can help get us out of our denominational bubbles. Indeed, the collaboration and cross-fertilisation of the twentieth-century liturgical renewal is one of the greatest moves toward authentic ecumenism in recent Church history. This achievement should not be given up, and challenges to it from shifting ecclesiastical norms must be met with reasoned resistance.

What's the point of liturgical change? Translating tradition and enabling community

Stephen Burns raises this question in his introduction to this book, and it was also raised in the process of implementing the new translation of *The Roman Missal* for English-speaking Roman Catholics. In the face of child sexual abuse, does it really matter? While refugees are detained indefinitely off shore by the Australian government, don't we have more important things to worry about?

Even if Christian revelation is universally relevant, its communication in particular times and places is still context-specific. It is also communal, and dependent upon past interpretations of revelation. Emphasising these dimensions of the Christian experience is crucial given the pervasiveness of individualism. One might be tempted to think understanding Christianity is the same as reading the Bible from cover to cover, or that liturgical translation is just a matter of sitting with the original text in one hand and a Latin-to-English dictionary in the other. But the Christian message is passed on through a tradition of interpretation, which itself must be translated into and imbued with the insights of the present. As we know from the oft-quoted axiom *lex orandi, lex credendi* our common worship is one of the most important interpreters and translators of tradition.

Perhaps a better way to phrase the question is, 'Why is ongoing liturgical renewal so important?' We can look to the distant past, noting the massive concern and effort put into liturgical matters at many times in history.[3] We can look to the recent past, noting how the Liturgical Movement and the Second Vatican Council tied the renewal of worship to the very heart of the Church's life and the possibility of its transformative mission enduring into the future.[4]

We can also look to the present, where it is clear that vital communities and vital worship are inseparable.[5] Mark Earey points to this relationship in his essay for this book on *Common Worship*. He points to a disjuncture in the Anglican understanding of the place of worship in

A Roman Catholic Response

the Christian life. A more traditional view is that worship leads to community, while a more progressive view is that community comes first. Both views make important points. On one hand, Christianity cannot exist without common worship. On the other, how do you get people to turn up in the first place in our post-Christian context? Both perspectives are true, and must be held in tension. The shared dimension is conversion, which comes through the action of the Holy Spirit. The fellowship of believers (the converted) comes first – without this it isn't (yet) Christianity – but fellowship is soon if not immediately constituted and maintained through worship and social action. The two views have different starting points: the traditional one assumes a community of believers, and the other seeks to form one.

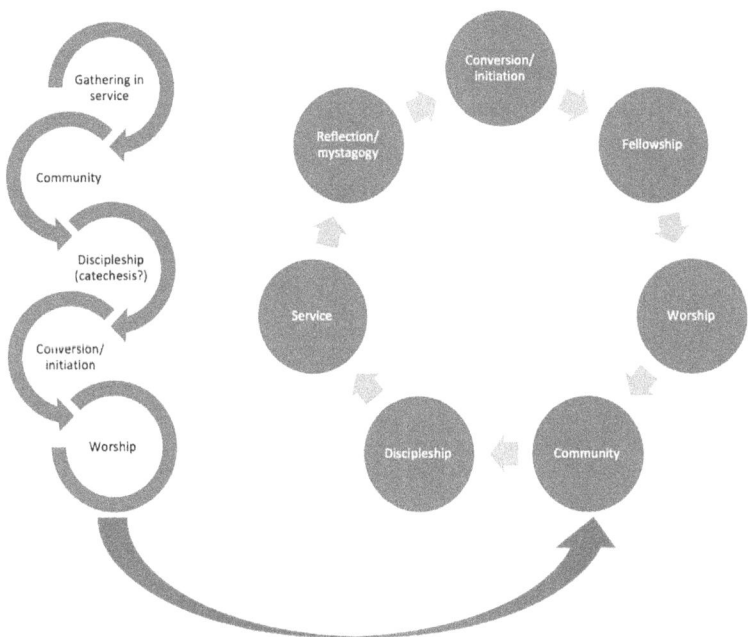

Most importantly, we can look to the future. If our forms of worship have allowed complacency among the faithful (ordained and lay alike) on matters like child sexual abuse, or have failed to form them to a stance diametrically opposed to and actively working against things like modern-day slavery and environmental destruction, or have allowed misogyny and marginalisation to endure unimpeded, then our forms of worship have failed to foster conversion and a Christian worldview and are in need of renewal. We would also have failed at connecting worship to life and justice, even though so doing was a central point of the Liturgical Movement and liturgical reform in the first place.

The dual challenges of connecting worship to life and forming vibrant worshipping communities in the first place are taken on by Amelia Koh-Butler in 'Becoming We: Exploring Liminality'. Liminality is a crucial concept in the study of ritual, and on the whole liturgical scholars have yet to utilise it to its full potential. It is clear that ritualising together is for Christians the normative way of forming a sense of *communitas*. As Koh-Butler states,

> *Communitas* sees people form community built through sharing together... Shared physical ritual can move community into *communitas*. People can overcome difference by sharing a 'sympathetic' sensation of mutual 'fellow-feeling.' They move beyond holding things 'in common' to experiencing community as sacred and blessed.

A Roman Catholic Response

She also asks several essential questions about mission, worship and community. We must work toward answers, but it is clear that *communitas* is key. Without it, worship (and community, service, etc.) is merely a gathering of individuals doing something together – thus opening fellowship to possible rupture when tensions and disagreements inevitably emerge – rather than the Body of Christ bearing all things together for the transformation of the world into the kingdom of God.

Roman longing

Through several of the essays in this collection, a minor but fascinating (and important) theme emerges—what one might call a Roman longing or a longing for tradition and authority in liturgical matters, which one rightly imagines is normatively the case in the Roman Catholic Church. Robert Gribben in 'The Spirit of Prayer Books Past' longs for 'The resources of the Church of Rome after Vatican II [which] were better marshalled than others' and 'had a tradition of authority in such matters the rest of us lack'.

And one can sense a bit of envy from Stephen Platten in 'Revolutionary Liturgy and the Prayer Book Tradition: What Revolution?' where he says, '... the centralised patterns of authority within the [Roman] Church have meant that such changes have been universally received. The recent over-literal revised version of the liturgy is a relatively small (albeit highly controversial) shift in contrast to the Vatican II reforms'. Here Platten justifiably simplifies the situation to make his point, e.g. the changes have been officially promulgated for liturgical use by all English-speaking Roman Catholics by the competent authorities, but some among the faithful would use the word 'imposed' rather than 'received'. In addition, the 2010 translation is also part of the Vatican II reforms in the sense that the process from the outset was envisaged as an ongoing one.

In Robyn Wrigley-Carr's 'Ecumenical Beauty: Evelyn Underhill's *Prayer Book*' she notes how Underhill, though assuredly an Anglican, often worshipped in Catholic Churches and likely was of the opinion that 'They order these things better in Rome' – 'these things' being forms of liturgy.

This emergent theme is, of course, a type of 'the grass is always greener on the other side' admiration for the Roman Church's ability to decide liturgical matters in a way that as a matter of course translates to actual liturgical praxis in local worshipping communities – whether it be happily or begrudgingly. This admiration is mutual; many in the Roman tradition look upon the freedom and flexibility exemplified in the Anglican, Episcopal, and Uniting traditions with some longing. Both sides, though, sometimes have an idealised notion of what's actually happening on the other.

From the Catholic perspective, the 'resources' are comparatively vast, but the 'tradition of authority' is both a boon to change and a hindrance if authority is not exercised charitably and the limited but crucial freedoms granted by *Sacrosanctum Concilium* are ignored. The Roman Catholic withdrawal from ecumenical bodies like the International Consultation on English Texts (ICET) and the English Language Liturgical Commission (ELLC) are examples of the limits of a wholly top-down approach. I think Gribben speaks well from the other perspective when he says, 'Nor... should we think the answers to our problems be bureaucratic, didactic, systematic, or the result of a program or curriculum.' Authority has limits, and so does freedom. Most can agree, though, that liturgical renewal must involve a careful well-informed plan, led by experts and assessed by the faithful in their participation in the liturgy over time.

The limits of freedom

Platten notes Prosper Guéranger's prophetic fear expressed in the 1840s about the dangers of liturgical variety; how, indeed, does *lex orandi, lex credendi* function without 'shared liturgical experience'? Indeed, as Paul Bradshaw argues (quoted by Platten), 'There is much more to be said for a shared liturgical experience than is often heard nowadays'.

Mark Earey speaks of two extreme views, both of which are untenable: 'On the one hand, [there are] a growing number of pioneers frustrated with... perceived restrictions... on the other, a frustration with a "no holds barred" irresponsible over-use of creativity and flexibility...' Each extreme creates a straw man of the other, though the motivation of each is the same: worship that connects with local assemblies of believers. Both views also neglect the fact that, as Platten says, 'the prayer book tradition was... born out of a *revolution*. In appreciating this, we can see that tradition as itself patient of development and subject to further revolution – as indeed in the case of the 20th century liturgical movement'. This is also the case for the post-Vatican II rites of the Catholic Church.

The value of liturgical stability

How our common worship should relate to our vast and complementary liturgical traditions is a concern addressed to some degree by all of authors who contributed to this collection. The value of liturgical stability is also a common theme. The sticking point is the *how* of it: how should local worship, which in fact is inseparable from liturgical tradition no matter how hard we try to make it fresh and new, interact with said tradition? Charles Sherlock, in 'The "Prayer Book Tradition": Back to the Liturgical Future', emphasises the essential benefits of stability in the form of a prayer book for worship: it makes 'the key resources of the Christian tradition available to all', and it constitutes 'an implicit "covenant" between clergy and people, which set "boundaries" to both clerical power and local idiosyncrasies'.

A Roman Catholic Response

If we take these benefits as a given, there are still many ways to interact with liturgical tradition:[6]

(1) Legitimate, officially approved opportunities for variation. Here the official rites are followed carefully and themselves provide specific opportunities for variation, e.g. where in *The Roman Missal* the rubrics state 'in these or similar words' or the use of entrance and communion hymns rather than the *introit* and *communio*. Such options, when deftly exercised, do create a local expression of a universal form.

(2) Deliberate variation in the spirit of the official rites. If possessing great skill, one might fruitfully engage in this kind of variation. Wrigley-Carr notes how Underhill 'drew upon liturgies from all branches of the Christian church' and used prayers from theologians throughout history. While her prayer book was for her personal use, it is worth considering how, with care, we might incorporate such prayers into our official rites when they communicate what the rites intend. In my view, this represents an openness to the enrichment of the tradition to the breadth of our shared tradition. Another example I have witnessed is the assembly's decision to stand rather than kneel during the Eucharistic Prayer.[7] One must be careful, however, that this sort of variation does not slip into clerical/local idiosyncrasy.

(3) Deliberate variation at odds with the spirit of the official rites. Distinguishing this way of interacting with tradition from the previous one is sometimes difficult, depending upon one's perspective, but generally speaking

I mean here doing things in the liturgy that the official rites clearly have not imagined possible, such as the entire assembly standing around the altar for the Eucharistic Prayer or the choir taking over the responses/prayers/songs that belong to the assembly. The motivations for such variation can be many: protest, concerns for justice and equality, nostalgia, convenience, taste, upending power structures, rejecting or challenging authority, and so on.

(4) Improvisation as the right way to do liturgy. In some manifestations of our common liturgical tradition, we start from scratch in our preparations for next Sunday. Here, rather than settling into given liturgical forms, we 'write the liturgy' each week. In the right hands, this type of interaction with tradition can result in truly vital worship, but it requires careful formation not only of the presiding celebrant, but also of the entire assembly. Otherwise, as Bosco Peters reminds us in 'The LORD's Song in a Foreign Land', '... our attention at worship is being held by the ever-changing words, but our attention is not being drawn to God or each other'. Peters also notes the 'inordinate time and energy expended in preparing creative, diverting services'. Few pastors have the limitless creativity required by the improvisatory model of worship, and, without such limitless creativity, improvisation sometimes has no apparent benefit other than diversion in our age of attention deficiency.

(5) Ill-informed variation. This is the most common form of interaction with liturgical tradition, most often engaged in unwittingly and with good motivations, simply because

a worshipping community lacks the necessary resources and formation.

(6) Ordered liberty / creative fidelity. Stephen Burns speaks of 'ordered liberty' in his introduction to this collection, which I and other have spoken of as 'creative fidelity'.[8] This is the soundest mode of interacting with liturgical tradition and should inform any of the previous modes already listed here. As Charles Sherlock states, 'Adopting a "common structure" and "classical shapes" approach carrie[s] forward the intention behind uniformity, replacing it with the harmony of a heritage-consistent, mission-shaped flexibility'.

'What we have failed to do'

There are several crucial matters deftly considered by some of the contributors to this collection, which, if our common worship is to endure, must be addressed. There is insufficient space here to take them up in detail, but I list them here in the hope that the authors will continue their work and that more of the academy will make them points of focus in their research.

Most critically, our processes for liturgical change must be enabled to take up these matters in a real and concrete way. Read liberally – as all liturgical norms and laws by their nature should be – Roman Catholic processes for liturgical change and renewal are able to address them, but this is possible only when there is real collaboration and trust between liturgical experts, organisations like ICEL, and ecclesiastical authorities.

(1) Sacramentality. Carmel Pilcher, drawing on the work of David Power, in her essay 'Creation Is also Our Prayer Book' emphasises how in our time people long for 'imaginative and symbolic language'. There has also been a 'loss of connection with creation as gift', she says. How can our common worship foster a sacramental worldview? Without it, symbol and sacrament are foreign language and become mere talisman and spell. Wrigley-Carr's excerpt from Underhill is perfectly suited to this dilemma:

> In the days that are coming, I am sure that Christianity will have to move out from the churches and chapels, or rather spread out far beyond the devotional focus of its life...telling the truth about God and man, and casting its transfiguring radiance on the whole of that world in which man has to live... Only those who have learned to look at the Eternal with the disinterested loving gaze, the objective unpossessive delight of worship, who do see the stuff of common life with the light shining through it, will be able to do that.

(2) Liturgy's connection to social transformation. This is an essential and foundational concern of the liturgical reform, now lost in many places. It must be a point of focus

and might ease some of the tension in current debates, i.e. if the aim of worship is the transformation of the world rather than personal piety or taste, then arguments over translation style, while still very important, are put in their proper place.

(3) Experimentation and inculturation. In the Roman Catholic sphere, the space to engage in liturgical experimentation, which is a necessary precursor to inculturation, has shrunk to almost nothing in the past two decades. I am speaking here of experimentation as permitted by the Conciliar and post-Conciliar liturgical norms, and an experimentation with deep respect for and ties to tradition and the corpus of liturgical rites and texts that have come down to us through the centuries, not of ill-informed anything-goes innovation. Carmel Pilcher, John Francis Fitz-Herbert, Stephen Burns and Bryan Cones point to urgent areas where experimentation leading to inculturation is of paramount importance in Part B of this collection.

Fitz-Herbert's 'Ritual Apologies and Reconciliation in Australian Society' for me emphasises the fact that for inculturation to even begin, lament and reconciliation need to come first or at least be facilitated through 'rites of becoming reconciled'. Here, the riches of the Christian liturgical tradition have a great deal to offer – Christianity is primarily about being reconciled, after all – but must themselves be transformed by indigenous insights. Pilcher rightly stresses the essential benefits (not least our relationship with and responsibility to our planet and fellow creatures) that might result from 'inculturating our liturgy with aspects of indigenous culture', but it will take experimentation and extreme care if it is to be an authentic mutual encounter and not cultural appropriation.

Burns and Cones provide more concrete examples of where our processes for liturgical change have so far failed us. '[I]n a wider culture that does not speak or perhaps not know how to talk theologically about sin', quoting Burns from 'Confessing More than Sin,' how is our common worship to reconcile? What do we do when many of the ways our liturgy talks about the central concepts of the faith are no longer comprehensible? If, as Cones says, our liturgy does not contain 'liturgical body language animated by the contention that baptism is the foundation of Christian ministry', how can our liturgy communicate anything other than an incorrect and, indeed, de-formative ecclesiology? Our current processes for liturgical change themselves need to change if they cannot cope with such urgent challenges.

(4) Liturgical formation and training. Possibly the most persistent problem today, which might also be the most easily addressed, is the fact that high-quality ongoing liturgical formation has ceased to be a priority in most places (parishes, seminaries, schools of theology, etc.). Given the fact that the post-Conciliar liturgy requires the engagement of the entire assembly, without such formation, the liturgy cannot function properly. Pre-

Conciliar sacramental theologies and ecclesiologies creep in, creating dissonance; the reasons for active participation become unclear and it begins to feel more comfortable to be spectators than co-celebrants. Both Glen O'Brien and Robert Gribben point to this problem in their essays. Gribben sums it up well saying, 'Who will speak for the liturgy, who have never studied it'?

The way forward

The range of solutions to the challenges posed by the process in liturgical change is multifaceted and context-specific, to be sure, but for those of us who worship in related liturgical traditions in English, we can look to the model of ICEL in its most productive and creative days – when the principles and demands of *Sacrosanctum Concilium* were met head on with enthusiasm and devotion rather than with suspicion and fear clinging to power and the past.

The goal is not constant change – indeed constant change would be as counterproductive to our common worship as stagnation. The goal put forward in the Holy See's establishment of mixed commissions like ICEL, rather, is an ongoing engagement with the cultures and contexts encompassed by a particular language so that they are capable of producing vernacular language editions of suitably adapted liturgical books. The principles of translation and adaptation are determined by the Holy See in documents like *Comme le prévoit* and *Liturgiam authenticam*, and the principles of *Sacrosanctum Concilium* and the Instructions on its proper implementation – bearing in mind that any instruction or requirement contrary to *Sacrosanctum Concilium* cannot hold the force of liturgical law.

ICEL's process is led by a governing body of bishops who represent the Conferences wherein English is a major language for worship, each bishop having been appointed by his respective Conference. This commission of bishops considers, approves and sometimes emends ICEL's work, and then provides the results to the member Conferences who then offer their own feedback to ICEL before final versions are produced and sent to the Holy See for confirmation. Such a process is a suitable and necessary exercise in ecclesiastical governance by the competent authorities – local and universal.

The nitty gritty of the process, however, is guided by ICEL's Secretariat – that small team of facilitators and experts of which for a time I was a part. The Secretariat engages committees of experts in various fields to do the brunt of the translation and adaptation work. The most useful elements reflected in and required by ICEL's work are a differentiation of roles, recognition of and respect for expertise, maintenance of sound organisational structures and processes, an ongoing revenue stream to fund the work, and most of all mutual trust.

It was a loss of this trust – along with healthy doses of clericalism, nostalgia, hunger for power, and sexism – that led to the disintegration and reconstitution of ICEL at the turn of the millennium. Differentiation of roles is key as well if Conferences of Bishops and their liturgical commissions are not to feel oppressed and overburdened (and out of their depth) by the nature and volume of work to be done, while at the same time being true shepherds of the process for the good of the faithful they lead. ICEL as an enduring and officially delegated organisation provides a framework for the ongoing and never-ending work, while at the same time providing and managing a stream of revenue to support the work through the collection of royalties for the use of its translations. Indeed, while any money ICEL makes belongs to its member Conferences of Bishops, its fiscal structure allows it to continue its work, self-funded in a sense, without any demands on the tight budgets of Conferences of Bishops.

The hoped for result in each new effort is a refreshed framework for worship. Sweeping change might happen every few generations, with properly authorised experimentation having taken place along the way. The process is by necessity both slow – it involves committees, compromise, and consensus, with multiple layers of approval and discernment – and bold-but-cautious – the matters at hand like cultural change, linguistics, the interpretation of ancient texts, the composition of new texts, etc., being essential to address but also extremely complex and interdisciplinary. A massive project like translating the *Missale Romanum* takes ten or even twenty years, but plans for the next phase begin even before the latest project is published.

From a certain perspective, we still have yet to realise the real fruits and potential of this process in Roman Catholic worship. The first wave of vernacular editions of liturgical books after the Council were produced with care but also in haste. Always in mind was the ongoing nature of liturgical change and the future opportunity to do it even better next time. In the *Order of Christian Funerals* (1989), *The Liturgical Psalter* (1994), and *The Sacramentary* (1998) we see a much fuller realisation of the potential of *Sacrosanctum Concilium*'s principles as well as ICEL's capacity for addressing the complex process of translation and adaptation. Only the first of these is officially approved for use in Roman Catholic worship, however, and even it is soon to be replaced by a new translation according to the principles of *Liturgiam authenticam*. Though the politics are complicated and recounted elsewhere,[9] in short, the problem isn't that it wasn't working but that we were afraid of the results. Collectively, we gave up. The project was abandoned. We faltered out of fear, nostalgia, and perhaps exhaustion. This begs the question, does the process need to be so hard, so fraught, so complicated, so lengthy? Yes, it does.

Even now ICEL's work continues, if diminished by the bridle of *Liturgiam authenticam*. There is some hope on the horizon now that this bridle has been loosened somewhat by Pope Francis's recent motu proprio *Magnum principium*.[10] We might see bolder efforts at experimentation and adaptation for particular contexts, and a more pastoral application of the principles of *Liturgiam authenticam*. In *Magnum principium*, Francis re-emphasises the need for liturgical translations to be comprehensible, and the previous requirement of the *recognitio* ('an attentive and detailed examination in order to judge the legitimacy and the conformity with the universal canonical and liturgical norms of the relevant texts which the Conference of Bishops desire to promulgate or publish'[11]) of the Congregation is now a simpler *confirmation* ('an authoritative act by which the competent Dicastery ratifies the approval of the bishops')[12] for translation. Substantial adaptations of the Latin models still require the *recognitio*, however, and the translation principles of *Liturgiam authenticam* remain in force. *The Sacramentary* (1998) will not be brought into use, and the multi-decade multi-million dollar project of *The Roman Missal* (2010) will not be abandoned.

All this is to be expected given the long arc of Church history, and the depth of ritual's function in human culture. Negotiation and conflict are inherent to the process of ritual change, and we should expect nothing different as we negotiate our worship today.[13] It is clear from Earey's essay that these Roman Catholic processual difficulties are also Anglican ones. In one of the best uses of understatement I have encountered recently, he says, 'There are several factors which combine to make it hard to move from seeing the problem to planning to improve the situation'. Indeed! He notes canonical revision is required if any sort of centrally-guided process is to be viable. '[Most] [p]eople don't understand the mechanisms for change', he says, and that, 'The long tortuous process of producing *Common Worship* has inoculated General

Synod against enthusiasm for liturgical business'. English-speaking Conferences of Roman Catholic bishops can surely relate.

The model for liturgical change offered by ICEL is infused with the realisation that our common liturgical prayer must meet the needs of our times and thus must be constantly renewed and adapted to particular contexts. This realisation also encompasses the fact that our worship must remain soundly rooted in tradition, while at the same time deconstructed and then refreshed to make room for the insights of particular cultures, subgroups of people, and languages left by the wayside of history and influence. The steamrollers of colonialism, capitalism, androcentrism and globalisation are not and cannot by their natures be good arbiters of what in the kaleidoscope of human cultures is of most value.

Collections of essays like this keep the liturgical conversation alive, which is essential, but the future of common prayer – *When We Pray* – depends on change, and thus on the establishment and ongoing support of robust, highly competent organisations like ICEL. Such organisations will look different in the Uniting and Anglican traditions than they do in the Roman Catholic one, of course. The work will continue to be hard and fraught, but it is essential... that is if our worship is to be anything other than a reliquary of venerable texts and ceremonies, the liturgy's riches hidden away in the language and ritual structures of a time now lost to our present-day modes of comprehension.

Endnotes

1. For some specific commentary on the document and its principles, see Jason J. McFarland, "Mass Antiphons and the Dialectic of Liturgical Genre and Translation," *Proceedings of the North American Academy of Liturgy* Annual Meeting, Montreal, 5-8 January 2012; McFarland, "An Overview of the *Ratio translationis for the English Language*," in *The Liturgy Documents*, Volume Three (Chicago, Ill.: Liturgy Training Publications, 2013) e-book edition; and Peter Jeffrey, *Translating Tradition: A Chant Historian Reads* LiturgiamAuthenticam (Collegeville, Minn.: Liturgical Press, 2005).
2. Whether the Curia has the authority to do so is a related but separate question. The impossibility of such a task being accomplished by the Curia is one of the primary reasons mixed commissions like ICEL were created in the first place.
3. The seventh-century creation of the Roman Mass Proper, the vast cultural adaptation of the Roman liturgy during the Carolingian renaissance, and the standardisation of liturgical books surrounding the Council of Trent are just three of many possible examples.
4. See Virgil Funk, "The Liturgical Movement (1830-1969)," in *The New Dictionary of Sacramental Worship*, ed. Peter Fink SJ (Collegeville, Minn.: Liturgical Press, 1990), 695-715.
5. The modes of connection between the two are complex and one should not oversimplify it, but it is indeed clear that the two go hand in hand, if we are speaking of a vital expression of Christianity.
6. N.B. only options 1 and 6 are officially possible for Roman Catholics.
7. This practice seems especially appropriate for Eucharistic Prayer II, which in the previous (more accurate in this case) translation read, "We thank you for counting us worthy to *stand* in your presence and serve you."
8. See Jason J. McFarland, *Announcing the Feast: The Entrance Song in the Mass of the Roman Rite* (Collegeville, Minn.: Liturgical Press, 2011), pp. xxxi, 196, 202.
9. Maurice Taylor, "A Cold Wind from Rome," in *It's the Eucharist, Thank God* (Suffolk: Decani Books, 2010).
10. Apostolic letter motu proprio *Magnum principium*, 3 September 2017.
11. Pontifical Council for Legislative Texts, *Nota esplicativa La natura giuridica e l'estensione della "redognitio" della santa Sede, Communicationes* 38 (2006): 10-17.
12. Arthur Roche, "A Key to Reading the motu proprio *Magnum principium*," *L'Osservatore romano*, 10 September 2017, 5.
13. See Ute Husken and Frank Neubert, *Negotiating Rites*. Oxford Ritual Studies. New York, NY: Oxford University Press, 2012.

www.ingramcontent.com/pod-product-compliance
Lightning Source LLC
Chambersburg PA
CBHW070247010526
44107CB00056B/2368